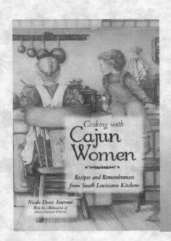

Cooking with Cajun Women

Nicole Denee Fontenot
Author & Historian

Phone: 337-370-1674   ndfontenot@aol.com
3524 W. Prien Lake Rd.,
Lake Charles, LA 70605

2003 Upcoming Book Signings & Appearances:

Jan 7   Good Morning Acadiana KATC

Jan 18   Barnes & Nobles @ Lafayette 1:00-3:00

Jan 24   Good Morning w/ John Bridges KPLC

Jan 25   Borders @ Metairie 2:00-4:00

Feb 1   Sam's Wholesale @ Lake Charles 12:00-2:00

Feb 8   Borders @ Kirby St., Houston 3:00-5:00

Mar 1   Weber Books @ Breckenridge 3:30-5:30

Mar 22 Barnes & Nobles @ Beaumont 2:00

Apr 12   Books-A-Million @ Lake Charles 2:00-4:00

May 3   Barnes & Nobles @ Metairie 2:00-4:00

May 10 Barnes & Nobles @ Baton Rouge 2:00-4:00

Contact the author to schedule an event or order signed copies (cost per book: $27.07 tax included plus $10.00 shipping & handling via UPS). For all other book orders contact your local bookstore, amazon.com, or hippocrenebooks.com. For sample recipes, a synopsis of & praise for the book see lisaekus.com.

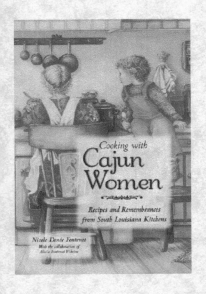

Author's Special
Old-Fashion Gumbo

2 pounds sausage, cut in 3 inch pieces
1/2 to 1 pound of tasso
1/4 to 1/2 cup oil
1 fryer (a young chicken of
2 1/2 to 3 pounds), cut in pieces
Salt to taste
Black & Red Pepper to taste
2 cloves garlic minced
2 onions chopped
Flour as desired
1 to 2 cups roux or
1/2 to 1 jar Kary's roux
3 to 4 bundles onion tops chopped

Brown sausage and tasso in a little oil in a large magnalite pot. Add chicken and brown on all sides. Then add onions and cook until wilted and a gravy begins to form. Add flour and thicken as desired forming a small roux base. (For the rest I add Kary's roux to keep the cooking time to 3 hours.) Fill pot with water and bring to a near boil, add Kary's roux and let continue cooking on medium heat for 1 hour. Add half of your onion tops, continue cooking for another 1/2 hour. Then add remaining onion tops and cook for 30 more minutes. In the last 10 minutes you can add 1 to 2 pounds fresh shrimp, if you want a little seafood, too. Serve over rice with potato salad. Serves 8 to 10. Bon Appetit!

Nicole Denee Fontenot
Author & Historian

Cooking With Cajun Women:
Recipes & Remembrances from
South Louisiana Kitchens
Published by Hippocrene Books

Cooking With Cajun Women

Recipes and Remembrances from South Louisiana Kitchens

Nicole Denée Fontenot

With the collaboration of
Alicia Fontenot Vidrine

Bon Appetit!
Nicole D. Fontenot

HIPPOCRENE BOOKS, INC.
NEW YORK

Cover art © Catherine Simpson.
For more information concerning Catherine Simpson's Original Watercolours,
Limited Edition Prints, Collector Plates, Figurines, and
her Forever Young Calendar, etc. please contact:
Forever Young Gallery
533 1/2 Richmond St. (at Kent)
London, Ontario Canada N6A3E9
TEL: (519) 438-6519
FAX: (519) 471-9680

Interior illustrations by Regina Meaux Fontenot.

Book and jacket design by Acme Klong Design, Inc.

For more information, address:
HIPPOCRENE BOOKS, INC.
171 Madison Avenue
New York, NY 10016

Library of Congress Cataloging-in-Publication Data

Fontenot, Nicole Denée
    Cooking with Cajun women : recipes and remembrances from
  South Louisiana kitchens / Nicole Denée Fontenot ; with the
  collaboration of Alicia Fontenot Vidrine.
       p. cm.
    Includes bibliographical references and index.
    ISBN 0-7818-0932-0
    1. Cookery, American--Louisiana style. 2. Cookery, Cajun.
  I. Vidrine, Alicia Fontenot. II. Title.

TX715.2.L68 .F66 2002
641.59763--dc21   2002032814

Printed in the United States of America.

Table of Contents

Cooking With Cajun Women

Recipes and Remembrances from
South Louisiana Kitchens

The Hippocrene International Cookbook Library

AFRICA AND OCEANIA
Best of Regional African Cooking
Traditional South African Cookery
Taste of Eritrea
Good Food from Australia

ASIA AND MIDDLE EAST
The Best of Taiwanese Cuisine
Imperial Mongolian Cooking
The Best of Regional Thai Cuisine
Japanese Home Cooking
The Best of Korean Cuisine
Egyptian Cooking
Sephardic Israeli Cuisine
Healthy South Indian Cooking
The Indian Spice Kitchen
The Cuisine of the Caucasus Mountains
Afghan Food and Cookery
The Art of Persian Cooking
The Art of Turkish Cooking
The Art of Uzbek Cooking

MEDITERRANEAN
Best of Greek Cuisine, Expanded Edition
Taste of Malta
A Spanish Family Cookbook
Tastes of North Africa

WESTERN EUROPE
Art of Dutch Cooking, Expanded Edition
A Belgian Cookbook
Cooking in the French Fashion (bilingual)
Cuisines of Portuguese Encounters
The Swiss Cookbook
The Art of Irish Cooking
Feasting Galore Irish-Style
Traditional Food from Scotland
Traditional Food from Wales
The Scottish-Irish Pub and Hearth Cookbook
A Treasury of Italian Cuisine (bilingual)

SCANDINAVIA
Best of Scandinavian Cooking
The Best of Finnish Cooking
The Best of Smorgasbord Cooking

Good Food from Sweden
Tastes & Tales of Norway
Icelandic Food & Cookery

CENTRAL EUROPE
All Along the Rhine
All Along the Danube
Best of Austrian Cuisine
Bavarian Cooking
The Best of Czech Cooking
The Best of Slovak Cooking
The Art of Hungarian Cooking
Hungarian Cookbook
Polish Heritage Cookery
The Best of Polish Cooking
Old Warsaw Cookbook
Old Polish Traditions
Treasury of Polish Cuisine (bilingual)
Poland's Gourmet Cuisine
The Polish Country Kitchen Cookbook

EASTERN EUROPE
Art of Lithuanian Cooking
Best of Albanian Cooking
Traditional Bulgarian Cooking
Best of Croatian Cooking
Taste of Romania
Taste of Latvia
The Best of Russian Cooking
The Best of Ukrainian Cuisine

AMERICAS
Argentina Cooks
A Taste of Haiti
A Taste of Quebec
Cooking With Cajun Women
Cooking the Caribbean Way
French Caribbean Cuisine
Mayan Cooking
The Honey Cookbook
The Art of Brazilian Cookery
The Art of South American Cookery
Old Havana Cookbook (bilingual)

Acknowledgements

Writing, compiling, and editing this historical cookbook proved a massive undertaking born out of my love for cooking, heritage, and history. This body of work represents my efforts along with that of others to bring Cajun cuisine, culture, and history from its most natural birthplace, the homes and kitchens of Cajun matriarchs, into your own homes. That being said, I owe my sincerest thanks and gratitude to many, most notably the women, who contributed to this book. I could not have written a narrative history, so many short stories nor documented so much quotable text without visiting dozens of Cajun women and collecting countless hours of oral history. Then nearly half of these women chose to take the added time and trouble to write down some of their favorite recipes and send them to me when I told them of my plans to create a cookbook that combined academic research collected for my master's thesis with recipes from established Cajun homes.

This book would have failed at its inception in 1998 without the cooperation of these Cajun women who generously opened their lives and their kitchens to me. I thank my grandmother, who inspired me to write about Cajun women because of the influence that she had on my daily life, particularly for my appreciation of my heritage, and for organizing a number of the initial interviews that I conducted. I thank the women, whose remembrances make Cajun culture come alive, for their candor, warmth, and wit, which made the interviewing process a pleasure rather than grueling work. Every time I listen to the tapes again and reread the transcripts I can visualize each woman, each distinctive personality, and I smile as I recall the stories they shared with me. The same warmth and richness of spirit emanates from their hand–written recipes. As I look over them sometimes for the tenth or even twentieth time, I still smirk every time I read their instructions. They not all too infrequently say something like "cook 'til done," and for them it's just that simple.

In addition to the willing assistance of the aforementioned Cajun women, I received support from my professional acquaintances as well. At the University of Louisiana at Lafayette's (formerly University of Southwestern Louisiana) History Department, where I worked on my master's degree for two years and where I taught for another two years; the Center for Louisiana Studies and the Center for Cultural and Eco-Tourism, where I was aided in all of my research and writing projects on Cajun women; and Kinder High School, where I now teach; the faculty and staff at each institution made me feel welcome, like part of a family. Some individuals from each institution, of a list too long to recognize all of them individually, helped guide, inspire, and motivate me at different

3

yet fundamental times in my academic and professional career and during the development of this cookbook.

For this work in particular I owe thanks to Dr. Chet Rzadkiewicz for introducing me to Anne McBride, who is now my editor at Hippocrene Books; to Dr. Baker, head of the UL Lafayette History Department, who insisted I sign with the New York-based press; and an extra special thanks to Dr. Brasseaux, formerly of the Center for Louisiana Studies and now the Director of the Center for Cultural and Eco-Tourism, who mentors me in all of my research and writing projects. His gentle nature, diligent editing of my previous historical writings, wealth of knowledge, and constant support and guidance have enabled me to dream and complete a work of this magnitude.

In order to complete a polished version of my manuscript that will find a national audience, I am indebted to Hippocrene Books for signing an author who was previously unpublished, with the exception of a few articles. Anne McBride, my editor, the copyeditor, and the book designer have diligently helped me succeed in producing a quality cookbook that is true to its purpose while proving fruitful for all involved. My endeavors would have fallen short without a beautiful painting to encapsulate the contents of the book and tantalize shoppers as they scan the bookshelves filled with hundreds of competing cookbooks. I greatly appreciate the generosity of Catherine Simpson, who so graciously allowed me to reprint one of her many pieces of artwork—entitled "Homemade Soup"—which will grace the covers of this cookbook.

Finally, I must also thank my family and friends who have listened to my incessant babbling about Cajun women, the interviews, the recipes, the writing, editing, and publishing process, and about finishing the cookbook, now entitled "Cooking with Cajun Women." My mother provided me with a sketch that captured the essence of the work and each time I looked at it while pulling another late night session, I found the inspiration to persevere. This was a project conceived while driving an hour-long commute to UL Lafayette and cultivated over four years late at night, on weekends, holidays, and over summer vacations. I needed all the coffee, motivation, and support that I could find. A special thanks to my sister for helping me by typing all the recipes, helping transcribe a few tapes, and accompanying me to a few of the many recorded interviews, and cutting stories from my typed notes, transcriptions, and narratives previously written for other projects and pasting them into the body of recipes. This endeavor began as an individual's idea, but it took the assistance of many to bring that concept to fruition and for that I Thank You All!

Author's Note

The individual stories that accompany the recipes were collected over a two-year period, from early 1998 to late 1999. I met and interviewed numerous Cajun women, who grew to maturity in the first half of the twentieth century and were willing to share their remembrances with me. The visits, recorded on audiotapes, lasted an average of two to three hours. Later, notes and transcriptions were made from the tape recordings. The stories found throughout the book originated from these oral histories and are written in one of two forms: either as direct quotations or as narratives that summarize a shared memory or depict something observed during the visit. As you read these reminiscences, written in first person, you will note that almost all of them begin with "I remember when;" yet, every word is not encapsulated in quotation marks. The women interviewed often used such phrases as "I remember when," "I can tell you about," or "I remember one time when" as they began to recall times past. I therefore chose to use "I remember" as the introductory statement to each memory. The repeated word pattern also serves as a clear break between recipe and story.

The paraphrased stories have been converted to first person in order to keep the personal connection that would otherwise be lost in a summary. For example, the statement "Mrs. Fontenot talked about how much she loved her grandchildren during the interview" lacks the personal feelings evoked by reminiscences shared during the visits with these women and in direct quotations. Paraphrasing is thus necessary to allow the whole story to be told in the limited amount of space provided. The absence or presence of quotation marks makes the reader aware of what is quoted and what is not.

Ellipses within directly quoted text indicate a gap between two quoted statements. The women often talked about one topic, then veered off to another related memory, and later returned to the initial story. In instances when I included a story verbatim, it was necessary to leave out moments of digression.

I am including these explanations regarding quotation marks and ellipses to explain what they mean and to let the reader know that I want to preserve the historical integrity of the book. In the end the purpose of including any and all of these stories is to give you a taste of Cajun culture as seen through women's eyes, more specifically through the eyes of twentieth-century Cajun matriarchs. I hope you enjoy the view.

Preface

Cooking With Cajun Women: Recipes And Remembrances From South Louisiana Kitchens, the title of this cookbook, directly reflects the treasures found inside. Beyond the cover lies a blend of history, culture, and cuisine. I attempt to illustrate how the seemingly simple culinary traditions of rural South Louisiana and the women who most frequently practice them affect familial and communal ties while simultaneously promoting cultural preservation. I do so primarily by letting the voices of the twentieth-century matriarchs illustrate the messages about their food, family, and folklore and add complementary historical data as needed.

Beyond the historical introduction lies a collection of the women's recipes and remembrances. The 300 recipes included were volunteered by dozens of Cajun women and reflect the constant interplay between old traditions and new techniques, foods, and modernizations; they result from the constantly changing influences on Cajun culture, especially as communities became less isolated and more Americanized. Although some look on in disgust at the innovations, these recipes are a representation of reality. Cajuns have nearly perfected the art of adaptability, which is key to their survival, by taking what they like from other cultures, absorbing borrowed elements into their repertoire, and somehow managing to make them uniquely their own. For instance, an ordinary sheet cake in America is a plain, fairly dry, store-bought mix, whereas a modernized Cajun sheet cake is something else entirely. It does sometimes contain a boxed cake mix, but the rest is a unique creation. Concoct a creamy mix, blend it well, then pour it on top of a warm cake so the two can meld into one, and *voilà*, now you have *mâche-pain*, or a Cajun sheet cake.

One of the thousand stories I have heard during oral interviews with Cajun women who were born in the first half of the twentieth century accompanies each recipe. Within these pages, memories are shared; remembrances of life in times past, which frequently inspire silent reflection, a warm smile of affection, or a smirk that often evolves into laughter. Take a look and see what response they evoke in you. Then, as you try the recipes and read the stories of these Cajun women with your children and grandchildren, always remember to tell them your own stories, teach them your favorite recipes, and share your history with them. Always stop and take time to say *"I remember when...."*

Twentieth-Century Cajun Women, Agents of Cultural Preservation

Cajun cuisine has earned a global reputation for its unique flavors, which are created from an array of spices that tantalize the senses of foreigners and natives alike. Yet, few people know about the treasures baked, fried, and stewed into every dish. Each morsel contains a part of Cajun culture, and if only the food could speak, what stories it could tell! Tales, not of secret recipes or seasonings, but of the people behind the food, their history of tight-knit families, who together worked the land for sustenance, placed their faith in God, and relished their *joie de vivre*. These values allowed them to survive persecution and separation in the *Grand Dérangement*, reunite in Louisiana, overcome economic hardships, and maintain cultural distinction amidst American society. Furthermore, the heart of a Cajun resides in the home, with the family. As a result, females, typically assigned the task of caring for the hearth and home, play pivotal roles in the development of everyday Cajun life, as well as the perpetuation of the community's heritage and family values. Cajun food ways, often deemed one of women's domestic duties, consequently reflect not only the history of Cajuns, but also the influential position women wield in Cajun society and cultural preservation.

This examination of women and old food ways in Cajun society is hampered by a lack of traditional documentation. Until recently, most Cajuns were illiterate and spoke only French; thus the community's lore and history were conveyed orally and transmission was restricted largely to Francophone Cajuns. Only in the last half-century have most Cajuns acquired a formal education, which came at the cost of their primary language. When dealing with the experiences of Louisiana's Acadian community in the early twentieth century, as when dealing with all non-literate or marginally literate peoples, historical researchers must rely heavily upon oral tradition to document everyday life in the community.

The informants who contributed to this historical investigation were raised primarily in working-class families, lived in South Louisiana's rural communities during the first half of the twentieth century, and shared common traditions. Cajun culture is a unique way of life and its peculiarities alert foreigners that they have ventured into a different world; yet, in Cajun society individuals are not altogether indistinguishable. For the purpose of this book, however, most of the informants were raised in agriculturally and environmentally based communities, most frequently on small farms, and lived a frontier-style childhood. The local economic crisis of the 1920s, the national Depression, World War II, and the advent of modernity molded the lives and personalities of the early twentieth-century Cajun women. This generation of Cajun women witnessed and participated in both unassimilated and Americanized Cajun society. Consequently, they hold the keys to the past, including culinary traditions, with their memories and continued practice of old customs. Often using food as a catalyst to bring their families together, they are role models of how future generations can survive further cultural erosion, while maintaining a distinctive cultural identity, familial unity, and a degree of social solidarity.

Until the World War II era and the modernizing effects of industrial and technological advancements, most socially insulated Cajuns of South Louisiana eked out a subsistence level of existence. Thus, their economic survival was based on subsistence farming, utilizing foodstuffs derived from the natural environment, and a communal system of interdependence. Each member of a family or larger community actively participated in some aspect of food preparation, but women undertook an integral role in almost every phase of home food production. For generations, food preparation included not only cooking, but also growing, harvesting, and slaughtering foodstuffs on small farms and supplementing the diet with wild game and seafood when available. On rural Cajun farms, almost everything consumed (except, sometimes, coffee, sugar, and flour) was homemade. Even the few store-bought items were often replaced by home-produced foodstuffs or needed further preparation before proving edible. The coffee was not always ready for consumption at the time of purchase, for many twentieth-century Cajun women bought green coffee beans, then parched and ground them at home. Flour was frequently supplemented with cornmeal ground from homegrown corn. In areas where sugarcane grew, small farmers often produced enough to provide their own syrup, and they either ground the cane at home or at the local mill. Furthermore, until modern transportation and refrigeration, the Cajun diet varied somewhat depending on the natural environment in which one lived, and Cajun women melded their culinary skills and traditions with the availability of local products. Five or ten miles might not seem like much in the motorized era, but when feet, buggies, and pirogues were the means of transportation, it made quite a difference. On land, travel was most challenging and limiting, thus a person who lived ten miles from the Mississippi River might not eat an abundance of seafood, whereas someone living on river road would benefit greatly from the fresh shrimp caught in shrimp boxes set along the river. Alternatively, people living on the prairie might expand their diet if they lived within walking distance of small canals, ponds, marshes, or woodlands areas. Some of the prairie-Cajuns consequently consumed crawfish, turtles, catfish, and waterfowl.

Although men typically farmed, trapped, hunted, and fished, some women actively participated in these activities. As for the women who focused more on in-house domestic tasks, they were involved in preparing harvested fruits, vegetables, meats, and seafood for human consumption. Everything from skinning a squirrel to plucking a duck, cleaning hog intestines before making *boudin* to gutting a fish, peeling shrimp to cleaning crabs, or even ringing the neck of a chicken and then plucking and cleaning it frequently fell under the category of domestic chores in early twentieth-century rural Cajun communities. Women also cooked most of the food served in the home for daily sustenance as well as the feasts for social events. According to Odile Hollier of Leonville, "My youngest son says he never saw my face 'til he was eighteen cause I was always at the sink or at the stove, cooking." Food played a central role in almost any family or social gathering, and as a result, the fruits of women's labor brought people together. Annie Taylor from Church Point said, "We had a long table. Everyone had a designated place and everybody sat there whether you were hungry or not." Odile Hollier commented, "That was the most beautiful thing of all." All of the elderly Cajun informants interviewed for this work confirm that meals were the centerpieces of social interaction.

Despite the different geographical regions or dietary regimens, one thing remains true: Cajun women played pivotal roles in food preparation. For example, women often grew a large portion of the food their families consumed in gardens and hen houses. Many women, especially those living in the prairie region, acquired the remainder of the household items by selling extra chicken eggs. Cajun women living on or near the waterways of South Louisiana, bartered seafood, pelts, moss, and fresh game caught by members of the family for fresh beef (which was not as prevalent outside the prairie region); any items not produced at home (for example, shoes, fabric, and sometimes soap); and occasionally for fruits and vegetables not cultivated at home (such as celery in some areas). In most small insular communities, families grew and exchanged fruits and vegetables with each other, giving everyone abundance and variety. Whatever one family lacked a relative supplied and vice versa.

Vegetables such as peas, tomatoes, and cabbage and a variety of fruits, including figs and wild blackberries, as well as potatoes and native pecans, added nutrients and diversity to the Cajun diet. Cajun women from every region canned vegetables and fruits in large quantities and saved them for use throughout the year. Edolia Dupré from Ville Platte remembers preserving over 400 quarts in one year. Viola Rider, 79, who is from Vidrine, still maintains a large garden and gives extra vegetables to her neighbors and friends. In rural prairie areas or on farms where a milk cow was available, dairy products were not bought at the local market. In many of the waterway areas, though, dairy products were more frequently purchased. Sometimes they had enough milk to drink, but were less inclined to make the additional dairy products more commonly produced at home in the Southwest prairies. Cajun women used the milk they collected for family consumption, baking, churning into butter, and making cream.

Whatever the tasks for home production were, they were not performed by one individual, but collectively by the family. Mothers and children, husbands and wives, and even entire extended families gathered to garden, cultivate a field, and harvest a crop, or set traps along the bayous, rivers, or in the woods, and process the meat and seafood together. These activities further solidified familial ties. The extended family, friends, and neighbors composed the social foundation of the Cajun community in the rural prairies. The main venues of social interaction were often organized for the specific purpose of procuring food, like working bees (a variety of group projects organized to complete a task as well as enjoy the company of friends and family, for example communal harvests). On other occasions, food was a key ingredient of the event, such as *veillées* (evening visits) and church-related activities. In the context of present-day America, the terms "social" and "work" typically represent diametrically opposed forces not to be conjoined; in Cajun communities they were intimately intertwined in institutions that were vestiges of widespread poverty and frontier life. Cajuns developed a communal system, which eliminated dependence on foreign cultures and their economic forces, promoted self-sufficiency, and solidified feelings of interdependence. This fostered harmonious relations among neighbors and allowed Cajuns to avoid cultural assimilation.

La boucherie de campagne (rural communal butcheries), collective harvesting, and *coups de main* ("helping hands") were a few of the many types of Cajun cooperatives. Cajuns living in rural South Louisianan communities participated in pork *boucheries* at each other's homes on a rotating basis. Beef *boucheries* were also a common occurrence, but more regionally specific to the prairies. Each time a family slaughtered a hog, the neighbors came over and helped. The implied promise of universal participation on butchery day was seen as part of a community workday. For pork *boucheries*, the men butchered a hog and made cracklings, whereas the women prepared sausage, *boudin*, bacon, and salted meat, which were preserved in jars of lard and were supposed to last all winter. According to Jean Brasseaux from Cankton and Marie "Ivy" Ortego from Grand Prairie, the men removed the hog's liver and brought it to the women inside. The liver was cooked first so that the men would have a hearty breakfast to sustain them during their long workday. The women then focused their energies on processing the rest of the meat and preparing lunch for all the participants. Every family left with a piece of meat, often a big roast, and a pack of *gratons* (cracklings) secure in the knowledge that when their turn came to host the *boucherie*, everyone in the community would again contribute to the communal effort. Beef *boucheries* usually were conducted on a weekly basis during the spring and summer, and each family generally received ten to fifteen pounds of meat, which was expected to last all week. These gatherings provided fresh meat year-round and served as an excuse to visit family and friends, catch up on the neighborhood gossip, tell jokes and stories, and, above all, eat fresh meat. In reference to *boucheries*, Jean Brasseaux comments, "I think they came for the food, to have a good meal." Annie Taylor said, "There was laughter and there was joking. It was just a fun day. It was a tiring day, but it was a fun day." Olga Manuel from Ville Platte enjoys the tradition so much that she organizes an annual family *boucherie* just for the camaraderie and to continue the Cajun ritual as a reminder of the old days for herself and her family's younger generations.

In the regions of South Louisiana where waterways limited the availability of grazing lands needed for cattle, seafood and wild game supplemented the protein needed in the family diet. Early twentieth-century Cajuns utilized the environment out of necessity. For example, families close enough to the gulf crabbed, along the Mississippi River family shrimp boxes were commonplace, and fresh fish and wild game caught and killed along the bayous, marshes, and swamps were welcome additions to a woman's ingredient list when she was deciding how to feed her large family.

Before the emergence of mechanized agriculture in the prairie country, small farmers often needed assistance to harvest their crops. They consequently pooled their labor supply, working on one field at a time until all of the neighborhood fields had been harvested. Gladys Hebert from Riceville, Belle Fontenot from Chataignier, and Lessie Deshotel from Vidrine, along with other farm wives, met at each others' homes, prepared hot lunches for their husbands, and then took turns taking meals to the fields. The expression *coups de main*, "helping hands" in Cajun French, describes the way a community supported anyone in a time of need. If someone was unable to harvest his crops, hoe his fields, or dig a well, his neighbors gathered and completed the task, while the woman of the house always fed the workers. No money was exchanged, for payment came later when the favor was returned in kind. A helping hand was given to anyone in need and was commonplace across regional divides, not specific to one group of Cajuns or another. If a hunter came home with a large kill such as a deer or alligator, family members and neighbors did not think twice about pitching in to skin and slaughter the animal.

After a hard day's work, families often left their home to "make a *veillée*." *Veillées*, now rapidly fading institutions among Cajuns, were informal visits during which oral traditions were preserved and perpetuated. Families and friends gathered on a neighbor's porch to visit, make homemade ice cream, and drink coffee. Olga Manuel remembers that there was always a good storyteller who told ghost stories, *defunt* tales (accounts of dead relatives), or Civil War stories about jayhawkers who raided local farmsteads. At these visits, the informants often witnessed a musical performance of some kind, including French songs accompanied by an accordion, a harmonica, or whatever was available. Annie Taylor stated, "One guy had a guitar which he couldn't play and we'd all grab our spoons, join in and sing and make our own music." Informal visits such as these were the highlights of the day. Annie Taylor recalls that, "If company came over, you just stopped what you were doing and cooked."

The connection between food, family, and religious festivities in the Cajun community is also readily evident. Sundays were reserved for God and family. The church provided a place for community involvement and an escape from the isolation of the farm or bayou. Jean Brasseaux recalled that her family would attend Mass on Sunday mornings and then eat dinner at her grandmother's home (next door to her own). The women cooked the meal, while the men visited or made a trip to her grandfather's racetrack in Mire. Her grandmother even attended Mass on Saturday so that she could have all morning on Sunday to prepare the elaborate meal. The other informants recount similar Sunday routines with some of the relatives even sleeping over on Saturday night. Pauline Langlinais and Rita Rodrigue of Vacherie remember that if they did not show up on Sunday for dinner, their parents would come and get them. Most of these women continued this practice as long as their health permitted.

Of the many celebrations linked to the ecclesiastical calendar, Christmas, Mardi Gras, and Easter foster the largest display of social interaction in Cajun communities. This was particularly important to the generations that lacked motorized transportation and felt the isolation of rural life. Religious rituals, such as Baptism, First Communion, Confirmation, weddings, and funerals, also foster familial and community relations as women prepare food for each event. For generations, these holidays served as a time for Cajuns to share religious beliefs, customs, and traditions. The matriarchy organized a large portion of these festivities; first by preparing the food, which is central to any Cajun gathering, and second by perpetuating numerous cultural and familial traditions.

Many families attend Mass as a group before returning home for a memorable celebration. Like most of the informants, Edolia Dupré remembered that for Christmas Eve, her family always decorated a tree with handmade ornaments and drank eggnog with a touch of whiskey. She also recalled that she received a small gift in her stocking. Patricia Ardoin from Mamou perpetuates a Christmas ritual that is unique to her family: she devotes a portion of the festivities to celebrate Jesus' birthday with a cake, candles, and singing.

Each year Cajuns throw one last party before entering the Lenten season of sacrifice: Mardi Gras. Participants often indulge in an excess of food, drink, and fun. Most of the informants remembered Mardi Gras horseback riders passing by and asking for a chicken, money, or supplies for the communal gumbo, which is prepared and eaten as the Fat Tuesday celebration comes to an end and the season of Lent begins. However, because most *krewes* (special groups of Mardi Gras riders) exclude women, only a few of the informants, such as Odile Hollier, actively participated and rode with the *krewe* in the *Courir de Mardi Gras* (running of the Mardi Gras). Behind the scenes, women often sewed the costumes, cooked the gumbos, and tried to keep rowdy riders in check. Utilizing the new bridges that Huey Long had built in the 1930s and traveling on the railroad system, some of the Cajuns on the west bank crossed the mighty Mississippi River and enjoyed an occasional trip to Mardi Gras in New Orleans.

Easter, like other religious holidays, provided an excuse to enjoy the religious ceremony and ensuing family celebration that followed. Because of its unique secular festivities, however, it stimulated more excitement, especially among prairie Cajuns. In addition to cooking a large meal, women gathered eggs over an extended period of time, and before the advent of commercial dyes, procured a variety of materials to decorate their eggs. Lois François from Eunice remembers gathering peach leaves to turn the eggs green, onion skins for a yellowish hue, and beets that stained the eggs a beautiful shade of burgundy. After the eggs were boiled and dyed and Easter Sunday arrived, egg hunting, *paqueing*, and feasting began. *Paqueing* remains an exclusively prairie Cajun Easter tradition. It is inextricably tied with the dependence on eggs as a primary means of monetary exchange in the prairies, thus giving them added value over and above that as a food item for human consumption. Olga Manuel explained that *paqueing* was not a casual game, but a serious competition between Cajuns of all ages. During this traditional event, family and friends take turns hitting each other's eggs until one cracks and the person with the stronger egg keeps both eggs. Viola Rider remembered, "Boy, when you broke one you didn't give it back." The competition has continued to this day with the same trickery of old, and a large potato salad or a tray of deviled eggs complements the family dinner.

These simple stories about food, family, and religion narrated by Cajun matriarchs, who nurture familial and communal relations, depict the way Cajun culture transcends through daily activities as well as the people who share in the experience. The value system comes alive as one reads about how rural South Louisiana Cajun communities rely on the land and all its bounty, on family and neighbors for work projects and social events, and on faith in God for strength and perseverance. What remains most important is that modernity and interaction between Cajuns and other cultural groups over the centuries of their existence failed to derail the trilogy of faith, family, and land as the core value system binding generations from the Cajuns' Acadian ancestors to the modern–day Americanized Cajun. Exposure has made Cajun daily life easier, and cultural absorption and adaptation, rather than assimilation, has culminated in rich blends of seasoning and culinary techniques from all regions and cultures still bearing the Cajun name. Today the environment does not dictate the diet of Cajuns within a region, nor is a family required to produce the sustenance for life at home or acquire it from nature (although they still frequently do), because modernity brought transportation, refrigeration, and new affordable products. Nonetheless, the families and communities still integrate remnants of the past traditions as subsistence farmers, trappers, hunters, fishermen, and cattle herdsmen with the benefits of modernity. As one drives down the scenic byways of South Louisiana today, truck-farming patches, small gardens, chickens, and crab and crawfish nets interspersed among the larger cane, rice, and oil fields symbol of a more commercial economy provide visible evidence that old traditions still hold firm. Better yet, venture into the homes and look inside the freezers: at the end of the summer, one will find the fresh vegetables blanched and frozen (replacing their canned counterparts) to last the winter season. After hunting season, one will find the deer-pork sausage mixed from wildlife slaughtered at home and processed at the local meat market or "The Corner Store," ducks and geese, as well as shrimp and crabs frozen in water until time to eat. The refrigerator and freezer end the regional limitations and the need for daily harvest and kills, but not the joy of the hunt, the fishing trip, or the garden and certainly not the love of fresh homegrown produce and livestock.

Cajun women maintain an emphasis on family cohesiveness with weekly Sunday dinners and larger event-oriented celebrations. They continue making homemade food products by choice, as a gift of love, insisting that there is no other way to cook correctly. Olga Manuel stated, "I am a stickler for the old-fashioned way. Don't give me a recipe that has a can of cream of mushroom soup and a can of Rotel tomatoes. That pisses me off!" Cajun women are very passionate about their cooking, and each woman has her own style. Olga Manuel frankly concedes that, "We all know our cooking is the best, we argue points of putting in there. [For instance], I don't like bay leaves, and I tell others it doesn't help." Cajun women are easily insulted when someone interferes with the preparation of a special recipe, or if a guest does not eat a hearty serving of each entrée. Edolia Dupré scolded, "I believe that the food we were cookin' in those days were much better for our kids than all those junks the kids are eatin' today." By continuing the emphasis on social gatherings and old culinary methods once necessary for survival on the farm and for sanity in lonely and somber environments, Cajun matriarchs bridge the gap between past traditions of frontier unassimilated Cajun life on Louisiana's prairies with the Americanized generations of Cajuns. In Cajun culture coffee is served by the *demitasse*, half-cup, because of its strong and rich flavor. As the *demitasse* portrays the potency of the coffee in Southwest Louisiana, Cajun women now epitomize the fervent spirit so representative of Cajun culture.

Acadian to Cajun in Brief

ACADIAN (in French: **Acadien** *m.*, **Acadienne** *f.*): a distinct ethnic group formed in the land of Acadia or Acadie (Canada), now known as Nova Scotia. The origin of the people called Acadians began when the first French settlers also known as *"engagés"*[1] (indentured servants "engaged" to resettle in Acadia) arrived on the Acadian coast in 1604. Acadians primarily trace their heritage to French Catholic ancestors of the peasant class. The ethnic characteristics ascribed to Acadians were cultivated over generations, as these people learned to live off the land, with the social support of family, and their faith in God. They increasingly fought assimilation and valued isolation, which fostered an even stronger sense of familial and communal interdependence.

GRAND DÉRANGEMENT: the Acadian Diaspora. The following quote best depicts what happened when the Acadians experienced the *Grand Dérangement*: "During the fall season of the year 1755, just at the onset of the great French and Indian War, a group of French-speaking Roman Catholic pastoralist/fishermen-trappers, some 6,000-8,000 in all, fell victim to British geopolitical strategy and military tactics."[2]

For over a hundred years, the Acadians had settled and developed their own unique way of life in Acadia. This group frequently came under attack by two dominant empirical regimes: the French and the British, who fought frequently and for generations over territory, including Acadia. The Acadians were not eager to choose sides in this bitter struggle, and as the pattern will prove, they only wanted to live their lives in peace and isolation. After the 1713 Treaty of Utrecht was signed, ending Queen Anne's War, Acadia became a British colony and the Acadians British colonials. The Acadians were then offered the option to either sign an oath of loyalty to Great Britain or to leave. In 1730, they finally agreed to sign the oath if it stated their neutrality. The British never included such a clause and the uneasy relations between British military leaders and Acadians continued.

In 1744, France and England engaged themselves in yet another battle: King George's war, which would threaten the Acadians' newly found peace. The British never trusted the Acadians and vice versa. Furthermore, as the British and French geared up for another imminent war (the French and Indian/Seven Years War), the British grew impatient, and the strategic location of Acadia made it premium value. Finally, a new British governor, Charles Lawrence, whose disdain for the Acadians was unequaled,

---

[1] James H. Dormon, *The People Called Cajuns: An Introduction to an Ethnohistory*, (Lafayette, LA: Center for Louisiana Studies, 1983), 8.

[2] Ibid, 7.

demanded that the Acadians sign an unconditional oath of loyalty or face deportment and loss of their land. "As expected and desired by Lawrence, the Acadians rejected the oath; the inevitable resulted: properties were confiscated, families were scattered, and the unhappy Acadians were loaded on ships destined for exile in the British colonies. Thus began the painful Acadian odyssey which historians refer to as the Grand Dérangement."[3] The Acadians were subsequently captured, separated by gender and age, and loaded onto ships, which brought them to the British colonies, and to France and England. This systematic attempt to expel them from their homeland continued for many years and was very successful. Yet, many escaped the grasp of English hands and abandoned theirs homes, opting for the refuge of the forests and other safer lands. The British's sole purpose was to confiscate the Acadian land and break the unity of this cultural group. For the most part, they succeeded in confiscating the land of Acadia, but could not conquer the Acadian spirit. The Acadians who survived the horrors of the ship ride were not welcome in many of the places in which they were deposited. Some attempted, often futilely, to return to their homeland, others ventured south to Saint-Domingue, in the French West Indies, and the greatest majority eventually sought refuge in the vast territory of Louisiana.

CAJUN (in French: **Cadien** *m.*, **Cadienne** *f.*): an ethnic group primarily composed of Acadian descendents or people having Acadian lineage, which has since been mixed with that of Germans, Spanish, Anglo-Americans, Irish, Scots, and French Creoles (an elite, distinct colonial group who were descendents of France and who helped establish Louisiana alongside Iberville and Bienville in 1699).[4] Although Acadians attempted social insularity, intermarriage and other avenues of cultural exchange did occur, often because of geographical proximity, and the Acadians frequently borrowed from other cultures without ceding their own heritage. For example "The emergence of gumbo in the Acadian culinary repertoire represented a new departure in Acadian cuisine, for it reflected the melding of cooking techniques developed by Franco-American, Indian, and African cultures."[5] The new culture that emerged from the blending of Acadians

---

[3] Jacqueline K. Voorhies, "The Acadians: The Search for the Promised Land," in *The Cajuns: Essays on Their History and Culture*, ed. Glenn R. Conrad, University of Southwestern Louisiana History Series, no. 11(Lafayette, LA: Center for Louisiana Studies, 1983), 82.

[4] Barry Jean Ancelet, Jay D. Edwards, and Glen Pitre, *Cajun Country*, ed. Jackson Montell (Jackson, MS: University Press of Mississippi, 1991), xvi.

[5] Carl A. Brasseaux, *The Foundings of New Acadia: The Beginnings of Acadian Life in Louisiana*, 1763-1803, (Baton Rouge, LA: Louisiana State University Press, 1987), 134.

with other ethnic groups came to be called Cajun (*Cadien*).

Acadians who ventured to Louisiana after the French and Indian War concluded in 1763, primarily to the southernmost parts of colonial Louisiana, built their communities with a premise of total isolation using the land, God, and family to keep them at or above a subsistence level of existence. This core value system and the social insularity that was partially self-imposed allowed the Acadians to avoid cultural assimilation. They adjusted to their new land and their new neighbors, and over generations evolved into a new, yet closely related ethnic group called Cajuns. When traveling across Acadia (Nova Scotia), one can observe that the names on the mailboxes, such as Arceneaux, Broussard, and Hébert among many others, mirror those found today in South Louisiana.

Cajuns did not truly suffer cultural assimilation until the twentieth century. Outside influences, such as mandatory education, the "Great Depression," World War II, modernization, and industrialization of the South facilitated the Americanization and penetration into Cajun culture. Cajuns have always battled with social and cultural changes that have threatened the cohesion of their society, but the transportation, industrial, and technological revolutions have made isolated territories that allowed for self-sufficient communities fading memories. But even if subsistence farming has lost out to commercial interests and French has been largely replaced by English, the emphasis on the traditional trinity of land, family, and faith has remained the cornerstone of Cajun cohesion and the perpetuation of a distinct cultural identity.

A Guide for Non-Cajuns

WHAT IS BOUDIN? *Boudin* today is made out of an artificial casing that is stuffed with ground pork, rice, and seasoning; what and how much depends on the local butcher. For instance some use a little liver as additional flavoring and others abhor the use of it in *boudin*. Then the *boudin* is boiled until cooked and the links are removed from the water and let cool a little so that they can be cut into pieces without the skin falling apart. *Boudin* is usually served warm. *Boudin*, as cooked in olden days, was made by using cleaned hog intestines as the casing and stuffing it with the pork and rice mixture. Cajuns made both *boudin blanc* and *boudin* rouge. *Boudin* blanc was made as previously noted, while *boudin rouge* included blood in the mixture thus the name that translates into red *boudin*.

HOW TO EAT BOUDIN? It can be eaten as a snack or a meal. To serve, cut into bite-sized slices or 3-inch links. As a meal, the average person eats a 1/2 pound of *boudin*. As an appetizer serve as slices with toothpicks or in links as a finger food.

WHAT ARE GRATONS? They are cracklings: fried pork skins that include a layer of fat and often times a small layer of meat as well. They are a good snack or appetizer and go well with *boudin*.

WHAT IS BOUILLIE? A homemade vanilla custard that makes a great pie filling for sweet dough pies, not to be confused with *bouilli*, which is a spicy stew made out of internal organs.

WHAT IS SAD CAKE? The reason Sad Cake is called Sad Cake is because when it is cooking the cake swells up and before it is finished baking it falls in the center and looks like a sad cake. According to Mrs. Gerri Brunet it doesn't look like much, but it tastes good.

WHAT IS MAKING THE VEILLÉE? This is having an evening visit with friends or family. *Veillées* originated long ago as a social custom. After a hard day's work, families often left their homes to "make the *veillée*."

WHAT IS A BOUCHERIE? It means communal butchery. *Boucheries* were once held as a necessary social activity in which neighbors and families gathered to slaughter one or more hogs or calves. They rotated turns to host the event and the meat was shared amongst the group. Nothing was wasted at these local butcheries. For instance the head of a hog was made into hog's head cheese, the intestines were used to make casing for the *boudin*, the stomach was used for *panse* or *chaudin*, and the skin and some fat was made into *gratons* or cracklings, while the rest of the fat was collected and made into hog lard. The meat was used to make sausage and pork stuffing, roasts, and chops.

WHAT IS HOT FAT? It was usually used to refer to the hog lard that was rendered from the hog at the local *boucherie*. The lard was used to preserve sausage and as the oil for frying foods and for making gravies and roux. Now people more frequently choose cooking oil as it is less fattening and better for your cholesterol level, but hog lard is still in circulation. You can find it at local meat markets and at local *boucheries*, which are still sometimes practiced more out of social tradition than a real necessity.

WHAT IS SAUSAGE? It is made by stuffing chopped pork meat and seasoning into a casing and cooking it. Every local community has a special meat market and some-times more than one. Each family has a favorite meat market and is a loyal customer.

WHAT IS GREEN SAUSAGE? Depending on the local area or family in which you grew up, you eat either smoked sausage or fresh sausage. When refrigeration was not an option, people often chose to smoke their sausage so that it would last longer. Sausage was also preserved in crock jars by covering it with hog lard. Green sausage is the name frequently used for unsmoked or fresh sausage by people who prefer smoked sausage. People who eat green sausage often call it fresh sausage, not green sausage. Entire local communities usually have a distinct preference for one or the other.

WHAT IS TASSO? It is the name commonly used to refer to a piece of smoked beef or pork meat. Tasso adds flavor and seasoning to any gravy, sauce, stew, or gumbo.

HOW TO COOK TASSO AND SAUSAGE? One easy way to cook smoked sausage and tasso is to fry them in a little oil in a Magnelite aluminum alloy pot, a cast iron pot, or an old black iron pot. Cut the sausage into 2 to 3 inch links and the tasso into 2 to 3 inch cubes. Place the pieces in the pot with some oil and season the meat. Brown the sausage and tasso on all sides. Then cover the meat with water and contin-ue cooking on a medium heat for another thirty minutes until the water cooks down to about 1 to 2 inches high in the pot. Add corn starch or flour to thicken the water and make a gravy. Serve over rice with a side of vegetables. Sausage is sometimes cooked in a gumbo or barbecued.

WHAT IS THE DIFFERENCE BETWEEN PANSE AND CHAUDIN?

Stuffed *Panse* is a stuffed pork stomach, also know as *Chaudin* in different locals. In some areas such as Vidrine it is called Stuffed *Panse* and in other places it is called *Chaudin*. The words are can be used interchangeably.

WHAT ARE TOES OF GARLIC? They are the same thing as cloves of garlic: the little individual pieces of garlic that you break off of the head/cluster of garlic.

HOW TO SMOTHER OKRA?

1 tablespoon oil
1 small to medium-sized onion, chopped
2 1/2 to 3 cups sliced fresh okra (because the okra will cook down you need to
*   start with a little bit more)*
1 whole tomato, cooked
salt and pepper to taste

Heat the oil in a pan. Sauté the onions until transparent and turning a light golden brown, but do not scorch or burn them or they will produce a strange sweet, burnt taste that ruins the mess/batch of okra. Add okra and tomato and season to taste. Cover and simmer for about 30 minutes. Watch it closely so that the okra does not burn or you will end up with the same result as scorching the onions. If you scorch okra, you will end up having to start over. You may have to add a little water intermittently and stir often so that it does not stick too much. The okra should cook down and become soft and velvety. Smothered okra cooks down in the same way that smothered potatoes do.

WHAT ARE ROTEL TOMATOES? Rotel tomatoes are a brand of canned tomatoes that have spices and green chili peppers mixed in with the diced tomatoes. Now with the convenience of grocery stores, Rotel tomatoes are sometimes used in place of homemade canned and seasoned tomatoes.

WHAT IS GUMBO FILÉ? Gumbo filé is made of sassafras leaves and spices, which is <u>sometimes</u> used as an additional seasoning placed in <u>either</u> a pot of gumbo while it is cooking <u>or</u> an individual bowl of gumbo while it is being served. The when and how once again depends on the region, the community, the family, and/or the individual.

WHAT ARE TRAITEURS AND HOME REMEDIES? Until modern medicine became affordable and more accessible in Cajun country, Cajun women employed home remedies handed down from their mothers, and other female relatives, and *traiteurs*,[1] only calling on doctors in mortal situations.[2] Dorothy Bryant remembers using kerosene and spider webs to heal open wounds.[3] When Odile Hollier returned home from a sleepover with lice, she lost her place in the house and was forced to sit outside in the sun with a "B" brand insect powder and Black Diamond tobacco salve in her hair. This was only one of her mother's many homemade concoctions.[4] In early twentieth-century rural prairie Cajun society *traiteurs* were important and many were women. For instance, when Pauline Langlinais was young, she fell on a water trough, cut her leg, and then played in the potato garden infecting the wound with mud. In lieu of modern-day antibiotics, Langlinais was treated by a female *traiteur*, who removed a piece of bone from her leg and applied a salve that burned the infected area. The demand for the healing powers of *traiteurs* and midwives (once used almost exclusively for birthing) has declined as a result of licensed practitioners, but they have not completely disappeared.[5] Probably the strongest evidence of this exists in the fact that Pauline Langlinais and Claire Bonin, two of the informants in this sampling of Cajun women, are practicing *traiteurs*.[6]

---

[1] A *traiteur* is a non-medical healer. Jules O. Daigle, *A Dictionary of the Cajun Language*, (Ann Arbor, Michigan, Edwards Brothers, 1984), p. 158, s.v. *traiteur*.

[2] Barry Jean Ancelet, Jay D. Edwards, and Glen Pitre, *Cajun Country*, ed. Jackson Montell, (Jackson, MS: University Press of Mississippi, 1991), pp. 95-100.

[3] Dorothy Mae Louviere Bryant, interview by author, tape recording, Lake Charles, Louisiana, 26 February 1998.

[4] Odile Doré Hollier, interview by author, tape recording, Vidrine, Louisiana, 4 June 1998.

[5] Patricia K. Rickels, "The Folklore of Sacraments and Sacramentals in South Louisiana," in *The Cajuns: Essays on Their History and Culture*, edited by Glenn R. Conrad, University of Southwestern Louisiana History Series, (Lafayette, LA: Center for Louisiana Studies, 1983), p. 42.

[6] Pauline Marie Bernard Langlinais, interview by author, tape recording, Broussard, Louisiana, 30 June 1998; and Claire Pauline Bernard Bonin, interview by author, tape recording, Broussard, Louisiana, 30 June 1998.

A Veillée at Grandma's

Ella Mae Fontenot, one of the Cajun women who contributed to this historical cookbook, has a granddaughter who wrote the following essay for a young author's contest when she was only sixteen. Alicia Lori Fontenot, Ella Mae's granddaughter and a collaborator of this cookbook, believed in what she wrote as a high school student. The essay went on to garner a Louisiana state young author's award in her age group. Now she wants to help spread the message of how Cajun culture is transferred from one generation to the next over the course of a woman's lifetime, not in some single lesson or school. Here is what she wrote long before the cookbook was planned and written. You can see what she discovered in her writing then and, after reviewing the cookbook, how it is written with the same thoughts in mind.

A VEILLÉE AT GRANDMA'S

My grandmother is a very strong and assertive woman, but when she is around her grandchildren, she is as gentle and kind as a summer's breeze on a warm face. I am the youngest of twelve grandchildren. She still thinks of me as her baby. She spoils me with food, hugs, and love. Even though I'm almost 17, I still try to sleep at her house as often as possible. Each time I go back to my grandmother's house I am reminded of all the times I had spent there when I was little.

I've spent most of my childhood in my grandmother's house. I slept at her house at least once a week. All of her rooms are cluttered with memories of the past: pictures of her departed husband, her mother, and her ten sisters and brothers. I used to look through the old pictures, trying to get an image of all the times that I was too young to remember.

When I was through with the pictures, I knew where to go for the toys—straight to the back of the hall in the linen closet. There was a xylophone that made lots of noise, a miniature tree house with Tigger and Pooh inside, and a little doll that was so ugly, tattered, and torn that it was cute. Those toys didn't last for long. Children get bored so easily.

The only thing that could hold my attention was playing cards with my grandmother. We'd play spades, casino, and gin rummy while watching *Wheel of Fortune*. We'd talk about what was going on in the family—weddings, babies, and those kinds of exciting events. I'd ask her questions about the past: "What was paw paw like?" "What did you do during the war?" and "How old were you when you got married?"

One question that would never escape her was, "Do you have anything to eat?" For most Cajuns, food is the way to the heart, and I am no different. I would sit on her counter watching her make homemade cinnamon rolls, bake a roast, or cook another one of her specialties.

Without even knowing it, my grandmother was showing me just a few aspects of my Cajun culture. In my visits, I have learned to have fun, cook, and give and receive love. Just imagine. All I thought I was doing was making the *veillée* (nighttime visit) with grandma.

Alicia Fontenot

Appetizers
and Drinks

Recipe For Happiness

2 heaping cups of patience
1 heartful of love
2 handfuls of generosity
1 headful of understanding
dash of laughter

Sprinkle generously with kindness. Add plenty of
faith and hope. Mix well. Spread over a period of a
lifetime. Serve generously to everyone you meet.

Velma Reaux

I Remember...

"when we raised chickens.
When someone would
come to buy a chicken, we
had to throw feed in the
pen and all the chickens
would come. Then the lady
would point out which
chicken she wanted and
we [the children] had to
catch it. We had to throw
ourselves forward and
catch them by the legs,
but I was pretty quick.
That was a funny sight."

Eva Mae Poirrier

Trail Mix

2 cups Chex cereal
1/4 cup raisins
1/4 cup dry roasted peanuts

Mix cereal, raisins, and peanuts in bowl.

Serves 4.
Verna Amedee

I Remember...

"One time, I went to see one of my daughters; one lives in Baton Rouge. I say, 'I'm sorry I couldn't give more when you were small.' Course I had less than naught but she say 'Mom you gave us plenty. You gave us an education; nobody can take that away from us.' She say, 'I don't know how you and daddy did. You can send eight children to school and live.' Well we stayed home. That's why we send them to school. We stayed home yeah, and they went to school. And [my husband] always told me, he say, 'I hope and pray that my children can graduate, and they don't have to work hard like me.'"

Henriette Richard

Cheese Hots

1 package (4 ounces) sharp cheese (New York)
1 stick butter
salt to taste
black pepper to taste
1/2 teaspoon red pepper or more if desired
3 or 4 dashes hot sauce (preferably Tabasco)
1 cup flour
1 cup crisp rice cereal (preferably Kellogg's Rice
   Krispies)

Preheat oven to 325 degrees. Grate cheese and mix
well with butter. Add salt, black pepper, red pepper,
hot sauce, and flour. Mix well. Add crisp rice cereal.
Mix well. Shape into 1-inch balls, and place on
ungreased cookie sheet. Bake in oven for 3 minutes. These keep well and are very good for enter-
taining.

Serves 8.
Rose Fontenot

I Remember...

living on a plantation after
I got married. We had a
big freezer; the men would
kill the hogs and put meat
in there. Before that, you
had to cook all your meat
and put it in a big Crock-
Pot and put grease on top,
so it wouldn't spoil.

Aimie Bergeron

Old-Fashioned Dip

I Remember...

when I was five my mother passed away and by the age of 10 my father could no longer afford to send me to school. I then moved in with my aunt and uncle who had no children of their own and they finished raising me. I managed to complete eight years of school.

Marie "Ivy" Ortego

1 container (8 ounces) cream cheese
  (room temperature)
1 package (8 ounces) American cheese
  (room temperature; preferably Velveeta)
1 container (8 ounces) sour cream
1 package (1 ounce) fried onion dip
1 teaspoon garlic juice
1 teaspoon onion juice
1 teaspoon yellow mustard
mayonnaise (as desired)
3 dill pickles, chopped
3 sweet pickles, chopped
1 jar (4 ounces) pimientos

Mix cream cheese, cheddar cheese, sour cream, onion dip, garlic juice, onion juice, and mustard. Add mayonnaise as desired until soggy. Mix in mixer until real creamy. Then add chopped dill pickles, sweet pickles, and pimientos to mixture and beat again a little. Chill and serve with chips or crackers. I learned this recipe from Phelma Brunet.

Serves 10 to 12.
Elva Ardoin

Chicken Dip

1 can (10 ounces) white chicken
  (preferably Swanson)
1 tablespoon instant diced onions
1 tablespoon bacon bits
1 tablespoon parsley flakes
6 tablespoons mayonnaise

Mix chicken, onions, bacon bits, parsley flakes, and mayonnaise. Stir well. Add more mayonnaise if needed, until mixture is soggy. Chill and serve with crackers, preferably Ritz. I learned this recipe from a friend, Gwen.

Serves 4 to 6.
Elva Ardoin

I Remember...

when my dad wanted to learn how to drive after he bought his first car but "...he never drove, never. He went to get a driver's, he wanted to get a permit, that's what he wanted and they told him they couldn't give him a permit at his age, that he had to get a driver's license. So he told the lady, 'if I can't get a permit to learn how to drive,' he said, 'I don't want it.' ... And he never drove, but he could raise the hood of the car and he could tell you everything that was wrong with the car."

Pauline Guidry

Shrimp Dip I

1 small to medium onion
2 cloves garlic
2 pounds shrimp, boiled and peeled
1 package (8 ounces) cream cheese (preferably Philadelphia)
1 small can (5 ounces) evaporated milk
1 cup mayonnaise
salt to taste
black pepper to taste
red pepper to taste
crackers (for serving)

Grind or finely chop onion, garlic, and shrimp. In a separate bowl mix cream cheese and milk until soft. Add mayonnaise, onions, garlic, and shrimp to the cream cheese and milk mixture and blend well. Season with salt, black pepper, and red pepper to your taste. Hint: If too thick add more mayonnaise until it makes the right consistency. Mix well, pour into serving dish, and chill. Best if prepared 8 hours before serving. You can serve this with appetizer–style crackers.

Serves 8 to 10.
Pauline Langlinais

I Remember...

when my future husband went to ask for my hand in marriage, "he was holding his straw hat and was so nervous he made a hole in it by the time he asked." Everyone laughed, my parents approved the match, and the marriage followed shortly thereafter.

Pauline Langlinais

Shrimp Dip II

1 package (8 ounces) cream cheese
1/2 onion, grated
1 cup mayonnaise
2 small cans (9 to 12 ounces total) shrimp
salt to taste
red pepper to taste

Mix cream cheese, onions, and mayonnaise well.
Gently fold in shrimp until you reach the desired
consistency. Season with salt and red pepper and
stir one last time. Keep refrigerated until ready to
serve. Serve with your favorite crackers.

Serves 8.
Alzena Miller

I Remember...

when I first started dating
my husband. "Aw well, we
were about 19, I guess. But
the thing is, no, but we
didn't visit each other;
there were no cars. He
didn't have a car. We didn't
have a telephone, you
know, to phone, or any-
thing. Well when we were
dating, we also wrote, cor-
responding, you imagine,
two miles apart. ... And the
mailman, sometimes I was
visiting a friend who lived
in the other lane over
there, then he would stop
over there and he knew us,
... when he passed and
he'd say, oh he said, 'I
brought a letter to your
house,' so then I was anxious to get back."

Helen Gravois

Shrimp Dip III

2 tablespoons lemon juice
1 container (8 ounces) sour cream
1 container (8 ounces) cream cheese
1 packet (.6 ounces) dry Italian dressing mix
1 can (4½ ounces) small shrimp, washed and
*   drained*

Mix lemon juice, sour cream, cream cheese, and
dressing mix until smooth. Gently stir in shrimp.
Refrigerate at least 3 hours before serving. I learned
this recipe from Hazel Deshotel.

Serves 4 to 6.
Elva Ardoin

I Remember...

"I was born in the house I
now live in. When I mar-
ried Thomas, we moved
into a small house for a
short time. When my dad
died, Thomas and I pur-
chased his house and I had
six children in the house. I
would have the doctor and
a midwife to assist with
the births. When I had a
baby, I would stay in the
house for nine weeks. My
husband would make a
ramp at the back door
when I was able to go
outside so I would have an
easier time walking down
to go outside."

Gertrude Stutes

Low-Calorie Shrimp Salad

8 ounces cottage cheese, with curd
1 pound shrimp, boiled, deveined, and chopped
2 eggs, boiled
$1/2$ cup chopped stuffed olives
salt to taste
black pepper to taste
red pepper to taste
paprika to taste
1 large tomato, sliced

Mix together cottage cheese and chopped shrimp. Peel eggs and mash until fine. Mix with cottage cheese and shrimp. Add olives. Season with salt, black pepper, and red pepper. Sprinkle with paprika for color. Arrange sliced tomato over top of shrimp mixture. Serve with crackers. (Great for a diet. Olives could be omitted, if desired.)

Serves 6.
Dorothy Bryant

I Remember...

asking for permission to marry. "Oh my God that was not funny. In those days we'd get so embarrassed for things like that, and today, I guess it's not more than chewing a gum."

Edolia Dupré

Shrimp Mold I

1 can (10³/₄ ounces) cream of mushroom soup
1 small onion, chopped
¹/₄ to ¹/₂ cup chopped celery
2 packets (.5 ounces total) unflavored gelatin
   (preferably Knox)
1 cup mayonnaise
2 tablespoons lemon juice
2 tablespoons Worcestershire sauce
1 or 2 tablespoons hot sauce (preferably Tabasco)
2 cups boiled shrimp

Simmer cream of mushroom soup, onion, and celery for 10 minutes. Dissolve gelatin in ¹/₄ cup water and add to soup mixture. Mix well. Add mayonnaise, lemon juice, Worcestershire sauce, and hot sauce. Let cool. Mash shrimp. Mix with sauce. Pour in well-greased mold and chill. I learned to make shrimp mold from my daughter, Gina Fontenot, who now lives with her family in Ville Platte, Louisiana.

Serves 8 to 10.
Etheleen Meaux

I Remember...

that at around 14 or 15 years old, I started working out of the house to help the family finances. One of my jobs was assisting Mr. and Mrs. Doucet with their new baby. One day while running an errand with Mr. Doucet, I met the man I would eventually marry. Mr. Doucet and I stopped in at Club Rendez-Vous for a coke, where Abbie Fontenot worked as a bartender. Although he was some seven years my senior, Abbie immediately noticed me and commented to a friend, "I wouldn't mind that girl putting her shoes under my bed."

Ella Mae Fontenot

Shrimp Mold II

¹/₂ cup chopped onions
1 can (10³/₄ ounces) tomato soup
1 bar (8 ounces) cream cheese
2 pounds shrimp, cleaned, deveined, and chopped
¹/₂ cup chopped celery
1 cup mayonnaise
salt to taste
black pepper to taste
red pepper to taste
2 packets (.5 ounces) Knox gelatin
1 box crackers (Ritz or Townhouse Classic)

Sauté onions, drain, and set aside. Put the tomato soup, cream cheese, and ¹/₂ soup can of water in a pot and cook on medium heat until dissolved. Then add onions, shrimp, celery, and mayonnaise. Season with salt, black pepper, and red pepper. Mix well. Dissolve the gelatin in ¹/₄ cup of water, and pour into the above mixture. Stir ingredients one last time, then pour into your mold and refrigerate. I recommend serving with crackers. This recipe was given to me by my daughter-in-law, Lois. She makes this around the holidays and feast days. They all go crazy over this and really enjoy it.

Serves 10 to 12.
Claire Bonin

I Remember...

"My grandmother used to tell us the story about the first time she saw a car. And she says, 'The chickens was wild. They would run all over and the horses would get so upset.' Just picture that. Try to visualize a car if you've never seen one before. Something moving like that you know, without nothing pulling it. And then we spoke about the airplane and I said, 'How did you feel the first time you saw an airplane?' Well it was just a simple plane then. 'How could it stay up there?' she'd say."

Anne Gros

Shrimp Mold III

3 pounds small shrimp, boiled and chopped
6 ounces cream cheese
³/4 cup chopped green onion tops
1 cup mayonnaise
salt to taste
black pepper to taste
red pepper to taste
hot sauce to taste (preferably Tabasco)

Mix shrimp, cream cheese, onion tops, and mayonnaise. Season with salt, black pepper, red pepper, and hot sauce. Pour into shrimp mold container and refrigerate until the next day.

Serves 6 to 8 with crackers.
Dorothy Bryant

I Remember...

having an outhouse with two holes in the ground that served as a bathroom facility. My sister and I spent time sitting on the commode looking at the Sears wish-book catalog, which often doubled as toilet paper. Ironically, I eventually worked as a sales clerk and then manager at Sears & Roebuck in Ville Platte until I retired. "Can you imagine hot like it was, the Sears wish-book catalog." Sometimes I would try to get out of doing dishes after dinner and I would go to the outhouse and look at the wish-book.

Rose Fontenot

Shrimp Cocktail Sauce

1 cup bottled chili sauce
2 to 4 tablespoons prepared horseradish sauce
3 teaspoons Worcestershire sauce
1 tablespoon vinegar
2/3 cup ketchup
3 tablespoons lemon juice
1/2 teaspoon salt
1 tablespoon grated fresh onion
red pepper to taste
1/2 teaspoon garlic powder
1 dash hot sauce (preferably Tabasco)

Combine chili sauce, horse radish, Worcestershire sauce, vinegar, ketchup, lemon juice, and salt. Add onion, red pepper, garlic powder, and hot sauce. Mix well. (This recipe can be altered by omitting onion, red pepper, garlic powder and hot sauce and adding 1/2 cup crushed pineapple with juice and enough sugar to get a sweet and sour taste.)

Serves 4.
Dorothy Bryant

I Remember...

when Morgan, who at the time was my boyfriend and later became my husband, requested permission to marry me. My mother knew that he was going to ask for my hand in marriage, but she still dropped the bowl that she was drying when he broached the subject after dinner.

Dorothy Bryant

Sauce for Crawfish Boil

¹/₂ cup tomato catsup
1 teaspoon prepared mustard
1 teaspoon prepared horseradish
2 teaspoons Worcestershire sauce

Mix together catsup, mustard, horseradish, and Worcestershire sauce well. Chill until ready to serve. Very good to dip clean crawfish tails in.

Serves 6 to 8.
Rose Fontenot

I Remember...

speaking French when I was young, learning my prayers in French, and learning English at school. I have continued to practice my French when conversing with older friends, my parents (until they passed away), and my children. Unlike many Cajuns who suffered from anti-French rules at school and were made to feel ashamed of their language, I spoke both French and English with my children. I had some relatives that couldn't speak English and by teaching my children English, I protected them from persecution. "I wanted them to know English before they started school."

Versie Meche

Sweet and Sour Sauce

1 jar (16 ounces) barbecue sauce (preferably Jack
    Miller's)
1 cup honey
1 can (10³/4 ounces) cream of mushroom soup

Mix barbecue sauce, honey, and cream of mushroom soup together well.

Makes 4 cups.
Joyce Brasseux

Tartar Sauce

2 to 4 heaping tablespoons mayonnaise
touch of mustard
dab of ketchup
$1/8$ onion, chopped
1 teaspoon relish
salt to taste
pepper to taste
1 teaspoon Worcestershire sauce

Mix mayonnaise, mustard, ketchup, onion, relish, salt, pepper, and Worcestershire sauce. Use for dipping.

Serves 8.
Regina Fontenot

I Remember...

"That's one thing I regret is not having an education. I regret that till today. But my kids educated me. I went out into the world with them. I did step by step with them. I was mother spoil. Everything they had, we were there. Every game they played, we were there. Anyhow I had dirty dishes in my sink, it didn't bother me. My kids came first. And I went all over the world with them playing football. I was with the richest people they had and the poorest people they had and it didn't make them any different and it didn't make me any difference. Because I never, this is the way I thought of myself, you know how some people lower themselves, they never say something good about themselves, well not me. I always said something good about myself. This is my level. I'm not there. I'm here. Pride."

Rita Rodrigue

Ham Ball

1 pound ground ham
1 package (8 ounces) cream cheese
2 packets (1.2 ounces total) Italian salad dressing
  mix
1 tablespoon fresh parsley
³/₄ to 1 cup mayonnaise
³/₄ to 1 cup chopped pecans

Mix ham, cream cheese, dressing mix, and parsley.
Gradually add mayonnaise until you reach a semi-
soft ball consistency. Put in icebox over night until
firm. Then put pecans around ball as a coating.
Place back in icebox until ready to use it.

Makes 1 large ball or 2 small balls.
Belle Fontenot

I Remember...

when I used to clean
houses. I often washed the
ceiling with dirty water
falling back on me, and
once the ceilings were
clean, I dusted. Finally all
the grime that fell from
the ceiling, dust that drift-
ed from the furniture and
walls, and dirt carried in
from outside commingled
on the wooden floors. The
task of cleaning the floors
was fourfold: take ashes
from fireplace and mix
with water to make a lye
and scrub the floors with
that, "and it was strong."
Then brush it, rinse it, and
dry it. "I'm telling you, we
had a tough life. ... I had to go to work. My momma and
daddy wouldn't give me nothing at that time and I was I
didn't even finish school." One time I was cleaning underneath a house and found a quarter. I immediately brought
it to the lady of the house. The lady I was cleaning for
paid me with the same quarter I had found.

Verna Amedee

Boudin

2 pork butts (25 to 30 pounds total)
1 pound pork liver
2 yellow onions, diced
1 bell pepper, diced
3 bunches onion tops, chopped
¹/₂ cup chopped parsley
1 case sausage casing
salt to taste
black pepper to taste
white pepper to taste
red pepper to taste
5 cups cooked white rice

In a stockpot, cook pork butts and liver with just enough water to cover on low to medium heat until tender. Reserve liquid.

Cook onions, bell peppers, onion tops, and parsley in approximately ¹/₄ cup of the reserved liquid. Soak sausage casings in water to remove the pre-serving salt. Grind pork butts and liver and place in a large mixing bowl. Add cooked vegetables with their liquid. Season with salt, black pepper, white pepper, and red pepper. Add small amounts of the reserved liquid, as needed, to keep the mixture moist. Add rice and mix thoroughly.

Clean sausage casings by allowing the water they have been soaking in to pass through the inside of the casing. Stuff casings with the sausage mixture. Return the links to the stock and cook for 5 to 10 minutes on medium heat. Remove and serve.

Makes about 30 pounds.
Evon Melancon

I Remember...

picking cotton with my family and friends, and singing the entire time, while we raced to see who could pick the most. The work was tiresome, but "it was fun."

Joyce Brasseux

Cooking With Cajun Women

Pork Cracklings

2 cups oil
2 pounds pork fat, cut up
salt to taste
black pepper to taste

In a deep pot, heat oil to a medium heat. Cut pork fat into 1-inch cubes. Put pieces in the pot and stir often. (Let cook for a good while.) When the cracklings are cooked they will float. When they are floating, they will brown. Take them out after they turn golden brown. Put a little salt and black pepper on them.

Serves 8 to 10.
Blanche Quebedeaux

I Remember...

"Oh my goodness..." At *boucheries*, the hogs were slaughtered in the winter and beef *boucheries* occurred in the summer. I considered the event both a party and a time of work. My husband remembers putting the hog in a barrel of boiling water in order to take the hair out of the pigskin, which would later be fried to make cracklings. I recall that the ladies cleaned out the intestine and stomach and made the stuffing for both. Women also cooked dressing, backbone stew, ribs, pork roast, and cracklings for the entire crew. At days end each family left with a five to ten pound pork roast and maybe even some '*tit salé*, sausage, or cracklings. Nothing was wasted at the local pork *boucheries*; the greasy scraps were mixed with lye to make the soap that was used to wash clothes, bathe, and wash hair. We were also one of 24 families that participated in weekly beef *boucheries* during the summer.

Belle Fontenot

Party Sausage

5 pounds sausage, cut bite size
1 box (1 pound) brown sugar
8 ounces pineapple juice
1 small can (8 ounces) crushed pineapple (optional)

Preheat oven to 375 degrees. Put sausage in a large roaster and set aside. Dissolve sugar in the pineapple juice and pour over sausage in the large roaster. You may add pineapples. Bake sausage uncovered about 1¹/2 hours. Stir sausage about every half hour.

When done, take sausage out and put them in a bowl. Leave the gravy or juice made by the sausage in the roaster. Set it in the icebox to cool. Then skim fat off the top and pour juice on the sausage.

You may freeze in gallon ziptop bags. Serve warm. Many years ago, I learned this recipe from my sister, Marie Deshotel.

Serves 16 to 20.
Elva Ardoin

I Remember...

that "my mother was, she was a real hustler. She used to, when we lived in St. James she used to have cows. She'd milk the cows and all that kind of stuff [*laughs*]. Daddy didn't do all that. Momma did anything she could to make money. She would raise chickens, and clean them and all, and sell them all cleaned. ... They'd call that a spring chicken when she'd dress them and all and sell them. ... She didn't sell eggs because we didn't have a lot of hens, not enough to sell, just enough for self."

Doris Poirrier

Hog's Head Cheese

4 pig's feet
1 pig's head
salt to taste
black pepper to taste
red pepper to taste
1 onion, finely chopped
1 to 2 tablespoons butter
1 bunch green onion tops, finely chopped

Boil pig's feet and head until tender and debone.
Set broth aside for later. Crush meat by hand or in
a meat grinder. Season with salt, black pepper, and
red pepper.

Sauté onion in separate pan in a little butter. Add
onion tops and continue cooking until they are
wilted. Add onion and onion tops to ground meat.
Add broth to meat to make it soft. Gel in the refrigerator on a platter overnight.

Serves 10.
Ella Mae Fontenot

I Remember...

that "the Depression never
bothered us. We had
everything we wanted to
eat. Daddy and them still
did well. ... People had to
have meat... and there was
no way to preserve it."
Because my father and
grandfather were butchers,
we always had meat and
enough money. "Dad and
grandfather each had a
route to go and peddle the
food. And the thing is you
knew exactly what every-
body wanted, you had
their meat fixed."

Doris Poirrier

Sausage Bread

1 package frozen bread loaves (3 in a pack)
2 or 3 pounds smoked sausage
1 stick margarine, melted
1 jar (14 ounces) pizza quick sauce
3 packs (24 ounces total) pepperoni slices
2 large packages (16 ounces total) shredded
    cheddar cheese
2 large packages (16 ounces total) shredded
    mozzarella cheese
jalapeño slices (optional)
flour

Thaw out dough while cooking sausage. Cook sausage in large pot on stove. Drain and grind or thinly slice. Cut bread loaves in half.

Preheat oven to 350 degrees. Roll out thawed dough on floured surface (7 by 9-inch rectangle). Spread margarine on center of dough leaving 1-inch margin all around. Spoon sausage on only 1/2 of dough. Add a few spoons of pizza quick sauce. Add pepperoni layer. Top with sprinkled cheddar and mozzarella cheese. Add a second layer of pepperoni. Place jalapeño slices on top, if desired. Fold other half of dough over meat and cheese. Bring edges of bottom dough over and seal with water. Moisten edges by dipping fingers in a cup of water. Pat seams with a little flour.

Place on cookie sheet. Repeat process. Two sausage breads will fit on 1 cookie sheet. Bake for about 30 minutes.

Makes 6 loaves.
Regina Fontenot

Swedish Meatballs

6 pounds ground meat
6 slices stale bread, broken into bread crumbs
3 eggs
garlic salt to taste
2 medium onions, chopped
$1/2$ cup parsley
$1/2$ cup chopped green onion tops
4 sticks celery, cut
2 quarts barbecue sauce (preferably Kraft)
2 cans (21.5 ounces total) cream of mushroom soup

Preheat oven to 350 degrees. Mix ground meat, bread, eggs, and garlic salt. Add onions, parsley, onion tops, and celery. Mix well. Make into bite-size balls and bake meatballs for 35 to 45 minutes until they are cooked through and through. Pour barbecue sauce and soup over the cooked meat-balls and warm up before serving.

Serves 8.
Dorothy Bryant

I Remember...

that in addition to the traditional sausage, *boudin,* and cracklings, my family made a batch of meatballs on the day of the *boucherie.* The meatballs were partially cooked before preserving them in big crocks and covered with lard. I also remember that the best way to cook salt meat is by boiling the piece of pork with potatoes or cabbage.

Blanche Quebedeaux

Chicken Salad Sandwiches I

¹/₂ cup mayonnaise
2 tablespoons lemon juice
1 cup minced celery
¹/₃ cup minced onion
¹/₄ cup chopped olives (optional)
8 cups diced chicken breast
6 eggs, boiled and chopped
1 teaspoon salt
¹/₄ teaspoon black pepper
¹/₄ teaspoon red pepper
2 to 2¹/₂ loaves day-old bread

Mix mayonnaise, lemon juice, celery, onions, and olives together. Then add chicken breast and eggs and toss lightly. Season with salt, black pepper, and red pepper. Remove crusts from the bread and diagonally halve the slices of bread. Fill with chicken salad. Keep refrigerated.

Makes 48 to 60 halved sandwiches or 24 to 30 whole sandwiches.
Rose Fontenot

I Remember...

"[My mom's] daddy got killed in World War I and her momma was widowed and [my grandmother would] tell us the story: she had two little children, you see. And she said she would tie 'em in the house while she'd go bilge the water; she had to walk to get her water, so the kids wouldn't get in anything or get hurt while she was gone. That's how she managed. ... She'd tie them with a sheet around them and put them by the bedpost so they couldn't get loose. And I said that was a clever idea she had."

Corinne Judice

Chicken Salad Sandwiches II

6 large fryers
1 bunch celery, chopped
4 onions, chopped
3 bell peppers, chopped
1 bunch parsley, chopped
salt to taste
black pepper to taste
red pepper to taste
1 dozen eggs, boiled
1 cup sweet pickles
1 can (10³/4 ounces) cream of mushroom soup
1 can (10³/4 ounces) cream of celery soup
mayonnaise (as desired)
20 loaves of day-old bread
butter

I Remember...

Mrs. Freddie Parent and Mona (my daughter-in-law's mother and aunt) used to make the best chicken salad sandwiches and this is the recipe I learned from them. These are especially good for weddings and special receptions.

Elva Ardoin

Boil fryers with celery, onions, bell peppers, parsley, and season with salt, black pepper, and red pepper. When done debone the chicken and save the broth for later.

Take the meat with the onions, bell pepper, celery, and parsley and run through meat grinder. Also grind boiled eggs and pickles at the same time. Mix ground ingredients with cream of mushroom and cream of celery soup. Add chicken broth. Then add mayonnaise until you reach a consistency that you like.

To make sandwiches, lightly butter bread before spreading chicken salad on it.

Makes about 220 whole sandwiches.
Elva Ardoin

Ham Salad Sandwiches

4 pounds cooked ham
1 dozen eggs, boiled
4 packs (32 ounces total) cream cheese
mayonnaise, as desired
oleo (margarine), as needed
11 loaves bread

Grind ham and eggs. Mix cream cheese, eggs, and ham. Add mayonnaise so it is easy to spread. Lightly spread soft oleo on bread first. Then fill sandwiches with ham salad mixture.

Makes 60 sandwiches.
Elva Ardoin

I Remember...

"[My mother] believed in education. She made sure we all went to college and finished, [well] not all our brothers didn't finish. ... When I graduated, there we were about 30, 35 in our class and only two of us went to college and finished and I was one of them."

Doris Poirrier

Irish Potato Soup

4 cups diced potatoes
1 cup chopped onions
1 cup chopped carrots
1 cup chopped celery
salt to taste
black pepper to taste
red pepper to taste
1 large can (12 ounces) evaporated milk
2 to 4 tablespoons flour

Mix potatoes, onions, carrots, celery, 4 cups water,
and seasoning in covered pot. Cook on medium
heat until tender. Add evaporated milk. Blend flour
with 1/2 cup of water and add to soup to help it
thicken. Simmer until heated thoroughly and soup
reaches desired thickness.

Serves 4 to 6.
Joyce Brasseux

I Remember...

that my parents spoke
French and that I only
learned English once I
attended school. "I often
say we speak *Cadien*,
because half English and
French. We mix it up."

Carrine "Yen" Fontenot

Corn Soup I

I Remember...

volunteering and promoting old Cajun traditions at home and by volunteering at the Jean Lafitte Center/ National Prairie Cajun History Museum in Eunice, Louisiana. I have demonstrated sewing, quilting, and cooking techniques for visitors of the museum. And of course, when we visit "we complain about our husbands or lack of. ... We brag about our grandkids; 'they're all little geniuses you know', compare aches and pains, exchange recipes, and go home and eat."

Olga Manuel

2 tablespoons fat or oil
1 large onion, chopped
1 cup chopped bell pepper
1 stalk celery, cut up
1 clove garlic, minced
2 cups shrimp
2 cups crabmeat
1 can (14.5 ounces) tomatoes
2 cups fresh corn
3 to 4 quarts hot water
salt to taste
black pepper to taste
red pepper to taste

Heat fat. Add onion, bell pepper, celery, and garlic together. Simmer for a while. Add shrimp, crabmeat, and tomatoes. Simmer on low heat. Add corn; simmer a while and add hot water. Season with salt, black pepper, and red pepper. Let boil a while until soup reaches desired thickness.

Serves 6 to 8.
Elma Oubre

Corn Soup II

6 ears corn or 2 cans (30.5 ounces total) whole
    kernel corn
1 pound ground beef
1 pound stew meat, cubed
2 small potatoes, cubed
2 cups chopped carrots
1/2 cup chopped onions
1/3 cup parsley
1/3 cup chopped celery
2 whole ripe tomatoes, cut
1 can (8 ounces) tomato sauce
1 can (8 ounces) tomato paste
salt to taste
black pepper to taste
red pepper to taste
1 tablespoon all-purpose flour

Cut kernels off of cob. Be sure to scrape the cob as
that is where the best milk of the corn is. Boil
ground beef, meat, corn, potatoes, and carrots in 3
quarts of water. Next add onions, parsley, celery,
tomatoes, tomato sauce, and tomato paste. Season
with salt, black pepper, and red pepper. When meat
is tender, cook on low fire or until soup thickens.
You may add the flour to thicken.

Serves 4 to 6.
Thelma Coles

I Remember...

when my brother went to
war; on D-Day he landed
with the heavy artillery. He
told me that when they
landed, they drove jeeps
and tanks in high water
and spent weeks in the
trenches to protect them-
selves. I kept all his old
letters. He said that
because of the shrapnel
every other guy was killed
and most of the others
were wounded.

Corinne Judice

Vegetable Soup

1¹/₂ pounds beef brisket, cubed
1¹/₂ pounds beef round, cubed
salt to taste
black pepper to taste
red pepper to taste
1 large onion, diced
1 bell pepper, diced
1 small tomato, diced
2 stalks celery, cut up
2 turnips, diced
2 carrots, cut up
2 cups chopped cabbage
1 large potato, diced
chopped celery leaves to taste
parsley to taste
1 to 2 cups chopped onion tops
1 cup vermicelli

Put beef in 3 to 4 quarts water; simmer slowly.
Season with salt, black pepper, and red pepper.
Gradually add onions, peppers, tomatoes, celery,
turnips, carrots, cabbage, and potatoes. Then add
celery leaves, parsley, and onion tops. Let boil until
meat is tender. Add the vermicelli. Let boil a while
until soup reaches desired thickness and vermicelli
are tender.

Serves 8 to 10.
Elma Oubre

Meat and Vegetable Soup

1 pound beef hocks
1 onion, chopped
1 clove garlic, minced
1 tablespoon salt
$1/3$ teaspoon red pepper
$1/2$ to $2/3$ teaspoon black pepper
1 teaspoon parsley
1 can (8 ounces) tomato sauce
3 Irish potatoes
2 cups corn, cut off the cob
4 cups cut up cabbage

Put hocks and 5 quarts water in a large stockpot and cook on medium heat. Bring to a boil. Add onion, garlic, salt, red pepper, black pepper, parsley, and tomato sauce. Cook until meat is tender, 30 to 45 minutes. Add potatoes, corn, and cabbage. Cook until all is tender, 20 to 30 minutes.

Serves 6 to 8.
Blanche Quebedeaux

I Remember...

that I learned to sew and cook at a young age from my mother. She sewed all of our clothes out of cotton and gingham; she used fertilizer sacks to make sheets; and she made featherbeds. "[My mom] was always the kind of person who taught us a lot of things to do in the house."

Evon Melancon

Old-Time Soup

1 beef soup bone (3 pounds)
salt to taste
black pepper to taste
red pepper to taste
2 cans (30.5 ounces total) whole corn
6 small Irish potatoes, quartered
2 cans (16 ounces total) tomato sauce

Season soup bone with salt, black pepper, and red pepper. Cook soup bone in a 6-quart pot with 1 gallon of water. When soup bone is tender, add corn, potatoes, and tomato sauce. Boil soup bone for 30 minutes more. When soup reaches desired thickness and potatoes are cooked, serve with crackers.

Serves 6 to 8.
Gladys Hebert

I Remember...

"When I first tried to ride a horse, I was eight years old. My dad had a store in Riceville. We had a milk cow. A friend of my dad would let dad drive the cow in his pasture. ... One afternoon I ask Dad to let me go get the cow on our old horse, Dutch. Well, he put me on the horse's back without a saddle. It was fun to go to the pasture. We had to open a gate. My girlfriend opened the gate. When we had the cows out, we had to close the gate. She asked me to help her close it. When we were ready to go, she jumped on her horse. I thought I could do the same. She helped me, and I landed on the other side of old Dutch. That was the end of that. I had to walk home."

Gladys Hebert

Deer and Vegetable Soup

1 deer shank or rib rack (3 to 4 pounds), bony part
  of the deer
salt to taste
black pepper to taste
red pepper to taste
2 onions, chopped
1 to 2 bell peppers, chopped
1 stalk celery, chopped
1 can (6 ounces) tomatoes
1 can (6 ounces) carrots
1 can (6 ounces) turnips
1 can (6 ounces) sweet peas
1 can (6 ounces) green beans
1 can (6 ounces) corn
1 package (16 ounces) vermicelli pasta

In a large soup pot add 2 gallons of water and deer.
Season with salt, black pepper, and red pepper. Boil
until meat comes apart from the bone. Add onions,
bell peppers, and celery while the water is boiling.
Add tomatoes, carrots, turnips, sweet peas, green
beans, and corn. Add extra water to soup, as needed.

After about 1¹/2 hours (when the meat pulls apart
from the bone) add vermicelli. Boil 20 minutes
more or until noodles are done and soup has
reached desired thickness.

Serves 6 to 8.
Verna Amedee

I Remember...

when my cousins from the
city gave me a big, old
coat. My mother and my
aunt took the coat apart,
and then washed and
pressed the material. They
turned the fabric inside
out and made me a little
coat and a hat to match
out of it.

Eva Mae Poirrier

Strawberry Fruit Punch

2 quarts ginger ale
1 quart carbonated water
16 ounces pineapple juice
3 cups sugar
1 can (6 ounces) concentrated frozen orange juice
1 pitcher tea
3 or 4 boxes (48 to 64 ounces) frozen strawberries

Mix ginger ale, carbonated water, pineapple juice, sugar, orange juice, and tea. Make sure the tea is real sweet and has lots of lemon juice in it. Chill, then pour into a punch bowl and add frozen strawberries. I learned this recipe from Thelma LaHaye. It is great for receptions.

Makes about 40 punch cups.
Elva Ardoin

Hawaiian Punch

1 bottle (32 ounces) concentrated fruit punch
   (preferably Hawaiian Punch)
$^{1}/_{2}$ gallon lime sherbet
1 gallon 7-up or Sprite

Mix fruit punch, sherbet, and 7-up or Sprite. Chill and serve over ice in a punch bowl. Mildred Bickley taught me how to make this punch. It is easy, delicious, and great for large get-togethers.

Makes 40 cups.
Elva Ardoin

I Remember...

when my husband passed away at the age of 53, only a month before my son was scheduled to wed. My son offered to postpone his wedding and move back to Ville Platte and help me adjust, but I said, "No. You planning to get married, and your life is just beginning and mine is ended." After his wedding my son ignored my wishes and moved back to take over the family meat market. Although my marriage was not always perfect, "I missed [my husband] something terrible, he was a good-hearted man."

Marie "Ivy" Ortego

Lime Sherbet Punch

2 bottles (4 liters total) ginger ale
3 bottles (6 liters total) 7-up or Sprite
1/2 gallon lime sherbet

Mix together 1 bottle of ginger ale with 1 1/2 bottles of 7-up or Sprite. Place the sherbet in the middle of the punch bowl. It should float. Chill and serve over ice in a punch bowl. Gradually add in remaining ginger ale and 7-up or Sprite, as needed to keep the punch bowl full. Make sure the 7-up or Sprite and ginger ale are already chilled before pouring them into the bowl. This cannot be made ahead of time. It must be served almost immediately or sherbet will melt.

Makes 40 to 60 cups.
Elva Ardoin

I Remember...

that "I always thought Momma was such a remarkable woman because she came from the back [Back Vacherie] ... and went up to tenth grade and really bettered herself ... unlike her sister; she only went to the fifth or sixth grade ... because she didn't care, you know."

Doris Poirrier

Cherry Bounce

1 quart wild cherries
2 quarts white port wine or whiskey
1 cup sugar

This recipe takes 2$^1/_2$ months to complete so you must plan ahead. Let cherries soak in wine or whiskey for 6 weeks. Keep in a cool, dry place. At the end of 6 weeks, draw the juice. Make a syrup with the sugar and 1 cup water. Do not cook. Add 1 cup syrup to 3 cups of cherry bounce juice. Let settle for 4 weeks. Ready to drink. You may use crushed ice for your drink.

Makes 2 quarts.
Elma Oubre

I Remember...

a time when people traveled in groups, sitting in the back of a flatbed truck in order to attend dances. Despite the fact that we often arrived all covered in dust and heavily chaperoned, I still have fond memories of my first dating experiences. I also remember that drinking and smoking were socially unacceptable for women, but Abbie (my future husband) occasionally poured a drink into a coke bottle for me so that I could have a little taste.

Ella Mae Fontenot

Root Beer

1 pack beer yeast
3 to 4 pounds white sugar
1 bottle (4 ounces) root beer extract (preferably
   Zatarain's)

I Remember...

This is the Zatarain's old-fashioned recipe that [my family and I] now use, but we used to make root beer when I was young. "[Root beer] is mostly what we drank. I remember when we used to make it. Used to call that, you'd make a stripe of it, you see; and you'd have these big demi-john's and they'd make it and then you would put it in the bottles and you would cap the bottles, and then you would put them out in the sun. You see, you'd make most of the time in the summertime. You'd put them out in the sun for about a week or so and it ended up, it tasted really good."

Doris Poirrier

Dissolve yeast in a glass of warm water. Mix 5 gallons water, yeast, sugar, and root beer extract. Put in clean glass bottles and cap. Lay them on their sides for 2 to 4 hours in the sun, then stand upright at room temperature for 24 hours. Check taste and carbonation. If done, refrigerate, but let stand a little longer if necessary. Be careful: if carbonation levels get too high, it can break the bottles. Keeps for months.

Makes about 40 pints.
Doris Poirrier

Meat

Roux

2 tablespoons flour
2 tablespoons cooking oil
¼ cup chopped onions

Brown flour in oil on low to medium heat until dark golden brown. Stir constantly until there is no white film showing in the roux. Turn heat down a little and watch not to burn the roux. Add chopped onions. Cook until onions are tender. Remove from burner and stir 2 or 3 minutes more. Roux may be stored in refrigerator for up to 6 weeks.

This is enough for a small fricassée. If you want to make enough roux for a gumbo or stew, use 1 cup of oil, 1 cup of onions, 1 cup of flour and follow the same cooking instructions.

Viola Rider

I Remember...

when I was young we ate a lot of white beans, salt pork, and chicken; and Dad hunted ducks, rabbits, and squirrels for us to eat. We didn't eat too much seafood. "Not too much seafood. Once in a while we'd get boiled crabs, buy crabs, or catfish, but not, we didn't have much seafood. A lot of wild game, whole lot, whole lot. Make rabbits, we used to smoke rabbits in the chimney. My brother would get on the roof of the house and put it on a pole and smoke rabbits or ducks."

Rose Thibodeaux

My Okra Gumbo

when I attended a one-room school and eventually graduated high school. The school did not have a "hot lunch kitchen;" therefore, I brought my lunch in a bucket from home. I usually ate sausage and a biscuit or rice.

Lessie Deshotel

1 hen (3 to 4 pounds)
1 tablespoon salt
black pepper to taste
red pepper to taste
onions chopped (optional)
$^1/_2$ cup oil
3 quarts cold water
2 cups smothered okra (see page 25 for instructions on smothering okra)
onion tops (optional)

Cut hen in usual pieces. Season with salt, black pepper, and red pepper. Place in a 5-quart or larger stockpot or black iron pot. Add onions and oil.

Cook hen on a medium flame or setting for 1 hour, until wing is tender. This will brown the meat nicely. Watch the meat browns well but does not burn. You can add a little ($^1/_2$ cup) water towards the end of the hour, only if necessary. After 1 hour, add the cold water and cook 10 to 15 minutes. Add okra. Hint: Never add okra until meat is tender. If you add okra too soon, it will make gumbo slimy. Add onion tops as desired and cook about 10 more minutes or until gumbo is ready to serve.

Serves 6.
Gladys Hebert

Chicken Gumbo I

½ cup roux
1 to 1½ teaspoons black pepper
1 teaspoon red pepper
2 tablespoons salt
1 onion, chopped
1 small clove garlic, minced
1 cup chopped green onion tops
1 whole chicken (3 to 4 pounds), cut up

In a large stockpot, bring roux and 3 to 5 quarts water to a boil. Add black pepper, red pepper, salt, onions, garlic, onion tops, and chicken. Cook for 1 hour.

Serves 6 to 8.
Blanche Quebedeaux

I Remember...

when my father bought his first car; I was already married with two children. "And you know why he bought it. He wanted to go on vacation so bad, poor thing, and he didn't know how to drive. And he asked my husband one day, he says, 'if I buy a car,' he say, 'would you go on vacation with us in Florida?' He wanted to go to Florida. And my husband said yes because he would have passed through hell for my daddy. ... So [my dad] bought his car, a '56 Chevy, ... and we went to Florida. That was the happiest man I've ever seen."

Rita Rodrigue

Chicken Gumbo II

1 whole chicken (3 to 4 pounds), cut up
1/2 cup chopped onions
1/2 cup chopped onion tops
1/2 tablespoon cut celery
3/4 cup parsley
2 teaspoons cut bell pepper
1 teaspoon minced garlic
1 teaspoon butter
1 teaspoon Worcestershire sauce
   (preferably Lea and Perrins)
1/2 tablespoon cooking oil
salt to taste
black pepper to taste
red pepper to taste
gumbo filé to taste

Roux:
1/2 cup cooking oil
1/4 cup all-purpose flour

Put all chicken, onions, onion tops, celery, parsley, bell pepper, garlic, butter, and Worcestershire sauce in your gumbo pot. Add the oil. Sauté for about 30 minutes.

While these ingredients are cooking down, make your roux. I use a cast-iron skillet. Heat oil and add flour. Stir until it is a medium brown. Turn burner off and keep stirring as it will keep cooking until it cools. After your chicken is medium brown, add 3 to 4 quarts water and roux. Also add salt, black pepper, red pepper, and gumbo filé and cook on a

"I did [make my own roux] up until about two years ago. Made with shortening and flour until it got dark enough on a low heat. Once it smokes it'll have a bitter taste. It's like a cake. You bake a cake, you bake it too long it's gonna get dry. If you don't it's gonna stay moist."

Corinne Judice

low fire. I recommend about 1 to 2 hours cooking time until the gumbo reaches desired thickness.

When it is cooked, turn fire off and cover with a tight lid until you are ready to serve with rice or crackers.

Serves 4 to 6.
Thelma Coles

I Remember...

going to a grove of oak trees and waiting to be called back inside when my mother was giving birth to one of my siblings. I saw the blood-stained blankets that my father took to the stream to wash afterwards. "They did not tell us anything, but we had eyes. We could see." My father wanted to protect us. One time he whipped my sisters and I for watching a pig giving birth to a litter. "All I knew was that if I lie with a man I could get pregnant and then he would leave me." And when I got married I knew that as a Catholic "[abstinence is] the only way they give you communion. If you take contraception, they'll refuse you. ... If you wanted to make a good confession, you'd have to tell [the priest]."

Ella Mae Fontenot

Turnips and Pork or Chicken

2 pounds pork or 1 fryer (2½ pounds)
½ cup oil
½ cup vinegar
1 tablespoon salt
black pepper to taste
red pepper to taste
2 to 3 turnips

Cook pork or chicken in oil until tender. Add vinegar to meat; it will help tenderize meat. Add salt and season with black pepper and red pepper. Cut turnips in bite-size pieces and add to meat. Cook in 250-degree oven in 1 cup of water until turnips are soft and all water is evaporated. Serve over rice.

Serves 4 to 6.
Gladys Hebert

I Remember...

when "Momma would cook a lot of, uh, they used to raise their own meat you see. Pork, we had a lot of pork. And she was a good cook. And she had a big garden. We'd have turnips and mustard greens, everything from the garden. ... They'd cut [the meat] up. We had to have a lot of salted meat because you see we didn't have refrigerators in those days, so we had a lot of boiled meat. She boiled vegetables, with mustard greens and turnips, with the meat. Wasn't too too good, but it wasn't bad. Ha ha ha."

Gladys Hebert

Quick Sweet- and- Sour Pork

1 pound boneless pork
2 tablespoons corn oil (preferably Mazola)
1 can (15¹/₄ ounces) pineapple chunks
¹/₂ cup dark corn syrup (preferably Karo)
¹/₄ cup vinegar
2 tablespoons catsup
2 tablespoons soy sauce
1 clove garlic, minced
2 tablespoons cornstarch (preferably Argo)
¹/₂ cup sliced bell pepper

Cut pork in 1-inch cubes. Heat oil in skillet. Brown pork. Add pineapple, syrup, vinegar, catsup, soy sauce, and garlic. Bring to a boil; simmer 10 minutes or until done. Mix cornstarch and 2 tablespoons water. Add to pork with bell pepper. Boil 2 minutes, stirring constantly. Serve over rice.

Serves 4.
Hazel Pousson

I Remember...

when I learned my catechism in French, attended Latin masses and made my First Communion at age 11. I also remember that my first cousin drank a little water after midnight on the eve of his First Communion. As a result, the priest refused him communion and my cousin had to wait until a later date to make his First Communion.

Lessie Deshotel

Pork Chop and Turnip Stew

4 pork chops (3 pounds)
salt to taste
black pepper to taste
red pepper to taste
1/4 to 1/2 cup oil
1 medium onion, chopped
1/2 cup flour
2 medium turnips, peeled and diced
1/2 cup onion tops, chopped

Season pork chops with salt, black pepper, and red pepper. Brown pork chops in small amount of oil (just enough to cover bottom of pot) in iron pot. When pork chops are brown, add chopped onion and sauté until onions are tender. Remove pork chops and set aside.

Add flour to onions and stir to brown lightly (add a little oil if needed). Pour in water (about 1 glass) and stir until oil is blended. Add pork chops and diced turnips. Make sure water covers pork chops. Cook on low heat until chops and turnips are tender. Add onion tops and continue cooking until they wilt and stew reaches desired thickness.

Serves 4.
Gertrude Stutes

I Remember . . .

that, "to tell you the truth, at my house, you couldn't find a stitch of liquor and my daddy liked his whiskey but only when he went out and when he came home he was a man. I mean he wasn't drunk; he wasn't."

Rita Rodrigue

Meatball Stew I

*1½ pounds ground meat (beef or pork, or mix
    50/50)*
salt to taste
black pepper to taste
red pepper to taste
1 medium onion, chopped
½ bell pepper, well chopped
1 egg
¾ cup bread crumbs or saltine cracker crumbs
flour
⅓ pint roux

Season ground meat with salt, black pepper, and
red pepper. Add onion, bell pepper, egg, and bread
crumbs. Mix well to make your meatballs. Pat well
with flour. Put about 1½ quarts and water in a 4-
quart pot and add your roux. If not thick enough to
your taste add a little more roux. Also add your
meatballs and cook on medium fire for about 2
hours. Serve on rice. Baked sweet potatoes go well
with stew.

Serves 6 to 8.
Ella Mae Fontenot

I Remember...

that my grandmother (who
lived with my parents)
would lead my siblings and
I in our nightly prayers. I
remember how important
that time was to me and
how we used to compete
for the opportunity to
sleep with our grandmoth-
er. When my own grand-
children were little and
they came to *la veillée*
[evening visit or sleep
over], my husband (who
has since passed away)
would give up his place in
the master bed so that
they could sleep with me.

Ella Mae Fontenot

Meatball Stew II

1 pound ground beef
1 egg
salt to taste
red pepper to taste
black pepper to taste
1 cup bread crumbs (old toast bread crushed)
1/4 to 1/2 cup oil
1 small onion, chopped
1 small green pepper, chopped
3 tablespoons roux
1 to 2 cups chopped onion tops

Mix ground beef, egg, salt, red pepper, black pepper, and bread crumbs well and form meatballs. Brown meatballs in small amount of oil in large iron pot. Remove meatballs and add onion, green pepper, roux, and extra seasoning to taste. Sauté until the onions are tender. Return meatballs to pot. Cover with water. Cook until meatballs are tender, about 1 hour. When almost done, add onion tops. Serve over rice.

Serves 4.
Gertrude Stutes

I Remember...

not having a lot of meat to eat when I was young. I loved chicken stew; it was one of my favorite family recipes. "That was a big thing, that was a feast when you had meat."

Elmina Landry

Chicken Stew

3 tablespoons roux
1 teaspoon salt
1/3 teaspoon red pepper
1/2 to 2/3 teaspoon black pepper
1 onion, chopped
1 clove garlic, minced
2 teaspoons parsley
1 whole chicken (3 to 4 pounds), cut up

Put roux and 2 quarts of water in a pot and cook
on medium heat. Bring roux to a boil. Add salt, red
pepper, black pepper, onion, garlic, parsley, and
chicken. Cook for 1 hour.

Serves 4 to 6.
Blanche Quebedeaux

I Remember...

that my mom had seven
children. For the first six
children, she paid a mid-
wife $3 per birth, and for
her last one, she paid $5.
"My momma used to say
she had seven children.
She'd say, 'I had seven
children for $23 and you
mean you had to pay
$3,000 to $4,000. You
think it's a change!'"

*Rita Rodrigue's husband,
Gaston Rodrigue*

Chicken Dumplings

1 cup flour
2 teaspoons baking powder
1/2 teaspoon salt
1 egg
1/2 cup milk
2 tablespoons minced onions
1 pinch parsley
1 pot chicken stew

Mix flour, baking powder, and salt. Blend in egg and milk. Add onions and parsley. Mix well into a soft batter. Set batter aside until your pan of chicken gravy or stew is almost done. Then drop by spoonful into the stew, while it is still cooking on a medium fire. Do not crowd dumplings as they expand as they cook. Finally, cover the pot and cook over low heat for 10 minutes. I make this every time I have a stew. It is very good. My mother and I had our own chickens so we could have stew often and the family would appreciate that.

Serves 6 to 8.
Claire Bonin

I Remember...

"My parents had chickens, pigs, and cows. We had our milk, eggs, and meat. It was wonderful when we would butcher an animal. Neighbors would get together to help one another. It was a day together. That was around 1927. What a wonderful time, and each neighbor would leave with a package of meat, boudin, and cracklings."

Claire Bonin

Rabbit Sauce Piquante

1 rabbit (3 pounds)
salt to taste
black pepper to taste
$1/2$ teaspoon red pepper
garlic powder to taste
$1/4$ to $1/2$ cup oil
$1/2$ stick butter
1 can (8 ounces) tomato sauce
1 tablespoon all-purpose flour
1 can (8 ounces) tomato paste
$1/2$ cup chopped onion
$1/2$ cup chopped bell pepper
$1/2$ cup chopped onion tops

The rabbit should be at least one year old, not a young tender one. Cut the rabbit in small pieces and season with salt, black pepper, red pepper, and garlic powder. Then put it in a black iron pot with oil and butter. Fry the rabbit down until browned. When browned, mix tomato sauce and flour and add tomato paste, onion, and bell pepper to the pot. Turn down your heat and let this simmer for 1 to $1^1/2$ hours to tenderize the rabbit. About 10 minutes before done, add the onion tops. Serve over rice.

Serves 4 to 5 if it is a big rabbit.
Dorothy Bryant

I Remember...

"Well I can remember that I couldn't go to school with the others because they had to walk too far. So I was nine years old before I went to school. It must have been a mile and a half, but they didn't have a good road; they had to walk on levees."

Gladys Hebert

Turtle Sauce Piquante

¹/₂ cup chopped onion
¹/₂ cup chopped bell pepper
¹/₄ to ¹/₂ cup oil
2 cans (16 ounces) tomato sauce
1¹/₂ pounds turtle meat (I suggest yellow
  belly turtle)
¹/₂ teaspoon red pepper
black pepper to taste
salt to taste
garlic powder to taste
¹/₂ cup chopped onion tops

Sauté onions and bell peppers in oil. Let simmer down, and add tomato sauce and turtle, and season with red pepper, black pepper, salt, and garlic powder. It takes an hour or more depending on tł tenderness of the turtle. Ten minutes before done add onion tops. When tender, serve over rice.

Serves 4 to 5.
Dorothy Bryant

I Remember...

when I quit school. "I went on until the ninth grade. When I was in the ninth grade I started wanting to quit school. Biggest mistake I ever made. My daddy didn't want me to stop. I told him afterward 'Why didn't you take a rope and beat me good?' 'No', he said, 'I couldn't do that. But I didn't want you to stop school.'"

Gladys Hebert

Chicken "Hen" Sauce Piquante

1 large hen (older chicken, 4 pounds)
salt to taste
black pepper to taste
red pepper to taste
3 tablespoons oil
2 large onions, chopped
4 cloves garlic, chopped
2 teaspoons chopped bell pepper
1 cup chopped celery
1 can (8 ounces) tomato sauce
1 large can (13.25 ounces) mushrooms
3 tablespoons Worcestershire sauce
1 teaspoon prepared mustard
2 tablespoons catsup
2 tablespoons chopped onion tops
3 tablespoons parsley

Cut hen into pieces. Season with salt, black pepper, and red pepper. Brown meat well in oil. Remove meat from pot and remove some fat. Add onions and garlic, and cook until clear. Return meat to the pot. Add bell pepper, celery, tomato sauce, mushrooms, Worcestershire sauce, mustard, and catsup. Cover pot while cooking. Cook meat until tender. Add onion tops and parsley and cook until onion tops are done and gravy is thick. Serve with rice.

Serves 6 to 8.
Doris Regan

Stuffed Panse

1 stuffed panse *(pork stomach; 3 1/2 to 4 pounds)*
salt to taste
black pepper to taste
red pepper to taste
garlic to taste

Preheat oven to 350 degrees. Season *panse* with salt, black pepper, red pepper, and garlic. Cook covered about 3 hours and then cook uncovered 1 hour more to brown. Then add water for gravy. Cook down a while until gravy is done, 20 to 30 minutes. Many years ago, I learned how to cook *panse* from Gladys Mayeux.

Serves 6.
Elva Ardoin

I Remember...

"Momma was crazy about Huey Long. Oh, she used to really love Huey Long, almost all the women around here did. Well the thing is, before the days of Huey Long, you couldn't get to Thibodaux. That was nothing. ... There was no roads there. He made the roads, gave the free schoolbooks." She would go to Baton Rouge to see Huey Long and Chep Morrison too. She could not stand Earl Long because he was crazy and she did not like Jimmy Davis either. "Dad didn't take part."

Doris Poirrier

Tongue

1 cow tongue (3 pounds)
3 to 4 cloves garlic
salt to taste
black pepper to taste
red pepper to taste
1/4 to 1/2 cup oil
flour or cornstarch, as needed

Stuff the tongue with cloves of garlic and season
with salt, black pepper, and red pepper. Season the
entire tongue, and brown well on all sides in oil.
Cover with water and cook on medium heat until
fully tender. The time varies depending on the age
of the tongue. Test with a fork for the tenderness. It
cooks like a roast. Thicken gravy with flour or
cornstarch. Serve with rice and vegetables.

Serves 6.
Ella Mae Fontenot

I Remember...

that I was the oldest of
the children and the oldest
of the grandchildren on
both sides. I was "spoiled
rotten."

Doris Poirrier

Jambalaya

1 can (14.5 ounces) chicken broth
1 can (10³/4 ounces) onion soup
1¹/2 cups uncooked rice
1 small can (5.5 ounces) V-8 juice (optional)
Meat or seafood of choice (for example if using left-
over chopped roast, put about 4 cups; if using
crawfish tails put about 2¹/2 pounds; or 3 pounds
sausage, cooked and cubed)
black pepper to taste
red pepper to taste
2 tablespoons butter, melted
2 tablespoons chopped celery
2 tablespoons chopped onion tops

Preheat oven to 350 degrees. In a 2-quart measuring cup, mix broth and onion soup. Add enough water to make liquid total 3³/4 cups. (The secret to this recipe is to use exact amount of liquid content—3³/4 cups liquid to 1¹/2 cups rice and cook in a black iron pot.) If you want rice to be red when using seafood, put small can of V-8 juice in liquid content and decrease the amount of water. Then add meat or seafood of choice. For seasoning, usually the chicken broth and onion soup make it salty enough. Season with black pepper and red pepper. Then add butter, celery, and onion tops to pot and cover. Bake in oven for 1 hour.

Serves 4 to 6, but this recipe can be doubled
for a larger group.
Eva Mae Poirrier

I Remember...

"If I am cooking for a lot of people I usually make two pots of jambalaya. I have two black iron Dutch ovens that will fit into my oven. ... You can use this recipe with any kind of meat, sausage, crawfish, or shrimp, etc. ... Quite often, when family of cousins come to my house for holidays, I make this Jambalaya with unsmoked sausage freshly made at a local meat market near my home. You cannot buy this sausage anywhere else."

Eva Mae Poirrier

Sausage Rice Jambalaya

³/₄ pound smoked sausage, thinly sliced
1 small eggplant, cubed
¹/₂ cup chopped onions
¹/₂ cup chopped bell pepper
²/₃ cup raw rice
1 cup chicken broth
1 cup chopped canned tomatoes, drained
¹/₄ teaspoon salt
ground black pepper to taste
1 small bay leaf

Preheat oven to 350 degrees. Cook sausage until lightly brown in oven-safe skillet. Add eggplant, onions, and bell pepper. Stir in rice, chicken broth, tomatoes, salt, pepper, and bay leaf. Bring to a boil, cover, and bake for 30 minutes or until rice is tender and the liquid is absorbed. Fluff lightly with a fork. Remove bay leaf before serving.

Serves 4.
Dorothy Bryant

I Remember...

that "I made every stitch of clothing [my children] wore." I used fertilizer sacks for dresses and I crocheted, embroidered, covered shoes for weddings, and made coats and hats. I even made patterns, but sometimes I used McCall patterns.

Odile Hollier

Meat Jambalaya

1 fryer (2½ pounds), cut in small pieces
2 pounds pork sausage, cut in 2-inch pieces
2 cups chicken broth
2 pounds raw rice
2 medium onions, chopped
1 tablespoon salt
black pepper to taste
red pepper to taste

Cook fryer and sausage in the oven at 350 degrees in a 4-quart pot. An iron pot is preferred. If meat sticks too much, add 2 ice cubes. When meat is browned, add broth, rice, onions, and salt. Season with black pepper and red pepper. Lower heat to 250 degrees. Cover pot and cook about 1 hour. If rice is too dry add ½ cup of water and cook until rice is soft (10 minutes).

Serves 14 to 16.
Gladys Hebert

I Remember...

the work ethic instilled in me as a child. "[My father] had three girls, and he made boys out of us." My sisters and I not only ironed and cleaned house for our mother, but we also helped our father outside with the hay, hoeing, and milking.

Blanche Quebedeaux

Oven-Crusted Chicken

1/2 cup butter, melted
1/3 cup all-purpose flour
1 1/2 teaspoon salt
1/8 teaspoon thyme
1/8 teaspoon crushed rosemary
1/8 teaspoon marjoram
5 cups corn flakes, crushed to 1 1/2 cups
1 chicken (2 1/2 to 3 pounds), cut up

Preheat oven to 375 degrees. Combine butter, flour, salt, thyme, rosemary, and marjoram. Use a shallow dish to place the cereal in. Dip chicken pieces in butter mixture. Roll in cereal to coat. Place on rack in shallow 10 by 12-inch baking pan. Bake for 55 to 60 minutes.

Serves 6 to 8.
Verna Amedee

I Remember...

how we used to visit family and friends often. "I think family is very important, myself. We use to go to my grandma's [on my mother's side] every day after [school] in the evening ... visit and drink coffee and eat cookies or whatever she's got to offer."

Gertrude Stutes

Baked Duck

4 ducks (6 to 7 pounds total)
salt to taste
black pepper to taste
red pepper to taste
1 onion, cut in strips
1 bell pepper, cut in strips
garlic (optional)
1 apple
flour

Season outside of duck with salt, black pepper, and red pepper. Take knife and slit breast from the neck, close to the bone on both sides. Make a pocket and put long strips of onion and bell pepper in it. (Season them first.) Use garlic if desired. Core the unpeeled apple and put 1/4 inside each cavity. Roast in a pot and flip until brown, 30 to 45 minutes. Add water and cover. Simmer on stove until legs detach when you twist them, 45 minutes to 1 hour. Use flour to thicken the gravy after you take the ducks out.

Serves 8.
Regina Fontenot

I Remember...

"Uncle Justin, I'm sure he went to heaven. He was a very good man, so good and kind. I never heard him fuss about anything. And we were there all the time."

Helen Gravois

Baked Goose

1 large goose (5 to 7 pounds), cleaned
salt to taste
black pepper to taste
red pepper to taste
1 small onion
¹/₄ to ¹/₂ cup oil

Preheat oven to 350 degrees. Season goose with salt, black pepper, and red pepper. Peel onion and place in cavity of goose. Pour a small amount of oil in bottom of Dutch oven, just enough to line the bottom of the pot. (Black iron pots were used.) Pour 1 glass of water in pot. Place goose in pot, cover, and bake until tender and browned for 2 to 2¹/₂ hours. We always ate baked goose for Christmas dinner.

Serves 8 to 12.
Gertrude Stutes

I Remember...

growing up that we did not always like what was being cooked for supper, but we had to "eat what you like, don't eat what you don't like. There wasn't say 'oh well go in the refrigerator and get what you want.' [My parents] had no refrigerator, my dear. [And we would] wash by washing board. Now they play music on the wash-board."

Rita Rodrigue

Baked Turkey

1 large turkey (15 to 20 pounds)
salt to taste
black pepper to taste
red pepper to taste
garlic powder to taste

Preheat oven to 425 degrees. Season turkey with salt, black pepper, red pepper, and garlic powder. Cook 4¹/2 hours. First, cook covered with foil for 1 hour. Uncover and brown on both sides for another hour. Cover again and cook for a third hour. Then for the final 1¹/2 hours uncover until brown and done. Baste often with turkey drippings. This is a recipe I learned from Linda Ardoin.

Serves 25.
Elva Ardoin

I Remember...

that my parents both went to the tenth grade. My dad stopped to help the family, and my mom stopped because she didn't have any transportation to go any further. "But Momma was a very smart woman. She could have gone on and continued [her education] because she was a go-getter. She couldn't get an education, but she made sure that we all got educated."

Doris Poirrier

Baked Ham

1 box (1 pound) brown sugar
8 ounces pineapple juice
1 ham (7½ pounds)
pineapple rings (as needed)

Preheat oven to 400 degrees. Mix brown sugar and
pineapple juice, make a thick paste, baste ham and
put pineapple rings on top. Wrap in foil and seal
tight. Put a little water in roaster, and steam,
uncovered, for about 2 hours or until tender. Test
with fork. Let cool and take skin off before slicing.

Serves 14 to 16.
Elva Ardoin

I Remember...

that "we went to school at
8:00 a.m. but our work
had to be done before we
left. We came back 3:45
p.m. and were busy 'till. In
the winter we had to have
enough wood for fireplace
and stove the next morn-
ing. And so it went. If we
had 15 to 20 minutes to
play hopscotch or jump
rope before supper that
was a luxury. After supper
was homework time. We
cooked a lot of rice, mostly
just plain. Sometimes rice
dressing. Fried a lot of
sweet potatoes. The pota-
toes were baked one day,
the next day we had fried
sweet potatoes. Another
big job was fixing a school
lunch for six people going
to school."

Vinice Sensat

Oven-Barbecued Lamb Ribs

6 to 8 lamb ribs (2 to 3 pounds)
salt to taste
black pepper to taste
red pepper to taste
¼ cup oil
barbecue sauce (as desired)

Preheat oven to 350 degrees. Season lamb ribs with salt, black pepper, and red pepper. Place in roaster with oil and ¼ cup water. Cover and bake for 45 minutes to 1 hour. Ten minutes before done, baste with barbecue sauce.

Serves 4 to 6.
Regina Fontenot

I Remember...

When my children come to my house, the first thing they ask is, "'What you cooking today?' If I would make a dinner and they coming over here [and] I wouldn't bake bread [they would ask], 'What's the matter, you didn't cook today?' And the moment they would come eat, they would start eating the bread, so they wasn't hungry for the dinner."

Verna Amedee

Lamb Round Steak

3 to 4 lamb round steaks (2 to 3 pounds)
salt to taste
black pepper to taste
red pepper to taste
barbecue sauce to taste

Preheat oven to 350 degrees. Line roaster with foil.
Season the meat with salt, black pepper, and red
pepper. Place in pan without overlapping the meat.
Bake for 45 to 60 minutes until they brown. When
almost done, uncover and baste with barbecue
sauce.

Serves 4.
Regina Fontenot

I Remember...

on Sunday afternoons "when we would leave in the car to go [to Grandma's house], [Mom] would say, 'Now remember, nobody ask. Ya'll eaten already. Don't ya'll go askin' for any food,' you see. And so when we'd get over there and our grandmother would say, 'You want something?' and it was, 'No thank you, Mama.' And they'd get so upset with us, you know. They said, 'We know.'" They knew Mom had told us not to ask for anything to eat. "Grandmother would get upset because we did want to eat."

Doris Poirrier

Roast for 50

37 pounds of meat
salt to taste
black pepper to taste
red pepper to taste
1 crown garlic, broken into cloves
3 to 4 large onions, cut in slivers
3 to 4 bell peppers, cut in slivers

Cut the meat into 4 roasts. Season meat thoroughly with salt, black pepper, and red pepper. Stuff with garlic cloves and shards of onion and bell pepper, as desired. Put the roast on two barbecue pits with rotisserie and cook several hours until done.

Serves 50.
Elva Ardoin

Roast Beef Hash

2 tablespoons all-purpose flour
3 tablespoons oil
1 large onion, chopped
1 clove garlic, chopped
1 teaspoon chili powder
1 teaspoon salt
1 teaspoon black pepper
1 cup broth or roast beef gravy
3 cups chopped cooked roast beef
2 potatoes, cubed

Make a roux of the flour and oil. Add onions when roux starts to brown. Add garlic, chili powder, salt, and pepper. Add broth to make a gravy (or use left-over gravy if you have enough) and bring to a boil. Add meat and potatoes and simmer until gravy thickens. Cook until potatoes are tender. Serve with rice.

Serves 3 to 4.
Doris Regan

I Remember...

"...that would come every year at the same time. Ok. You had for instance, you had crabs, you had craw-fish, there were certain times of the year certain seasonal. And then the first thing you know the blackberries would come around. Well momma would make the blackberry pie and the custard pies, that would go together. That was a season thing. And then if, ok, the chickens you'd set your chickens so that around they'd be about six months, six months old by the time the okra was due. Then you'd make your gumbos. The different seasons for things, the corn, you'd make your corn soups when the corn would uh you know. You wouldn't have it all year round like you have it now and I think we appreciated it more that way because you looked forward to it you know.

Verda Bellina

Beef Casserole

1 pound ground beef
1/4 cup chopped bell pepper
1/4 cup chopped onion
2 cups canned whole tomatoes
1 tablespoon catsup
1 tablespoon Worcestershire sauce
2 tablespoons parsley
salt to taste
black pepper to taste
red pepper to taste
1 package (8 ounces) macaroni
1 can (10 3/4 ounces) mushroom soup
1 cup grated cheddar cheese

Cook beef on medium heat until red color disappears.
Add bell pepper, onion, tomatoes, catsup,
Worcestershire sauce, and parsley. Season with salt,
black pepper, and red pepper. Simmer for 30 minutes.

Preheat oven to 350 degrees. Boil macaroni on high
for 10 to 15 minutes or until tender. Then add to
meat mixture. Gently spoon in mushroom soup
until well blended. Put mixture into a casserole
dish. Top with grated cheese and bake in oven until
hot. Hint: Do not overcook or cheddar cheese will
burn.

Serves 8.
Belle Fontenot

I Remember...

at 10 years old I started
cooking meals, and I have
enjoyed cooking ever
since. "I believe that the
food we were cookin' in
those days were much
better for our kids than all
those junks the kids are
eatin' today."

Edolia Dupré

Meal-in-One-Dish Steak Casserole

1 steak (1½ pounds)
salt to taste
black pepper to taste
red pepper to taste
4 tablespoons butter
4 tablespoons Worcestershire sauce
4 medium potatoes, sliced
1 large onion, chopped
5 carrots, whole or sliced
1 bell pepper, sliced

Preheat oven to 350 degrees. Place steak and ¼ cup water in 13 by 9-inch baking dish. Season with salt, black pepper, and red pepper. Dot with butter. Add Worcestershire sauce, potatoes, onions, carrots, and bell peppers. Cover with foil and bake for 1½ hours. This is a wonderful meal. You don't have to cook anything else; only a green salad if you wish.

Serves 4 to 5.
Claire Bonin

I Remember...

We had an outside bathroom when I was growing up and I raised eight kids with one bathroom and three bedrooms. This was before we built our new house when my last child was born. I was so anxious to get in the bigger house. "It was like, 'Oh my God.' I can't wait until I get into the house where I have more than one bathroom, and I wanted to get in that house so bad and my husband would not let me because it wasn't six weeks. At that time you had to take care of yourself six weeks, you know you didn't do anything. ... He says 'no if we move you gonna be lifting heavy stuff you gonna ta da da na. No [on and on].'"

Winnie Fernandez

Leftover Pot Pie

¹/₄ cup boiling water
¹/₂ cup shortening
1¹/₂ cups all-purpose flour
¹/₂ teaspoon baking powder
¹/₂ teaspoon salt
1 to 2 pounds leftover cooked meat (chicken, roast, sausage)
1 onion, chopped
¹/₄ cup margarine
1 can (10³/₄ ounces) cream of mushroom soup
leftover vegetables or 1 can (16 ounces) Veg-All

To make crust: Pour boiling water over shortening and beat until creamy. Sift in flour, baking powder, and salt. Stir until dough forms a ball. Roll a little more than half the dough on lightly floured wax paper. Place in pie pan. You can also use unbaked crust found in frozen foods.

Preheat oven to 375 degrees. Cube the meat. Sauté onion in margarine. Add meat, cream of mushroom soup and vegetables. Pour into pie shell. Roll remaining dough to cover pie. Crimp edges. Bake until brown, 20 to 25 minutes.

Makes 1 pie.
Regina Fontenot

Tamale Pie

1½ pounds lean ground meat
3 tablespoons bacon drippings or oil
½ cup minced onion, parsley, and garlic, mixed
*   together*
1 to 2 chili peppers or mild peppers, chopped
chili powder to taste
salt to taste
1 can (14.5 ounces) tomatoes (preferably Rotel)
2 packs Mexican corn bread mix (preferably
*   Martha White)*
8 ounces shredded cheddar or American cheese

Brown ground meat in bacon drippings in a black iron skillet. Add onions, parsley, garlic, peppers, chili powder, and salt. Cook until meat is brown and onions are wilted down. Add tomatoes. Cook on medium heat about 10 minutes. Let it dry out.

Preheat oven to 350 degrees. Pour one layer of dry corn bread mix into a pie pan, and one layer of meat mixture alternately into an oblong 9 by 13-inch glass baking dish. When you have used all mixture, top with grated cheese and bake until corn bread is cooked, 25 to 35 minutes.

Makes 5 to 6 slices.
Thelma Coles

I Remember...

when "we'd grow all our popcorn, grows like corn only smaller and dry it and shuck it, and peanuts, grows in the ground as a root crop, pull them and let them dry in a bin in the barn and replant every year. Sometimes the neighborhood kids would come and we'd have popcorn parties and we used to make syrup candy and boy we'd have fun."

Corinne Judice

My husband asked permission to marry me. "My daddy wasn't so pleased. Well I was helping in the house: washing the dern dishes after momma died [when I was 14]." I got married at almost 25. My dad tried to put me off. "I made me a little hope chest. I had embroidered some little pillow cases and scarves. ...We took the train for the honeymoon, went to Lake Charles, stayed at a hotel where they served breakfast. We were big shots."

Gertrude Stutes

Hot Tamales

Meat mixture:
2 pounds ground meat
4 garlic cloves, minced
1/2 cup cornmeal
1 1/2 cups tomato sauce
2 medium onions, minced
2 1/4 ounces hot chili powder
salt to taste
black pepper to taste
red pepper to taste

Batter:
3 cups cornmeal
2 teaspoons salt
18 to 24 wet corn shucks or hot tamale peppers
1 can (8 ounces) tomato sauce
4 tablespoons regular chili powder

Make a meat mixture out of the ground meat, garlic, cornmeal, tomato sauce, onions, 1/2 cup water, and hot chili powder. Add salt, black pepper, and red pepper. Mix well. (Hint: If you prefer mild tamales use half hot and half mild chili powder.)

In a separate bowl, make the batter. Mix the cornmeal and salt. Then spread 1/2 teaspoon cornmeal mixture on wet corn shucks or on hot tamale peppers on a sheet of wax paper. Form a roll of the meat mixture about thumb size and place over cornmeal. Add another 1/2 teaspoon cornmeal mixture. Roll in shucks or wax paper (if using peppers) and stack each tamale in a heavy pot.

Cover tamales with water. Add tomato sauce, regular chili powder, and a little salt. Weigh down tamales with something heavy. Let tamales come to a boil. Turn down to a simmer and cook for 1 hour and 15 minutes, covered.

Hope you enjoy these old-time tamales as they are very good and can be put in freezer when cold for another day's celebration.

Makes 18 to 24 tamales.
Claire Bonin

I Remember...

The competition of *paqueing* has continued to this day with the same trickery of old. At my Easter celebration my children, their spouses, and my grandchildren try to find new ways to out-fox one another. They have tried substituting chicken eggs with guinea eggs, coating the eggs with fingernail polish, and if all else fails, they pull out a plastic egg. Another tradition I remember is that at a wedding, if one of the newlyweds has an older unwed sibling, he must dance barefoot in a tub with a mop. When one of my granddaughters was married, her older brother was forced to dance in the bucket. One of his aunts set out months in advance decorating the perfect mop, which included hair and makeup.

Ella Mae Fontenot

Mrs. Verna's Chili

5 onions, chopped
1 celery stalk, chopped
4 medium to large bell peppers, chopped
8 to 10 pounds ground meat, as desired
salt to taste
black pepper to taste
red pepper to taste
1 gallon tomato paste
1 gallon tomato sauce
1 gallon catsup

Sauté onions, celery, and bell peppers. Add meat and season with salt, black pepper, and red pepper. Cook down a few minutes until meat browns. Add tomato paste and a little water. Cook down for 10 minutes. Add tomato sauce and a little water. Cook down for 10 minutes. Add catsup and a little water. Cook down for 10 minutes. Continue cooking until the chili reaches your desired thickness. Add water and continue cooking until you have a good thick sauce. Divide by 4 if you want to make less.

Serves 20 to 25.
Verna Amedee

I Remember...

"Well, when they ask me, I tell them. They come, my grandchildren, my children come they say, 'Mama I try. It don't come out like yours.' And I make chili but I don't put chili in it, and everybody take my recipe but they say it don't come out like mine. I say 'because ya'll don't put the amount I tell ya'll.'"

Verna Amedee

Spaghetti and Meatballs with a Cajun Twist

Meatballs:
10 pounds ground meat
garlic powder to taste
red pepper to taste
black pepper to taste
salt to taste
1/2 cup dried parsley
1 onion, chopped
1 bell pepper, chopped

Meat sauce:
2 onions, chopped
2 bell peppers, chopped
1 bundle onion tops, chopped
1/2 cup dried parsley
2 to 3 tablespoons oil
8 ounces roux (preferably Kary's)
1 can (15 ounces) stewed diced tomatoes
6 ounces button mushrooms
2 cans (16 ounces total) tomato sauce
2 to 3 teaspoons minced garlic
red pepper to taste
black pepper to taste
salt to taste
cornstarch (preferably Argo)

Noodles:
2 to 3 pounds spaghetti noodles
salt, as needed
1/2 stick butter

Preheat oven to 350 degrees. Make the meatballs:
Mix ground meat with garlic powder, red pepper,
black pepper, salt, dried parsley, onions, and bell peppers. Shape ground meat into good-sized meatballs.

when I was young and life was simpler. "It was a good life ... compared to today." Families were better and neighbors would help each other. "Just having family coming over makes you feel good when you are old."

Odile Hollier

Makes about 30. Place in 1 large or 2 smaller deep pans and cook in oven for 1 hour. Let cool. Drain and remove meatballs. Place in ziptop bags. You may freeze meatballs and use with spaghetti meat sauce at any time.

Make meat sauce in a large roaster. Sauté onions, bell peppers, onion tops, and parsley in cooking oil. Then add water as follows: Fill pot to half full with water. Add roux to water (it will dissolve). Add more if sauce needs thickening toward end of cooking time. Add stewed diced tomatoes, mushrooms, and 1 can of tomato sauce. (Add a second can of tomato sauce once all is dissolved if need be.) Add the garlic. Season with red pepper, black pepper, and salt to taste throughout cooking.

After mixture is well heated (about 45 minutes), cook for 1 to 1½ hours more over medium heat. Add more water as needed to have enough sauce. Stir often. Add meatballs. Add more roux if needed now. Let dissolve. If need be, just before all is cooked, thicken gravy with cornstarch dissolved in water. Stir into pot a little at a time until it gets a good consistency.

Cook spaghetti noodles with salt, water, and butter for about 20 minutes or until tender on medium-high heat.

Serve meatballs and sauce over spaghetti. Serve with salad and garlic bread. Great meatballs with a Cajun twist.

Serves 15 hearty eaters.
Freddie Parent

Spaghetti Sauce

1 pound ground meat
salt to taste
black pepper to taste
red pepper to taste
1 tablespoon oil
1 onion, chopped
1 bell pepper, chopped
1 clove garlic, minced
1 rib celery, cut up
1 can (8 ounces) tomato paste
2 cans (29 ounces total) tomatoes (preferably Rotel)
1 can (13.25 ounces) mushrooms

Season meat with salt, black pepper, and red pepper. Brown meat in oil until redness is gone. Add onions, peppers, garlic, and celery. Cook until withered. Add tomato paste and cook 10 minutes longer. Add tomatoes, and simmer for 3 to 4 hours, stirring occasionally. Add mushrooms last.

Serves 6 to 8.
Doris Regan

I Remember...

when "this recipe was told to me about 30 years ago when our children were small and we belonged to a camping club. This spaghetti sauce could be made ahead and brought along with us. All we had to do was boil a pot of spaghetti. ... This is a very good sauce."

Doris Regan

Lasagne

2 cloves garlic, chopped
1 large onion, chopped
1 small bell pepper, chopped
1 to 2 tablespoons oil
1 can (16 ounces) tomatoes
1 can (8 ounces) tomato sauce
1 can (8 ounces) tomato paste
2 1/2 to 3 pounds ground meat
salt to taste
black pepper to taste
red pepper to taste
1 can (13.25 ounces) mushroom pieces
1 box (16 ounces) curly edge lasagna noodles
1 large container (24 ounces) cottage cheese
3 packages (12 ounces total) shredded mozzarella
  cheese

The process takes a couple of hours and can be
done ahead of time, frozen, and then baked. Wilt
garlic, onion, and bell pepper in grease over medium heat. Add tomatoes, tomato sauce, and tomato
paste. Cook slowly until thick (1 to 1 1/2 hours).
Brown ground meat and season with salt, black
pepper, and red pepper. Add mushroom pieces and
add tomato sauce to meat. Boil lasagna noodles.

Preheat oven to 350 degrees. Then begin layering in
1 large pot or roaster or in two 9 by 13-inch casserole dishes. Put 1/3 meat in bottom of a large pot,
then 1/3 cottage cheese and 1 pack of mozzarella
cheese. Then put 1/2 noodles. Repeat with 1/3 meat,

⅓ cottage cheese, 1 pack mozzarella cheese, last ½ of noodles. Finish with meat, cottage cheese, and mozzarella cheese. Cover. Bake for ½ to 1 hour.

Makes 1 extra large or 2 medium-size lasagnas.
Regina Fontenot

Seafood

Oyster Dressing

2 tablespoons all-purpose flour
2 tablespoons oil
1 small onion, chopped
1 small bell pepper, chopped
salt to taste
red pepper to taste
2 jars (20 ounces total) oysters
1 cup chopped onion tops
2 cups cooked rice

Make a light roux with the flour and oil (the color
of peanut butter). Add chopped onion, bell pepper,
and season with salt and red pepper. Stir until
onions are becoming soft. Add 1 glass of water.
Cook about 30 minutes. Add oysters with juice.
Cook 15 minutes. Turn off heat. Add onion tops.
Add rice; stir to combine. Serve hot.

Serves 6 to 8.
Gertrude Stutes

I Remember...

what I like to cook. "Oh
Lord, quite a few. I make a
lot of gumbos, seafood
gumbos, chicken and
andouille gumbos, and
crawfish stews, stuffed
crabs, a lot of seafood."
We ate a lot of seafood
growing up next to the
river. "Yeah pretty much.
Well way, way back we
used to have shrimp boxes.
We used to get the river
shrimp, you know. I tell
you they tasted different
from the, I like to taste
shrimp. That's all the
shrimp that you could find
around here. But then
when Christmas time came
along, we used to have
things brought by boat or
maybe by train."

Hilda Waguespack

Boiled Crabs in Ice Chest

1 box (26 ounces) salt
4 ounces red pepper
4 dozen live crabs

1 Styrofoam ice chest

Fill an extra large stockpot with water 1/2 to 3/4 of the way full. Start boiling your water so that it is ready when you put the crabs in the pot. You can boil the crabs outside using a butane burner and then eat them outside at a picnic table. This makes cleanup easier. Mix salt and red pepper and set aside. Purge crabs in a tub of water. Then dump out the dirty water and place crabs in the stockpot of boiling water. Make sure the crabs are covered with water. Boil crabs for 20 minutes. When done, remove crabs and immediately place 1 layer of crabs in the bottom of your ice chest. Sprinkle with seasoning (the mixture of red pepper and salt). Then add another layer of crabs and repeat the seasoning. Cover with newspaper and close tightly. Heat will steam and melt seasoning for flavor. After 1 hour, take out and eat. Will stay hot for 5 to 6 hours.

Makes 4 dozen crabs. Servings vary greatly depending on the company you are serving.
Mazel Lassiegne

I Remember...

"And the first cotton mattress that I had was from cotton corded by hand like we were talking about a while ago, and we were a bunch of ladies that day. I can see us, we were in a big room in the big house and we had, I mean we had cotton everywhere." I can remember a cousin who would fix it to the right thickness. Then we had the material all done.

Delna Hebert

Barnes & Noble Bookseller
626 106th Ave NE
Bellevue, WA 98004
(425) 451-8463
10-29-03 501915 R003

Cooking with Cajun Women   24.95
0781809320
A

SUB TOTAL   24.95
SALES TAX   2.20
TOTAL   27.15
AMOUNT TENDERED
CASH   2.25
GIFT CARD REDEEM   25.00
Card # 504507145065442
AUTH CODE: #000000
BALANCE REMAINING   .00

Creole Gumbo (Crabmeat and Shrimp or Chicken)

4 tablespoons lard or oil
4 tablespoons all-purpose flour
1 large onion, chopped
1 clove garlic, minced
1/4 cup chopped bell pepper
1/4 cup chopped celery
1 bay leaf
1/2 dozen crabs, shelled (add claws)
1 1/2 pounds shrimp, peeled and deveined or 3 to 4
    pound fryer (young chicken), cut up
salt to taste
black pepper to taste
red pepper to taste
2 1/2 cups very warm water
1/2 teaspoon gumbo filé

I Remember...

when we used boxes to catch big river shrimp for Mom to boil, make okra gumbo, or shrimp jambalaya.

Eva Mae Poirrier

Brown fat and flour together until it makes a golden brown roux. Add onion, garlic, bell pepper, celery, and bay leaf. Sauté until golden brown. Add crabs, and shrimp or fryer. Let cook. Also add salt, black pepper, and red pepper. Simmer 20 to 30 minutes.

Add water. Let cook for about 45 minutes to 1 hour on low heat. Last add gumbo filé. Turn off heat. Serve with steamed rice.

Serves 6 to 8.
Elma Oubre

Seafood Gumbo Cajun-Style

5 tablespoons Cajun roux
2 medium onions, chopped
3/4 cup chopped onion tops
1 can (6 ounces) crabmeat
1 tablespoon salt
1/2 teaspoon black pepper
1/2 teaspoon red pepper
1 pound fresh shrimp, peeled and deveined
1 pint oysters

Place 1 gallon of water in a large pot and boil. When boiling, add roux, onions, onion tops, and crabmeat. Season with salt, black pepper, and red pepper. Boil for 45 minutes, stirring frequently. Then add shrimp and oysters. Bring back to a boil and simmer for 15 minutes. I remember when I learned this recipe from my old aunt.

Serves 8 to 10 over rice.
Ella Mae Fontenot

I Remember...

when I was young, "Mom did it all [raising the children]; except Dad played with the kids a little and Mom used him as a threat for punishment." Similarly, my husband, like most men of my generation, did not help with the children; "it just wasn't the thing to do, and a man couldn't change a diaper, my God!"

Olga Manuel

Seafood Gumbo

1 pint roux
2 large onions, chopped
2 bundles onion tops, chopped
parsley to taste
8 pounds shrimp, peeled and deveined
2 dozen crabs, shelled (add claws)
2 pints oysters
2 pints crabmeat
salt to taste
black pepper to taste
red pepper to taste

Fill large gumbo-size pot half full of water. Add
roux, onions, onion tops, and parsley. Bring to a
boil; boil for at least 30 to 40 minutes. Then add
shrimp and crabs. Let come to a rolling boil again.
Then turn heat low and cook for 20 minutes more.
Finally add oysters and crabmeat. Let simmer for
10 to 15 minutes. Turn off heat. Add seasoning a
little at a time throughout cooking. I learned this
recipe from Ti-Gus and my Mom.

Serves 16 to 20.
Pat Ardoin

I Remember...

when my mom and 'Ti-Gus
used to make seafood
gumbo. This is really their
recipe and it is a "no-fail
recipe! 'Ti-Gus and Mom
were first cousins, but they
were more like sisters.
They were both great
cooks and often cooked
big meals together for
family. They were a
blessing to us!"

Pat Ardoin

Crawfish Fettuccini

1 large onion, chopped
1 bell pepper, chopped
1 stick margarine
2 pounds crawfish, peeled and deveined tails only
1 can (10¾ ounces) cream of mushroom soup
1 pound Velveeta jalapeño cheese
1 package (12 ounces) fettuccini noodles

Sauté onions, bell peppers, and margarine. Add crawfish. Then add soup and cheese. Cook on medium heat until cheese is melted.

In a separate pot boil noodles until tender. After noodles are done, mix with crawfish. Ready to eat. Freezes well.

Serves 14.
Ella Mae Fontenot

I Remember...

when my sisters, my mother, and I spent many days in the field hoeing, picking cotton, and digging potatoes. All year long my parents and later my husband and I would live on credit until the cash crops were harvested and then the debts were settled. "Life was hard, very hard, but it was simple, and good, happy."

Versie Meche

Crawfish Patties

1 bottle (48 ounces) oil
1 pound crawfish, peeled and deveined tails only
1 bell pepper, chopped
1 large onion, chopped
1 large potato, chopped
2 cloves garlic, minced
1 stalk celery, chopped
2 tablespoons finely chopped parsley
salt to taste
black pepper to taste
red pepper to taste
1 to 2 eggs, as needed
3 tablespoons bread crumbs

Place oil in deep pot over medium heat. Grind together the crawfish, bell pepper, onion, potato, garlic, and celery. Add parsley. Season with salt, black pepper, and red pepper. Add eggs and mix. Form into patties and roll in bread crumbs. Fry in hot oil until cooked and golden brown.

Serves 4 to 6.
Hilda Waguespack

I Remember...

that my mother cooked Sunday dinners as long as her health permitted. My mom had 13 children and when each one got married they lived with her until they could make their own homes. "We were lucky to have parents who tend to us and help us." When my parents fell ill, I returned the favor by caring for them until they passed away. "I'm glad I did it because I was right there until both of them died."

Carrine "Yen" Fontenot

Crawfish Etouffée I

1 onion, chopped
1 bell pepper, chopped
1 stick margarine
1 tablespoon paprika powder
1 pound crawfish tails, peeled and cleaned
salt to taste
black pepper to taste
red pepper to taste
1 to 2 tablespoons cornstarch

Cook down onion and bell pepper in margarine until wilted. Add water so as not to burn the onions. Add paprika and crawfish. Season with salt, black pepper, and red pepper. Cook for 20 minutes. Take out a little gravy and put cornstarch in it. Replace the gravy. Serve over rice.

Serves 3.
Regina Fontenot

I Remember...

that "[My mother] always had a pretty good meal at night. To me I was always happy when I know the relatives would come, because she'd fry some eggs and she'd cook some Irish potatoes. She didn't cook that too often. She'd make a big, an etouffée."

Gladys Hebert

Crawfish Etouffée II

1 stick margarine
1/2 bell pepper, chopped
1 medium onion, chopped
1 pound crawfish, peeled and deveined tails only
1 can (10 3/4 ounces) cream of mushroom soup

Sauté margarine, bell pepper, and onion well. Then add crawfish and soup. Cook on medium heat for about 20 minutes. When ready to eat, serve over rice.

Serves 4.
Ella Mae Fontenot

I Remember...

"This I remember, Daddy used to go fishing. Then he'd catch some turtles and put 'em in barrels and ... then Momma'd cook 'em for us. But they'd put 'em in barrels and feed 'em some bread and keep 'em fat. ... Then Daddy would go in the gully and he'd catch catfish with his hand underneath the water in some holes. ... He'd fool 'em. He'd go under there and he'd feel 'em with his hands and he'd pull 'em out. Some were pretty big. And that's a lot of the seafood that we ate."

Dorothy Bryant

Crawfish Bisque

2^1/$_2$ *cups (5 sticks) butter or margarine*
2^1/$_2$ *cups all-purpose flour*
6 cups chopped onions
2 cups chopped bell pepper
1 cup chopped celery
^{1}/$_2$ cup chopped garlic
1 teaspoon sugar
1 tablespoon salt
2 teaspoons black pepper
1 teaspoon red pepper
1 can (8 ounces) tomato paste
1 cup chicken broth
2 pounds crawfish tails

Make roux by heating butter and flour until dark brown. Do not burn. Add onions, bell pepper, celery, garlic, and sugar. Season with salt, black pepper, and red pepper. Sauté for about 10 minutes. Add tomato paste, broth, 1 quart water, and crawfish. Boil for 10 minutes. Turn down your heat and let gravy thicken a little, but not too long or the crawfish will overcook, about 10 minutes at most. The boys had a commercial crawfish farm so I had plenty and experimented.

Serves 4.
Rose Fontenot

I Remember...

that "Poppa, Momma had a big old crock jar about this big around and Poppa would, we'd get the sugar by the hundred pounds. And to keep the ants from it, see, [Momma would] put a kerosene rag around it, and it would keep the ants from taking the sugar in the summertime."

Corinne Judice

Crawfish Casserole I

1 pound crawfish or shrimp, peeled
1¹/2 cups uncooked rice
1 can (10³/4 ounces) French onion soup
1 can (10³/4 ounces) cream of mushroom soup
1 can (14.5 ounces) tomatoes
¹/3 can (5 ounces) Rotel tomatoes
¹/2 cup chopped bell pepper
¹/2 cup (1 stick) margarine
Cajun seasoning to taste (salt, black pepper, and red
    pepper)
green chives (as desired)

Preheat oven to 350 degrees. Combine crawfish or
shrimp, rice, French onion soup, cream of mushroom soup, tomatoes, Rotel, bell pepper, margarine,
Cajun seasoning, and green chives. Mix well. Place
in a greased 4-quart casserole dish. Bake for 1 hour.

Serves 3 to 4.
Verna Amedee

I Remember...

that "my mother-in-law,
to me, was like my mother.
A lot of people I used to
hear say 'oh mother-in-
law.' Oh, they hated their
mother-in-law, not me. I
never hated that woman.
She was so good, so kind,
so loving. You could not
help yourself from liking
her. And she taught me a
lot, too."

Rita Rodrigue

Crawfish Casserole II

1 stick butter or margarine
1/4 cup finely chopped bell pepper
1 large onion, finely chopped
1 stalk celery, finely chopped
1 pound crawfish tails
1/4 cup finely chopped onion tops
2 cups cooked rice
1 can (10 3/4 ounces) cream of mushroom soup
1 can (10 3/4 ounces) cream of celery soup
salt to taste
black pepper to taste
red pepper to taste

Preheat oven to 350 degrees. Melt butter or margarine in a saucepan. Add bell peppers, onions, and celery into the saucepan and sauté until onions are clear. Add crawfish tails, onion tops, rice, cream of mushroom soup, and cream of celery soup. Season with salt, black pepper, and red pepper. Mix well. Pour ingredients into a well-greased 2- or 3-quart casserole dish. Bake for 30 to 40 minutes. This is my own experimental recipe.

Serves 4 to 5.
Rose Fontenot

I Remember...

when my father owned a couple hundred acres of woodland. "All farmers at that time bought woodland because everybody heated with fireplaces and wood stoves and they cooked on wood stoves. ... We had to haul that wood in for 'em to, for Mama to have wood during the day and then for us to burn at night; but that was our chore after school."

Corinne Judice

Shrimp Creole

1 tablespoon all-purpose flour
1/4 to 1/2 cup oil
1/2 cup chopped onion
1/2 cup chopped bell pepper
2 pounds shrimp, peeled and deveined
1/2 teaspoon red pepper
black pepper to taste
salt to taste
garlic powder to taste
1 can (8 ounces) tomato sauce
1 can (8 ounces) tomato paste
1/2 cup chopped onion tops
1 dash thyme (optional)

Put flour, oil, onions, and bell pepper in a pot and brown until onions are cooked. Add shrimp. Season with red pepper, black pepper, salt, and garlic powder; and let cook 10 minutes on medium heat, stirring occasionally. Add tomato sauce and paste and onion tops. Turn down the heat, and let simmer for 1 1/2 hours so that the flavors can gel. Right before you finish cooking, add thyme and cook 10 more minutes. Serve over rice.

Serves 5.
Dorothy Bryant

I Remember...

when "I had my baby in 1930, the first little girl. And she lived three and a half months, January 19 until March 30; we found her dead. That was the hardest thing to face. The doctor said he didn't know what it was and she was a sweet little girl. She was a red head, big brown eyes; she was precious."

Gladys Hebert

My Shrimp Creole

I Remember...

learning needlework from my mother and have since made a lot of quilts and afghans in my life, "all of my relatives have a piece of my crochet. I sew pieces of scraps together and then give the large piece I create to a friend of mine, Ella Mae Fontenot, to quilt. When we have time Ella Mae and I and a few other ladies enjoy quilting together. "It was always like a party when we'd go [to Ella Mae's], four or five women."

Viola Rider

1 medium onion, chopped
1/2 bell pepper, chopped
1 stick margarine
1 pound shrimp, peeled and deveined
salt to taste
black pepper to taste
red pepper to taste
1 can (10³/4 ounces) cream of shrimp soup

On medium heat, cook onion and bell pepper in margarine. Add shrimp and season with salt, black pepper, and red pepper. Cook about 10 minutes then add shrimp soup. Add about a half of a soup can of water when you add the shrimp soup. Cook about another 10 minutes. Serve over rice when done. I made this recipe on my own. I have a friend and he enjoys it very much.

Serves 3 to 4.
Ella Mae Fontenot

Shrimp Casserole

1 stick margarine
1 onion, chopped
1 bell pepper, chopped
$^{1}/_{2}$ jalapeño pepper, chopped
1 can (13.25 ounces) sliced mushrooms
1 large can (14.5 ounces) chicken broth
1 dash salt
$^{1}/_{2}$ pound shrimp, peeled, deveined, and coarsely chopped
1 cup and 2 tablespoons uncooked rice

Cut margarine in fourths. Add onion, bell pepper, and jalapeño pepper. Then add mushrooms with juice, chicken broth, salt, and shrimp. Put all ingredients in rice cooker with raw rice. Swish around until well mixed. Cook in the rice cooker as you would rice. A friend had given me this some years ago.

Serves 4.
Claire Bonin

I Remember...

tales of *fricaleurs* (dead little angels) at night who were trapped between the physical world on earth and the spiritual world in heaven. There is a special prayer for those who have miscarriages, so that the baby's soul will not haunt the mother.

Olga Manuel

Deep-Fat Fried Shrimp

2 quarts cooking oil
3 pounds shrimp, peeled and deveined
1 tablespoon salt
1 teaspoon red pepper
1 teaspoon black pepper
1 cup self-rising flour

Preheat oil. Set deep-fat fryer on 400 degrees and add oil. Set aside. Season shrimp with salt, red pepper, and black pepper. Then roll in self-rising flour. Drop floured shrimp in ice water for 3 to 4 minutes. Remove from ice water, and roll again in self-rising flour. Drop in hot oil and cook for 5 to 7 minutes. If you use jumbo shrimp, cut the shrimp on top so they will be butterfly shrimp. This batter can be used for fryers (young chickens) also.

Serves 6 to 8.
Belle Fontenot

I Remember...

when a few unmarried great uncles lived at the house during harvest time or construction projects; they made me dolls and little furniture. When an old maid aunt's visit might last five years, when she came to help with a new baby.

Olga Manuel

Fried Shrimp or Chicken

*2 to 3 pounds medium to large shrimp, peeled and
    deveined or 1 chicken (2 to 3 pounds)*
salt to taste
red pepper to taste
black pepper to taste
garlic powder to taste
1 bottle (48 ounces) cooking oil
1 cup milk
2 eggs
all-purpose flour, as needed

Place shrimp or chicken in a pan. Season with salt,
red pepper, black pepper, and garlic powder; and
set aside. Pour oil 4 inches thick into deep pot or
deep-fat fryer (preferably Fry Daddy). Turn on your
Fry Daddy or put deep pot over medium heat and
let oil heat up. Mix milk, eggs, salt, red pepper,
black pepper, and garlic powder in a bowl. Dip a
handful of preseasoned shrimp or chicken in this
mixture. Have flour in a paper plate. Take the
shrimp or chicken out of the milk batter and roll in
the flour. Fry that batch until the shrimp float to
the top of the grease and are golden brown. Repeat
the entire process until finished. For chicken, cook
until there is no more blood.

Serves 4.
Dorothy Bryant

I Remember...

when "outside, we has two
tubs, one tub was to wash
and the other one was to
rinse. So in the rinse water,
we'd put a little bluing.
And like the clothes, the
men's clothes we'd boil
that in a big pot. And
when I'd first married, I
didn't know how to wash.
I hadn't washed when I
was at home. My sister
would do the wash."

Gladys Hebert

Salmon Gumbo

4 to 6 tablespoons roux (preferably Savoie's)
1 large onion, chopped
1 bell pepper, chopped
1 clove garlic, minced (optional)
1 bundle onion tops, chopped (optional)
salt to taste
black pepper to taste
red pepper to taste
Tony Chachere's Creole Seasoning (optional)
1 large can (14.75 ounces) salmon
4 eggs

For roux, I used to cook flour in oil on a medium fire until it formed a roux and reached the desired color of brown. I now use ready mix dark roux. Cook roux, onion, bell pepper, garlic, and onion tops in 3 to 4 cups of water for about 1 hour at medium heat.

While this is cooking down, season with salt, black pepper, red pepper, and Creole seasoning. Then add salmon. Cook about 20 minutes longer. Then you gently break eggs into gumbo. Cook until eggs are done. Serve with rice and good homemade potato salad.

Serves 3 to 4.
Joyce Brasseux

I Remember...

that "I grew up in a Catholic family, and we did not eat meat on Fridays. So living on a farm we grew our own foods: chicken, vegetables, and beef. Some of my favorite meals was salmon gumbo, then tomato gravy with dropped eggs served on rice, then potato fricassée with boiled eggs served on rice. Rice and potatoes were very much used every day in some way."

Joyce Brasseux

Stuffed Catfish

2 1/2 cups corn bread stuffing mix
1/2 cup diced cooking apples
1/2 cup crushed walnuts
1/2 cup white raisins
1/2 cup evaporated milk
2 tablespoons brown sugar
1 large egg
1 1/2 sticks butter
1/2 cup French style salad dressing
1 tablespoon Worcestershire sauce
3 tablespoons lemon juice
6 farm-raised catfish (12 pounds total, cleaned fillets or whole)
6 lemon slices (optional)

Preheat oven to 350 degrees. Combine corn bread mix, apples, walnuts, raisins, milk, brown sugar, egg, and 1/2 stick of butter. Cook on low heat for 10 minutes. Add salad dressing to the stuffing mixture.

Mix together Worcestershire sauce, 1 stick butter, and lemon juice to make basting sauce.

For whole fish baste the inside of the fish, then stuff. For fillets, baste inside of fillet, place stuffing in middle of fillet and roll with seam side down securing with toothpicks.

Bake fillets 15 minutes and whole fish 40 minutes. Baste afterward and broil for 5 minutes. Garnish with lemon slices, if desired.

Serves 8 to 10.
Dorothy Bryant

I Remember...

when, "we used to love to go to the store [that my dad owned], and then when we got old enough, well, he would let us help around. If someone wanted a spool of thread or something that, you know, wasn't too important well he'd let us wait on the people, serve the people. ... Well now some people, who had a lot of chickens, they would bring their eggs to the store; and whatever the eggs were worth well they would keep a record of that, you know, and they would trade it for merchandise."

Jeanne Arceneaux

Perch

1 bottle (48 ounces) oil (preferably canola)
8 small perch (8 pounds total), cleaned
salt to taste
black pepper to taste
red pepper to taste
garlic powder to taste
cornmeal as needed

Pour oil 4 inches deep into large pot or deep-fat fryer. Heat oil in pot over medium heat or turn on deep-fat fryer. Season perch with salt, black pepper, red pepper, and garlic powder. Roll in cornmeal and fry in hot oil until they float.

Serves 4.
Dorothy Bryant

Tuna Fish

1 can (6 ounces) tuna fish
3 eggs, boiled and mashed
1 Irish potato, boiled and mashed
3 tablespoons mayonnaise
$^1/_2$ cup pickle relish
salt to taste
black pepper to taste
red pepper to taste

Mix tuna fish, eggs, potato, mayonnaise, and relish.
Stir well and season with salt, black pepper, and
red pepper. This makes a good filler for a sandwich
or as a side with macaroni.

Serves 3 to 4.
Blanche Quebedeaux

I Remember...

that at *veillées*, we often
witnessed a musical per-
formance of some kind,
which included French
songs accompanied by an
accordion, a harmonica, or
whatever was available.
"One guy had a guitar
which he couldn't play but
he'd try and we'd all grab
our spoons, join in and
sing and make our own
music." Informal visits
such as these were the
highlight of the day, and
"If company came over,
you just stopped what you
were doing and cooked."

Annie Taylor

Side Dishes

Sauce Des Pommes De Terre (Potato Stew)

2 pounds sausage
5 pounds potatoes, peeled and cut in chunks
1 bell pepper, chopped
2 onions, chopped
3 ribs celery, chopped
3 to 4 cloves garlic (optional)
salt to taste
black pepper to taste
red pepper to taste
onion tops (optional)
parsley (optional)

Chop sausage in 1/2-inch slices and brown in a Dutch oven over medium heat. Add potatoes, bell peppers, onions, celery, and garlic. Season with salt, black pepper, and red pepper. Sauté until light brown. Add water to reach a level of 1 inch. Reduce heat, add onion tops and parsley, simmer for about 20 minutes. Allow potatoes to begin to break apart to thicken gravy. Serve over rice.

Serves 8.
Velma Reaux

I Remember. . .

that my family's property never changed hands. My family originally got the land through land grants many generations ago. After the Civil War, the property was almost lost, because my great great grandfather's Confederate money was worthless. So my great grandmother went to her father (from Illinois) and asked for her inheritance early so she could save her father-in-law's property. And that's what saved the property.

Eva Mae Poirrier

Stewed Potatoes

6 Irish potatoes
¼ cup oil
1 onion, sliced
salt to taste
sausage (optional)

Peel and slice potatoes. Put them in a pot with a little oil. Add onion, salt, and 1 cup water. Cover and cook, stirring occasionally to keep potatoes from sticking. Add more water if needed and cook until potatoes are tender. This is very good with sausage. If using sausage, slice and fry it first. Then add other ingredients as described above.

Serves 5 to 6.
Doris Regan

I Remember...

when "we went to school with one teacher, with one room, seven grades. And we had to walk, well it was over a mile that we walked and uh when it was dry, you was in dust that deep, and when it was wet, it was raining plenty, you was in mud that deep."

Rita Rodrigue's husband, Gaston Rodrigue

Potato Fricassée

4 to 6 tablespoons dark roux (preferably Savoie's)
1 onion, chopped
1 cup chopped celery
1 bell pepper, chopped
5 or 6 large potatoes, cubed
6 eggs, boiled

For roux, I used to cook flour in oil on a medium
fire until it formed a roux and reached the desired
color of brown. I now use ready mix dark roux.

To make potato fricassée cook as you would gumbo
only it's much thicker. Cook roux, onions, celery,
and peppers in 3 cups of water for 30 to 45 minutes
at medium heat. Add potatoes. Continue cooking
until the potatoes are done then add boiled eggs.
Cook another 10 minutes. Serve on rice when done.
I have eaten many starches in years gone by.

Serves 6 to 8.
Joyce Brasseux

I Remember...

when I learned to cut hair
from my mother, who cut
all of her children's hair. I
would go on to do the
same including cutting my
own hair.

Carrine "Yen" Fontenot

I Remember...

"When I was young, my parents didn't have much to offer us to eat. We ate a lot of potatoes and rice. I will offer a couple of recipes for potatoes that was used during Lent."

Doris Regan

Potatoes Gravy

2/3 cup oil
2/3 cup all-purpose flour
1 onion, chopped
5 Irish potatoes, peeled and quartered
salt to taste
black pepper to taste
red pepper to taste
3 eggs, boiled (optional)
shrimp (optional)

Make a roux of the oil and flour. After roux is made, add 2 cups water, onion, and potatoes. Season with salt, black pepper, and red pepper. On a medium flame cook down until potatoes are tender and gravy reaches desired thickness. You may add 2 or 3 boiled eggs that have been peeled and sliced.

This gravy is also good with shrimp. If using shrimp, add them to the gravy when it is almost done and cook until shrimp are done.

Serves 3 to 4.
Doris Regan

Smothered Irish Potatoes

6 medium-size potatoes
1/3 cup cooking oil
1 big onion, chopped
1/2 bell pepper, chopped
salt to taste
black pepper to taste
red pepper to taste

Peel your potatoes. Cut them up in pieces. Put your oil in a thick pot. Add onion and bell pepper. Season with salt, black pepper, and red pepper. Cook for 1 hour on low fire and stir often. Add water as needed.

Serves 6 to 8.
Ella Mae Fontenot

Irish Potato Casserole

1 can (10³/4 ounces) celery soup
¹/2 cup milk
salt to taste
black pepper to taste
red pepper to taste
4 cups thinly sliced potatoes
¹/2 cup chopped onions
¹/2 cup grated American cheese

Preheat oven to 350 degrees. Heat can of soup and milk. Butter casserole dish. (Use ¹/3 to ¹/4 of your ingredients to make each layer; season with salt, black pepper, and red pepper between layers.) Arrange 1 layer of potatoes, 1 layer of onions, 1 layer of soup, and 1 layer of cheese. Repeat this process three to four times. Cover casserole and cook for about 30 minutes.

Serves 6.
Ella Mae Fontenot

I Remember...

"I was the oldest in family, and naturally, my momma and daddy, my momma didn't even have a washing machine, and that's when I went to work to get her first washing machine. I worked at the cigar factory, I used to cellophane cigars at the cigar factory in Donaldsonville, which manufactured King Rubin cigars." Also "When I was growing up, they had a rolling store come in front of the house with a bus, like with shelves. I tell you even when I first got married it was easy because we had grocery. We had our bread man, we had our vegetables and fruits, the meat man. What else? We'd get everything. I'd tell my kids that all the time, how we never had to go to grocery. They'd come two or three times a week, well the fruit man would come once a week."

Winnie Fernandez

Cooking With Cajun Women

Potato Casserole

1 bag (12 ounces) hash browns, thawed
1 can (10³/₄ ounces) cream of chicken soup
1 container (8 ounces) sour cream
2 ounces shredded cheddar cheese
¹/₂ cup butter, melted
1 onion, minced

Preheat oven to 350 degrees. Line greased 9 by 13-inch casserole dish with hash browns. Mix chicken soup, sour cream, cheddar cheese, butter, and onion together and pour over hash browns. Bake for 45 minutes.

Serves 4 to 5.
Dorothy Bryant

I Remember...

when I went to dances as a young girl. Boys and girls sat on separate walls and when we danced, the chaperones always watched. And that was a big thing for a guy to walk a girl back to her buggy or car. "Grandma researched all eligible young men with other moms and let you know who was O.K."

Olga Manuel

Stuffed Potatoes

2 Irish potatoes
salt to taste
red pepper to taste
black pepper to taste
2 cloves garlic, peeled
1 to 2 tablespoons oil

After paring the potatoes, drill a "hole" in each potato. I use a slender blade for drilling. (If holes are too large, stuffing will not remain in potatoes during cooking.) Mix salt, red pepper, and black pepper in a separate container. Using a small spoon, put desired amount of seasoning into each opening. Add a small piece of garlic into each opening. Replace potato drillings into each opening. Press firmly into holes so that stuffing will not fall out during cooking.

Brown potatoes in pot in a small amount of oil. Add water to cover potatoes. Bring to a boil, then lower burner and simmer until tender.

Serves 1 (*I usually figure 2 potatoes per serving.*)
Evon Melancon

I Remember...

when "I learned to prepare these potatoes from my mother. It's a recipe she created for using the fresh Irish potatoes from her garden. She was always careful to select uniform-sized potatoes. They cooked evenly, and it made the finished dish more attractive."

Evon Melancon

Stuffed Red Potatoes

4 or 5 large red potatoes
salt to taste
black pepper to taste
1/2 cup chopped onion tops
1 small white onion, chopped
1/2 cup parsley
1 celery rib, chopped
1/2 cup chopped bell pepper
2 teaspoons minced garlic or
  1 teaspoon garlic powder
2 tablespoons oil
4 to 5 strips bacon

Wash and dry the red potatoes. You may peel or scrape off peelings. With sharp knife, scrape out the center and mix with salt and pepper to taste. Add onion tops, onions, parsley, celery, bell pepper, and garlic together and stuff the potatoes.

Preheat oven to 375 degrees. Next in a pan or pot, add 2 tablespoons water and oil together. Place the stuffed potatoes in the oil and cover each one with a strip of bacon. Bake for 1 1/2 hours or until brown and tender.

You can cook on stovetop or bake. "This was always served on Sundays. My mother would add to every Sunday dinner as everyone loved it."

Serves 5.
Thelma Coles

I Remember...

that I was the one who cooked all the meals when my husband was alive. "Oh yeah and I still cook. ... [My husband] made coffee and made toast for the kids when I was sick that's about it." Pat, my son, added, "Oh Poppa never cooked, Momma said he'd never, we'd have starved to death if we waited to eat what he cooked."

Corinne Judice

Tomato Gravy and Eggs

1 can (8 ounces) tomato sauce
1 small can (8 ounces) tomato paste
1 onion, chopped
salt to taste
black pepper to taste
red pepper to taste
2 to 3 eggs

Cook down tomato sauce and paste at medium heat for 15 to 20 minutes. If too thick add water. Add onion and season with salt, black pepper, and red pepper. Cook 20 to 30 minutes. Break eggs into gravy. Cook 15 minutes. Serve with rice and vegetables.

Serves 2 to 3.
Joyce Brasseux

I Remember...

when all of the family celebrations were held at my parents' house until they passed on and then I took over as the event host and coordinator. For Easter, all the neighbors would come over and *paque* eggs. I remember that one year I was so busy visiting I forgot to put my rice on and dinner was ready before I remembered. I enjoyed dying my eggs with old material, weeds, and whatever I could find around the yard that would stain the eggs a nice color. Mardi Gras was merely another excuse for a family gathering at my house.

Carrine "Yen" Fontenot

Maque Choux Corn

6 to 10 ears corn
1 onion, chopped
1 small clove garlic, minced
1/3 cup oil
1/2 can (4 ounces) tomato sauce
1 tablespoon salt
1/2 teaspoon black pepper
1/4 teaspoon red pepper
1 bell pepper, chopped

Cut corn off of the cob. Put corn in a medium-size pot. Add onion, garlic, oil, tomato sauce, salt, black pepper, red pepper, and bell pepper. Cook all together on medium to low heat for 1 hour. Add water as needed to avoid burning. When done, serve.

Serves approximately 8.
Blanche Quebedeaux

I Remember...

when I was young, I was taught to always fast everytime we take communion, to make confession before receiving communion, and to never eat meat on Fridays. Since we could not eat meat on Fridays and we could not afford fish, we ate tomato gravy, Irish potatoes, black-eyed peas, or eggs instead.

Jean Brasseaux

Casserole

1 cup uncooked rice
1 cup whole kernel corn
salt to taste
black pepper to taste
red pepper to taste
2 cans (16 ounces total) tomato sauce
1/2 cup chopped onions
1/2 cup chopped bell peppers
3/4 pound ground beef
5 bacon strips

Preheat oven to 350 degrees. Put all ingredients in a large casserole dish in this order—rice at bottom of dish, next corn, salt, black pepper, red pepper, 1 can tomato sauce, and 1/2 cup water. Add onions and peppers. Next, add the ground beef and second can of tomato sauce and 1/4 cup water. Cover with bacon strips. Bake for 1 hour. Take cover off of dish and bake about 30 minutes or until bacon is crisp.

Serves 4.
Thelma Coles

I Remember . . .

when "I used to watch [my mom], but Momma was just like I am. I didn't let my kids cook in the kitchen; they'd help me, but I was always the leader and Momma was the same way. I guess all Mommas are that way. And you miss that help when they leave. ... But now my daughters that are married are very good cooks."

Corinne Judice

Corn Bread Dressing I

3 boxes (25.5 ounces total) corn bread mix
  (preferably Jiffy)
4 packs (6 to 7½ pounds total) gizzard, chopped
1 cup chopped onion tops
½ cup chopped celery
1 cup chopped bell pepper
1 dozen eggs, boiled and chopped
3 cans (43.5 ounces total) chicken broth
salt to taste
black pepper to taste
red pepper to taste
garlic powder to taste

Following the directions on the corn bread box,
make 3 corn breads and set them aside for later.
Boil gizzards in a 5-quart pot until tender. Remove
the gizzards and keep the gizzard broth in the pot.
Chop the gizzards in a mixer and put back in the
broth. Then add onion tops, celery, and bell pepper
to the gizzards and broth. Cook on a medium heat
until onion tops and bell peppers are tender.

Preheat oven to 350 degrees. Crumble corn bread in
a large roaster and add eggs. Add the gizzard mixture to the corn bread and mix well. Then gradually
add chicken broth as needed for moisture. Season
with salt, black pepper, red pepper, and garlic powder until you reach desired taste. Mix well.

Bake uncovered in a large roaster in the oven for ½
hour. Stir twice while baking and add water if necessary to keep from sticking.

Serves 12.
Dorothy Bryant

I Remember...

meeting my husband while
I was dating his cousin.
My would-be husband
kept picking at my date
and me. In his defense, my
husband, John comments,
"Well, he couldn't dance
and I could. I wanted to
make you dance and we've
been dancing ever since."

Joyce Brasseux

Corn Bread Dressing II

1 corn bread, prepared
1 fryer, boiled and cut up
6 cups bread crumbs
3 raw eggs
2 cups chopped bell pepper
2 cups chopped onion
chicken broth (from cooked fryer)
milk (as needed)

Preheat oven to 350 degrees. Crumble corn bread. Add fryer, bread crumbs, eggs, bell peppers, and onions. Mix. Add chicken broth, and enough milk to moisten mixture. Bake in a 9 by 13-inch pan or large casserole dish for 25 to 35 minutes and light brown in color.

Serves 6 to 8.
Viola Rider

I Remember...

for the *boucheries* we'd use the fat, "cause fat is good in some foods. You need fat, you need some fat in foods. And then [my mother would] always make uh, uh, we called it *café au lait* but it's actually brown sugar. You brown your sugar and put milk in it, Pet milk or whatever. That was *café au lait*. My mother would make her own ketchup and she'd make syrup."

Rose Thibodeaux

Corn Bread Dressing III

2 cloves garlic, minced
1 large onion, diced
2 or 3 stalks celery, minced
1 cup minced bell pepper
3 tablespoons oil
1 pound ground beef
1 pound ground pork or seasoned sausage
salt to taste
black pepper to taste
red pepper to taste
1 cup broth or water
1 or 2 cups chopped onion tops
1 cup parsley
1 pan (9 by 12-inch) cooked corn bread
10 to 12 Ritz crackers, crushed
6 to 8 eggs, boiled and chopped
1 or 2 raw eggs, slightly beaten
mushrooms (optional)

Boiled eggs and corn bread may be cooked the day before. Also chop vegetables day before and store in plastic bags (preferably Ziploc) in the refrigerator.

Preheat oven to 300 degrees. Place garlic, onions, celery, and bell pepper with oil in a large skillet. Brown lightly. Season ground beef and ground pork or sausage with salt, black pepper, and red pepper. Add the seasoned meat to the skillet. Brown slowly and thoroughly stirring often (until all pink is out of the meat). Add broth (or water) to the meat and cover. Cook over low heat for about 15 minutes.

I Remember...

when times were harder. "We rich now. We rich by what we were raised... I tell you the truth, now we a millionaire by what we were raised."

Henriette Richard

that "we were raised on rice and gravy and potatoes. We had to stir in the pot as soon as we were tall enough. Our mother had too many other thing to do besides. Setting the table then cleaning and washing dishes was the same: one would wash, one would wash, one would dry. Sweep the kitchen and dining room was the job of the dishwasher and dryer, a set of two, cleaning the rest of the rooms, [and] washing and hanging out clothes were for the older ones."

Vinice Sensat

Add onion tops and parsley. In large baking pan, crumble corn bread, crackers, and boiled eggs. Add meat mixture. Mix well. Dressing should be moist, add broth or water if needed. Next add raw eggs and mix well.

Place dressing in oven and bake for about 20 minutes. Serve with brown gravy. If desired, mushrooms may be added. Recipe originally from Miss Genuso.

Serves 8 to 10.
Etheleen Meaux

Eggplant Dressing

2 eggplants
2 pounds ground beef
1 tablespoon salt
black pepper to taste
red pepper to taste
1 medium onion, chopped
1 can (14.5 ounces) chicken broth
2 or 3 cups cooked rice

Cube and cook eggplant down in boiling water until tender. Drain and set aside. Brown ground beef in a 4-quart iron pot or larger. Season with salt, black pepper, and red pepper. When your meat is almost cooked, add onions and eggplant. Continue cooking until onions wilt. Then pour in chicken broth and cook down. Stir in rice. Mix well and cook for 2 minutes. Ready to serve.

Serves 6 to 8.
Gladys Hebert

I Remember...

that my mother made all of the family's clothes, "underwear and all," out of rice sacks and cotton. I remember that my mother loved to sew more than anything else. When I was just a child, my mother started letting me sew the hems. I would make shirts out of feed sacks for my own husband and children. My mother not only taught me how to sew, but how to embroider as well.

Blanche Quebedeaux

Eggplant Fritters

1 bottle (48 ounces) oil
1 or 2 eggplants
1 small onion, chopped
1 egg
1 teaspoon baking powder
1/2 bar (8 ounces) mild cheddar cheese, grated
1 pack saltine crackers, crushed
salt to taste
black pepper to taste
red pepper to taste
flour

Heat oil in a deep pot over medium heat. Peel, quarter, and boil eggplants in water until tender. Mash eggplants after softened. Drain off extra water. Sauté onions in microwave until clear. Add to eggplant. Add egg, baking powder, cheese, and crackers. Season with salt, black pepper, and red pepper. Add flour until thick enough to roll into balls. Roll in flour. Fry in hot oil until brown. Fry last: cheese will mess up your grease.

Serves 8.
Regina Fontenot

I Remember...

how close my father and my husband were. "If I would have gone home and left my husband, [my father] would have taken a strap and beat me back until I get back over here... He would have taken up for my husband more than he would have taken up for me."

Rita Rodrigue

Eggplant Casserole I

1 large eggplant
1 onion, finely chopped
1 1/2 pounds ground meat
salt to taste
black pepper to taste
red pepper to taste
1/2 teaspoon garlic powder
3 slices bread, crumbled
2 eggs
1 small jar (4 ounces) pimientos, chopped
grated cheddar cheese (as desired)

Preheat oven to 350 degrees. Peel, cube, and cook eggplant in salted water. While it is cooking, sauté onion and meat. Season with salt, black pepper, red pepper, and garlic powder.

Drain and mash eggplant. Add bread crumbs, eggs, and pimientos. Stir, then add to meat mixture. Put in greased 9 by 13-inch casserole dish. Cover with grated cheese. Bake for 25 to 30 minutes.

Serves 6 to 8.
Regina Fontenot

I Remember...

"You see, my neighborhood where I live there, we're about five ladies... We sit on my car porch and we stay there for three or four hours and we talk, almost every night. That's a *soirée*. ... But I mean it's nice. It passes the time and some-times the men's gonna come. We just talk; we just visit; we tell stories and we know all the news from New Orleans to Baton Rouge to Lafayette."

Pauline Guidry

Eggplant Casserole II

2 medium-size eggplants
2 cups ground meat
1 tablespoon shortening
1 onion, chopped
1 bell pepper, chopped
$^1/_2$ cup Italian seasoned bread crumbs plus extra for
    topping, or 1 cup cooked rice
4 to 6 tablespoons Parmesan cheese
1 teaspoon Italian seasoning
1 teaspoon garlic powder
salt to taste
black pepper to taste
red pepper to taste

Peel eggplants. Cut in 1-inch cubes and cook in a small amount of water until tender. Drain and set aside.

In a skillet, brown ground meat with shortening. Add chopped onion and bell pepper. Sauté until tender and juicy. Add eggplant to skillet plus bread crumbs or rice, 3 to 4 tablespoons Parmesan cheese, Italian seasoning, and garlic powder. Season with salt, black pepper, and red pepper.

Transfer to 3-quart casserole dish. Top with desired amount of bread crumbs and 1 to 2 tablespoons of Parmesan cheese.

Serves 6.
Rose Fontenot

Eggplant Casserole III

3 medium eggplants, cubed
1 stick butter
1 large onion, chopped
1 bell pepper, chopped
1 clove garlic, minced
salt to taste
black pepper to taste
red pepper to taste
2 cups shrimp, chopped coarse
1/2 cup seasoned Italian bread crumbs

Boil eggplants until tender and set aside. Melt 1/2 stick butter in pot. Add chopped onion, bell pepper, and garlic. Season with salt, black pepper, and red pepper. Let simmer down. Add scalded eggplants. Let cook for 10 minutes. Add shrimp. Let cook 30 to 45 minutes. Add a little bread crumbs while cooking.

Preheat oven to 350 degrees. When cooked, pour in casserole dish. Sprinkle with rest of bread crumbs and 1/2 stick butter cut into small pats. Bake in oven for 20 minutes.

Serves 4 to 6.
Elma Oubre

I Remember...

"when my little sister had polio, 76 years ago. The doctor in Crowley didn't know and then she went to New Orleans, they didn't know anything either. It would take her an hour to eat just soft foods. Poppa went to see if there wasn't a chair he could get, kind of like a recliner and it lays all the way back and a footstool comes out. He ordered one and "her chair came in the day she died, so she didn't use her chair." I still have my sister's chair. "Mama said the doctor's was as dumb as them. They didn't know what to do for that you see and Mama said they never did state it was polio but she figured that's what it was after so many others had polio."

Corinne Judice

Stuffed Bell Peppers I

4 large whole bell peppers
2 pounds shrimp
1 large onion, chopped
2 tablespoons finely chopped parsley
1/2 cup chopped celery
1/2 cup chopped bell peppers
2 cooking spoons oil
2 tablespoons butter
2 slices bread, dampened
salt to taste
black pepper to taste
red pepper to taste
1 egg
2 to 4 tablespoons butter, melted
1/4 to 1/2 cup bread crumbs

Preheat oven to 350 degrees. Cut whole peppers in halves, lengthwise. Remove stems, seeds, and membranes. Parboil for 10 or 15 minutes. Then drain. Cook the shrimp and grind them. Set aside.

Sauté onions, parsley, celery, and chopped bell peppers in oil and 2 tablespoons butter for about 8 minutes. Mix with the shrimp. Crumble the dampened bread into the mixture. Season with salt, black pepper, and red pepper. Beat the egg and add to the mixture. Mix well.

Then stuff the bell peppers and place them in a 9 by 13-inch casserole dish with a touch of water lining the pan. Spread melted butter on top of stuffed peppers and cover with bread crumbs. Bake until bell peppers are fully cooked and bread crumbs brown.
Makes 8.
Hilda Waguespack

Stuffed Bell Peppers II

5 large bell peppers, halved
2 tablespoons olive oil or cooking oil
1 large onion, chopped
1 bell pepper, chopped
2 stalks celery, cut up
1 clove garlic, minced
1 bunch onion tops, chopped
$1/2$ loaf bread
2 eggs
$1/2$ teaspoon salt
$1/4$ teaspoon black pepper
1 pound shrimp, peeled and deveined
1 pound fresh crabmeat
$1/2$ cup Italian bread crumbs
$1/2$ stick butter
1 bunch parsley

Boil the halved bell peppers until tender. In large skillet, heat oil. When warm add onion, chopped bell pepper, celery, garlic, and onion tops. Simmer down until tender.

Soften bread in a bowl of water. Squeeze bread from water and dispose of the water. Return bread to the bowl and mix well with eggs, salt, and black pepper. Then add this to the skillet with shrimp and crabmeat. Mix well and cook on low heat for 10 minutes.

Preheat oven to 350 degrees. Stuff bell pepper with this mixture. Sprinkle with bread crumbs and a pat of butter each. Bake for approximately 15 minutes. Garnish with parsley. Serve with salad and hot garlic bread.
Makes 10.
Elma Oubre

1 pound ground meat
1 can (10³/4 ounces) cream of mushroom soup
1 can (8 ounces) mushroom steak sauce
1 can (10³/4 ounces) French onion soup
1 cube beef bouillon
1 cup raw rice
1/2 cup chopped onion tops
1/2 cup chopped bell pepper
1/2 cup chopped celery

Preheat oven to 375 degrees. Brown ground meat and drain. Add cream of mushroom soup, mushroom steak sauce, French onion soup, beef bouillon cube, rice, onion tops, bell pepper, and celery. Mix well.

Cook in a black iron pot in the oven for 1/2 hour, covered. Then uncover and cook 1/2 hour more.

Serves 4. If you want to make it for a large family of 8 to 10 double all the measurements. Dorothy Bryant

I Remember...

when I met my husband. He was from Mamou, and I was from just down the road near Chataignier, in Lanse Aux Paille. Back then "Cajun married Cajun, because we never looked outside our society, our friends, our kind of people. I didn't know everybody couldn't speak French. ... My generation was the last generation in a totally French culture. Everybody spoke French."

Olga Manuel

Rice Dressing II

1 large eggplant
1 medium onion, chopped
$1/2$ pound ground beef
$1/2$ pound ground pork
$1/2$ cup cooking oil
2 tablespoons salt
2 teaspoons black pepper
1 teaspoon red pepper
1 clove garlic, minced
3 cups cooked rice

Peel, cube, and cook eggplant in salted water until they float and soften, approximately 10 minutes.

While eggplant is cooking, sauté onion and meat with oil in a separate pot. Season with salt, pepper, and garlic. Drain and mash eggplant. Add to meat mixture. Cook down a little. Add water if necessary to keep from sticking. Then add cooked rice and stir. Cook 3 to 5 minutes longer before serving.

Serves 4 to 6.
Blanche Quebedeaux

I Remember...

when we could call our cows by name and they would come. They would graze all day along the bank of the Mississippi River and they knew when to come home. When one wouldn't come down from the levee, we knew that it had gotten bogged in the mud near the river. The men would have to get ropes and pull the cow out. "If the cows got sick and they lost their ability to chew, we had to fix an old rag with different things on it and get them to chew."

Eva Mae Poirrier

Baked Rice Dressing

1¹/4 cups raw rice
1 pound ground beef
1 can (10³/4 ounces) onion soup
1 can (10³/4 ounces) cream of chicken soup
1 large can (13.25 ounces) mushrooms, stems and
*   pieces drained*
1 bell pepper, finely minced
1 onion, finely minced
salt, to taste
black pepper, to taste
red pepper, to taste

Preheat oven to 350 degrees. Mix raw rice and meat well with hands. Then add onion soup, chicken soup, mushrooms, bell peppers, and onions. Add salt, black pepper, and red pepper. Mix well. Place in well-greased 10 by 14-inch pan and cover tightly with aluminum foil. Bake for 1 hour and 20 minutes.

Serves 8 to 10.
Belle Fontenot

Cajun Rice

1 cup uncooked rice
¼ teaspoon hot sauce (preferably Tabasco)
1 can (10¾ ounces) cheddar cheese soup
1 can (10¾ ounces) mushroom soup
¼ cup chopped bell pepper
1 teaspoon salt
1 small onion, chopped
*1 can (6 ounces) drained crabmeat or drained
   shrimp (fresh shrimp will do)*

Preheat oven to 350 degrees. Mix rice, hot sauce,
cheddar cheese soup, and mushroom soup. Add
bell pepper, salt, 1 soup can of water, onion, and
crabmeat or shrimp. Mix well. Bake in a 4-quart
casserole dish, covered, for 1 hour or until done.
Stir once during baking.

Serves 4.
Dorothy Bryant

I Remember...

when we used to make our
own soap and washing
clothes was an all-day
affair. We did not have
indoor plumbing, washing
machines, and air-condi-
tioning. "I always say,
'thank the good Lord we
have warm houses during
the winter and cool houses
during the summer,
because I know what it's
like to do without.'"

Rose Fontenot

Stuffed White Round Squash

1 or 2 large squash
1/2 pound ground meat, browned
1 cup bread crumbs or cooked rice
1/2 cup chopped onion and parsley mixed together
2 slices bacon, cut in small pieces
salt to taste
black pepper to taste
red pepper to taste

Preheat oven to 350 degrees. Wash and dry squash. Peel skin off. Take all seeds out of squash and scoop out most of the flesh, leaving a "shell." Mix the meats of the squash you take out with ground meat, bread crumbs or rice, onion, and parsley, and bacon. Season with salt, black pepper, and red pepper. Put back in squash and bake in a casserole dish with a little water in the bottom for about 45 minutes or 1 hour.

Serves 3 or 4.
Thelma Coles

I Remember...

We used to make our own toys: bottles were horses. We would make a a wagon and play under the house and under the trees. "When it would rain and we was outside we'd take a twine and we'd make a loop... and put some feed for the chickens and we'd pull that and catch the chickens by the feet and see how many we could catch. It didn't take a whole lot to make us happy."

Corinne Judice

Squash

2 to 3 yellow squash
1/2 stick butter
1 bell pepper, chopped
1 onion, chopped
bread crumbs to taste

Preheat oven to 350 degrees. Peel squash, scoop out seeds, and slice. Sauté butter, bell pepper, and onions until they turn clear. Do not burn. Add squash in and cook on stove for 10 to 15 minutes at medium to low heat. Add bread crumbs and put in a medium-size casserole dish. Bake for 15 minutes.

Serves 4.
Regina Fontenot

I Remember...

when I was dating Jim [my future husband] that we always went out as a group or had chaperones. One time my mother sternly warned me, "Don't let Jim touch you or date you, because then he's not gonna marry you." Even at home, we were carefully watched, whether we knew it or not. "I noticed one time in [my mother's] bedroom door there was a little peephole, and one time I saw a little stool there, and I'm sure [my parents] would sit there sometimes."

Rose Fontenot

Mirliton Casserole

8 good-size mirliton (chayote squash)
1 onion, chopped
²/3 cup chopped celery
¹/4 teaspoon oil
1¹/2 pounds ground beef or shrimp
³/4 cup crumbled crackers (preferably Hi-Ho)
4 cloves garlic, minced
seasoned bread crumbs to taste
2 teaspoon season-all
2 to 4 tablespoons butter, melted

Boil mirliton until tender. Take out of water and let cool. Peel and mash pulp with fork and place in colander to drain.

Wilt onion and celery in little oil. Then add ground beef or shrimp to this and cook until meat is well brown or shrimp tails are curled. Add drained mirliton, then crackers, garlic, bread crumbs, and season-all. Let cook down for ¹/2 hour.

Preheat oven to 350 degrees. Take off fire and let it cool and then put in a casserole dish. Dust with bread crumbs and melted butter on top of entire casserole. Bake for about 20 minutes.

Serves 8.
Eva Mae Poirrier

I Remember...

"When I first started making this I used to fry bacon crisp and crumble fine to put in it but I do not do that any more since bacon is not healthy to eat. ... I really like to take young mirliton and stuff them but the young people do not eat the shell of the mirliton so I only fix those for myself like that. I do not scrape the pulp down to the skin when I stuff them. I leave a little bit pulp and I eat shell and all."

Eva Mae Poirrier

Broccoli Casserole

1 medium onion, chopped
3 tablespoons oil
2 packages (2 pounds total) frozen broccoli,
   chopped
1 package (6 ounces) garlic cheese (preferably
   Kraft)
1 can (10¾ ounces) cream of mushroom soup
1½ cups bread or cracker crumbs
1 stick oleo (margarine), melted

Preheat oven to 350 degrees. Sauté onion in oil
until clear. Add broccoli. Continue cooking about
10 minutes. Remove from heat and spoon ½ of
broccoli in casserole dish. Slice ½ of garlic cheese
over broccoli. Add ½ can cream of mushroom soup
over cheese. Combine crumbs with oleo until well
coated, and spoon ½ of crumbs over mixture in
dish. Repeat procedure and finish with crumbs.
Bake for 30 minutes.

Serves 8 to 10.
Ella Mae Fontenot

I Remember...

that in the midst of the
Depression my family had
made the biggest crop of
potatoes ever, but we fed
them to the pigs because
we could not find buyers.
"We'd call ourselves poor
but yet we never did suffer
from [not] having some-
thing to eat."

Blanche Quebedeaux

I Remember...

that my mother taught me to respect all other religions. When my brothers and sisters and I asked to watch the Baptist people's baptisms in the Mississippi River, my mother told us not to laugh at the black ladies who would baptize their people in the river. She warned, "They might holler and scream and cry and sing as their way of praising their God. ... And let me tell ya'll, they might get to heaven before ya'll."

Eva Mae Poirrier

Broccoli Rice

2 medium onions, chopped
3/4 cup chopped bell pepper
1 to 2 stalks celery, chopped
4 cloves garlic, chopped
4 tablespoons oleo (margarine)
2 packages (20 ounces total) chopped broccoli
salt to taste
black pepper to taste
red pepper to taste
1 jar (8 ounces) soft cheese (preferably Cheese Whiz)
1 can (3 ounces) chopped mushrooms
1 can (10³/4 ounces) golden mushroom soup
1 can (10³/4 ounces) cream of chicken soup
2 cups cooked rice

Sauté onions, bell peppers, celery, and garlic in oleo. When onions are clear and tender, put sautéed vegetables in a 9 by 13-inch casserole dish.

Preheat oven to 350 degrees. Boil broccoli, drain, and add to the mix. Then season with salt, black pepper, and red pepper. Add soft cheese, mushrooms, golden mushroom soup, and cream of chicken soup. Fold in cooked rice. Bake 15 to 20 minutes or until light brown.

Serves 6 to 8.
Verna Amedee

Broccoli Rice Casserole

1 stick butter
1 large onion, chopped
1 broccoli crown, boiled
salt to taste
black pepper to taste
red pepper to taste
1/2 pound Velveeta cheese
1 can (10 3/4 ounces) cream of mushroom soup
2 cups cooked rice
1/4 jar (13.25 ounces) mushroom pieces
1/2 cup Italian bread crumbs
1 dab butter

Preheat oven to 350 degrees. Melt butter in pot. Add onion to butter. Cook until clear. Add broccoli and cook on medium heat until tender. Season with salt, black pepper, and red pepper. Then add Velveeta cheese and cream of mushroom soup. Add rice and mushroom pieces. Pour into casserole dish. Sprinkle bread crumbs on top with dab of butter. Bake 25 to 30 minutes or until bubbling.

Serves 6 to 8.
Elma Oubre

I Remember...

that my cousin, Doré, was a judge and congressman; and on one trip to see him, I met Huey Long. He just happened to be in my cousin's office. I also went to a LSU football game against [Alabama's] Crimson Tide, while visiting my cousin, and this time I sat right behind Huey Long. "He was very loud." Later in life I met Huey's brother Earl Long; "He was off his rocker."

Odile Hollier

Rice-Cabbage Casserole

1 pound ground beef
¼ cup dried minced onions
¼ cup chopped bell pepper
¼ cup chopped celery
¼ teaspoon black pepper
1 teaspoon salt
1 small head cabbage
2 tablespoons cooking oil
3 cups cooked rice
1 can (8 ounces) tomato sauce
¾ cup shredded cheese
½ cup cracker crumbs
½ cup crumbled fried bacon

Preheat oven to 300 degrees. Brown meat, onions, peppers, and celery. Add seasoning to taste. Set aside.

Wash and coarsely shred cabbage. Steam in oil and ¼ cup water for 15 minutes. Grease 9 by 13-inch casserole dish and put cabbage, cooked rice, and meat mixture in layers. Pour 1 can tomato sauce and ½ can water over all. Bake for 20 minutes covered.

Top with cheese, cracker crumbs, and bacon. Heat until cheese is melted. Can be prepared ahead of time and reheated.

Serves 6.
Lola Belle Foret

Cabbage Casserole

1 pound ground meat
1 pound sausage, cut in bite-size pieces
1 large head cabbage, cut in wedges
1 medium onion, chopped
1 cup uncooked rice
1 medium bell pepper, chopped
1 pinch onion tops
1 can (14.5 ounces) Rotel tomatoes
salt to taste
black pepper to taste
red pepper to taste

In a large bowl or pot, mix ground meat, sausage, cabbage, onion, rice, bell pepper, onion tops, and tomatoes together with your hands. Season with salt, black pepper, and red pepper. Pack loosely into 8- or 10-cup rice cooker. Set on cook. When the bell rings signifying that it has finished cooking allow it to set on warm for $1/2$ to 1 hour.

Serves 14 to 16.
Ella Mae Fontenot

I Remember...

When I think about World War I and II, "I always remember those people that had some kids that went to war." I prayed nonstop for Abbie's [Ella Mae Fontenot's husband's] mother and father, because they had five boys at war. "As soon as I finished praying for one it was time to pray for another and they all came back." In addition to prayers I sent letters to servicemen, and trying to give them a good home cooked meal and a reminder of the holidays, I even sent them a fryer and dyed eggs for Easter. Although the eggs rotted on their way to Europe and the meal was ruined, my message of love reached the soldiers, nonetheless.

Carrine "Yen" Fontenot

Smothered Cabbage

I Remember...

"the old way, the true Cajun way" of cooking, and I enjoy researching old recipes. "I am a stickler for the old-fashioned way. ... Don't give me a recipe that has a can of cream of mushroom soup and a can of Rotel tomatoes. That pisses me off!"

Olga Manuel

1 large cabbage, with core removed, cut into large pieces
1 tablespoon oil
1 large onion, chopped
1/4 teaspoon baking soda
about 1/2 teaspoon salt
black pepper to taste
red pepper to taste

Place cabbage, oil, onions, and baking soda in a heavy saucepan. Add salt, black pepper, and red pepper. Add water to come halfway up cabbage. Boil until all of the water evaporates. Reduce heat and continue cooking cabbage until it starts to brown. Cabbage will have the appearance of mashed vegetables.

Serves 8 to 10.
Belle Fontenot

Cabbage Rolls

1 large cabbage head
1/2 cup uncooked rice
1 pound ground meat
1 onion, chopped
1 bunch onion tops, cut
parsley
1 can (10 3/4 ounces) cream of mushroom soup
salt to taste
black pepper to taste
red pepper to taste

Preheat oven to 375 degrees. Remove tough outer leaves from cabbage. Cut out core and place in a large pot of water. Boil for about 10 minutes. Rinse rice and let soak for about 5 minutes. Mix ground meat, rice, onion, onion tops, parsley, and 1/2 can cream of mushroom soup to make a meat mixture. Season with salt, black pepper, and red pepper. Set it aside for later.

Cut rib out of the cabbage leaves. Place about 1 tablespoon (or more) of meat mixture on each leaf. Roll up and place in large greased skillet. Add small amount of water to soup can and pour remaining cream of mushroom soup over cabbage rolls. Cover and bake in oven for at least 1 hour. Make sure the meat and rice are cooked.

Makes 12 to 18.
Etheleen Meaux

I Remember...

hat I used to cook for my children all the time. Now that I can't, they cook for me, "but I don't want to depend on them too much." I still cook and bake for them, but not as much as I used to do.

Rose Fontenot

Fresh Mustard Greens

1 large bunch mustard greens
1 cup chopped salt pork
1 small onion, chopped

Clean and chop mustard greens. Place greens, salt pork, and onion in stockpot. Cover with water and bring to a boil. Boil until tender, making sure water is over greens.

Serves 2.
Gertrude Stutes

I Remember...

how much I love to cook for my family and still do. My son comes by every day after work. "You wanna eat? What you wanna eat? That's my first words. What you wanna eat? You ate? My husband, my husband says, he says 'I don't know when that restaurant's gonna close.' I say as long as those eyes are open, and those hands can work, and those legs can walk, that's not gonna close, not for my children or my grandchildren. That's what we living for."

Rita Rodrigue

Peas Jambalaya

3 pounds smoked sausage
4 ounces bacon
1 quart fresh field peas
3 onions, chopped
1 bell pepper, chopped
1 stalk celery, chopped
2 to 3 cups cooked rice

Cut sausage and bacon in small pieces and brown. Add peas. Cook at medium heat. Add onions, bell pepper, and celery. Blend together with meat until well cooked. Add water as needed. When completely cooked and smothered down, add rice and mix well. Let simmer for a few minutes and serve when done.

Serves 6 to 8.
Verna Amedee

I Remember...

some home remedies that we used to use. "But one favorite 'concoction' I would call it, that we would make for colds would be, I still do that sometimes, lemon juice, olive oil, and honey. Now some people would use a few drops of ammonia in there and some people would use a little vinegar, like a teaspoonful. In fact I used some the other day. It's even better with whiskey. You can feel the warmth."

Hilda Waguespack

Black-Eyed Peas

2 large onions
2 large bell peppers
1 bunch green onion tops
1 pound dried black-eyed peas
1 pound pork sausage, beef tasso, ham, or mix of all
2 teaspoons minced garlic
salt to taste
black pepper to taste
red pepper to taste

Finely chop onions, bell peppers, and onion tops. Place peas, onions, bell peppers, onion tops, meat of choice, and garlic in 6-quart heavy duty pot. Season with salt, black pepper, and red pepper. Fill pot with water 1 inch from top of pot. Bring to a boil. Lower heat to medium (or more) and cook for 2 hours. Stir often and gently move spoon so as not to mash the peas. Important: Add water throughout cooking process so as to keep water level or level of contents in pot 1 to 2 inches from top of pot. Season as you cook to taste.

Serves 12 to 16.
Freddie Parent

Optional: Serve with rice and pork roast. Can soak black-eyed peas in water for 30 minutes to 1 hour before cooking; speeds up cooking time. Freezes quite well. Patricia Ardoin sent this recipe in for her mother, who passed away last year. Patricia's attached note said, "Enjoy Mom's Specialty. Freddie Frugé Parent: a great Mom, a great cook, a great friend."

I Remember...

that "Mardi Gras was always a big celebration." My family would always watch the riders and give them a chicken or some rice for the gumbo.

Versie Meche

Fresh Black-Eyed Peas

1 pound fresh black-eyed peas
1 small onion, chopped
$1/2$ pound salt pork, chopped
salt to taste
black pepper to taste
red pepper to taste

Place peas, onions, and pork in a medium stock-pot. Season with salt, black pepper, and red pepper. Cover with water until pot is $3/4$ full. Boil until beans are tender (about 1 hour). Add water as needed to keep beans from sticking. Peas should be tender in a thick gravy.

Serves 6.
Gertrude Stutes

I Remember...

"when I was young, there were no local supermarkets. We grew our own vegetables. These vegetables were a large part of our diet. Because we were a large family, gravies made with roux were used almost on a daily basis. Beans were also a large part of our diet. ... Well I tell you what, we ate a lot of ground meat because Momma used to make a lot of meatballs and long gravies [roux]. ... And Mom made her own roux with flour."

Gertrude Stutes

Green Bean Casserole

1 can (10³/4 ounces) cream of mushroom soup
³/4 cup milk
¹/8 teaspoon black or red pepper
2 cans (29 ounces total) green beans
1¹/3 cups French-fried onions

Preheat oven to 350 degrees. In 1¹/2-quart casserole dish, combine soup, milk, and pepper. Stir until well blended. Stir in drained beans and ²/3 cup French fried onions. Bake uncovered for 30 minutes or until hot. Stir. Sprinkle remaining ²/3 cup onions. Bake 5 minutes or until onions are golden brown. It's very good.

Serves 12.
Ella Mae Fontenot

I Remember...

that "in olden times we'd believe [in *traiteurs*] cause doctors probably there were very few and probably we didn't have the money to go. ... If it don't help, it can't hurt." One of my personal encounters with a *traiteur* occurred when I had 19 warts on my hands. My doctor said that he could not burn 19 holes in my hand and then asked if I believed in *traiteurs*. I told him, "I believe in anything if that could go away." Because scientific medicine failed me and at the suggestion of a doctor, I decided to use alternative medicine. During the second visit with the *traiteur*, Alexis Comeaux, he said that I would be cured, because the moon was full. "And you better believe those warts went away."

Pauline Langlinais

Cooking With Cajun Women

Boiled Okra

2 pounds small okra
1 tablespoon salt, plus additional to taste
black pepper to taste
red pepper to taste
vinegar

Wash the okra. Cook in water that covers the okra. Add I tablespoon salt. Cook about 10 minutes, let cool, put in a deep dish or bowl. Season with salt, black pepper, and red pepper. Add vinegar to cover okra. Very good to serve as a salad.

Serves 4 to 6.
Gladys Hebert

I Remember...

when I enrolled in school for the first time, I knew very little English and had trouble adjusting to English. I remember "if we'd let a French word out that was write 100 lines, 'I must not talk French.' And now they teach it in school."

Lessie Deshotel

Candied Yams

6 Louisiana golden yams, cooked and peeled
½ cup sugar
1 teaspoon cinnamon
4 tablespoons butter
1 cup cold water

Preheat oven to 350 degrees. Slice yams and arrange in a shallow 9 by 13-inch casserole dish. Sprinkle with sugar and cinnamon. Dot with pats of butter and pour water over all ingredients. Cover and bake for 30 minutes. Remove cover and bake 15 minutes more.

Serves 6 to 8.
Viola Rider

I Remember...

when First Communion and Confirmation were nice with nice big ceremonies. "The first mass was at 7:00. We'd receive Communion, and then we'd go and have breakfast. Everyone would bring cake and something to drink. Some would drink milk. We'd go outside under they'd call it the shed here at that time... the Parish Hall now. We'd eat breakfast, then go back in church, stay there about half hour, 45 minutes I guess, go back in church. And then we'd have all the, you know, the talks that they had. I don't know what they used to call them. ... And then they had angels also. The girls dressed as angels. It was nice, much nicer. They don't do that anymore"

Rose Thibodeaux

Glazed Carrots

2 tablespoons butter
¹/₄ cup packed brown sugar
3 cups sliced and cooked carrots

Blend butter, sugar, and 1 tablespoon water in a heavy fry pan. Cook over low heat, until sugar dissolves. Add carrots, and cook over low heat for 5 to 10 minutes, turning carrots to coat all sides with syrup. Keep heat low to prevent scorching.

Serves 6.
Pauline Langlinais

I Remember...

when my brother was wounded in World War II and spent six weeks behind the firing line in emergency tents before getting to a hospital to be sewed up. "They went through hell those boys, I feel for these kids that has to go to service. But he survived. They have nightmares when they get back, they don't sleep and they think about the war."

Corrine Judice

Candied Carrots

2 pounds carrots
2 cups boiling water
2 tablespoons oleo (margarine)
1/2 cup syrup (preferably Mrs. Butterworth's)

I Remember...

when "... we raised everything from chickens, ducks,
geese, all our stuff and we
butchered in the winter,
we made our sausage and
we had our little house
where we smoke and they
stayed there until we used
the rest, our sausage and
bacon, big old slabs of
bacon and we raised all
our potatoes, both kinds
[sweet and Irish]. ... We
didn't suffer for nothing,
now we weren't rich, but
we weren't, didn't suffer
for anything."

Corrinne Judice

Wash, peel, and cut carrots diagonally into 1-inch
slices. Then place in 2-quart saucepan. Add boiling
water to measure 1 inch high. Cover and simmer 20
minutes until tender. Drain, add oleo, and toss
until carrots are well coated. Add syrup, heat, and
roll carrots in syrup until evenly glazed. Cook over
medium heat until well glazed. Watch carefully to
prevent scorching.

Serves 4.
Dorothy Bryant

Marinated Carrots I

1 medium onion, chopped
1 can (10¾ ounces) cream of tomato soup
1 cup sugar
¾ cup vinegar
1 teaspoon salt
1 teaspoon black pepper
1 teaspoon Worcestershire sauce
5 cups sliced cooked carrots

Mix onion, tomato soup, sugar, vinegar, salt, black pepper, and Worcestershire sauce. Pour over carrots. Refrigerate overnight before serving. These will keep in refrigerator for 2 weeks. Fresh carrots are better than canned or frozen. I've fixed these for church suppers numerous times and my dish always returns empty!

Serves 10 to 15.
Jane Hoffpauir

I Remember...

"But you know I don't ever remember having, getting a doll. A doll, I don't remember. My momma used to make us you know the sacks, the flour sacks, they had what you call and she'd stuff it. But I mean you know a real doll. ... My sister Catherine was younger and I'll never forget this. It stayed in my memory. She, her godfather had given her a doll and she was so happy with her doll. She was young and she, I shouldn't say this but she went to the, we had outside toilets, and she went to the outside toilet and dropped her doll in the hole. [She] cried and cried. [She] wanted my daddy to go get it, but it was impossible. We still laugh and talk about that doll. ... We were poor, not like now."

Elmina Landry

Marinated Carrots II

1 cup vinegar
1 cup sugar
1 onion, sliced
$\frac{1}{2}$ cup chopped celery
1 bell pepper, sliced
1 dash salt
6 cups sliced boiled carrots

Heat vinegar and sugar. When boiling, turn off heat. Drop in onions, celery, peppers, and salt. Then add carrots. Mix well. Then pour into pint-sized jars and cover with lids. Will keep well in refrigerator.

Makes 2 pints.
Rose Fontenot

I Remember...

that my father spoiled the children more "because Mom didn't have time, poor thing." I remember the time my father took us children to a swimming hole "for men," when the men were gone, and unsuccessfully tried to teach us how to swim. My father also took us fishing and we used worms dug from the yard as bait. I would go fishing and camping frequently with my own children and husband, but I refused to bait the hook myself.

Versie Meche

Marinated Beets

10 beets
2 cups sugar
2 cups vinegar
1 dash salt

Boil the beets. When cooked, peel and quarter or slice them, and place in pint jars. Bring sugar, vinegar, 1 cup water, and salt to a boil until sugar is dissolved. Then pour over the beets. Put lids on the jars. Keeps well in the refrigerator.

Makes 2 pints.
Rose Fontenot

I Remember...

"old recipes I have been having maybe 50 years. Country women collect everything they can get. My aunt was a home economics teacher and old maid so she helped me a lots to cook. I have her recipe box with many recipes in [it]."

Rose Fontenot

Harvard Beets

2 tablespoons butter
1 tablespoon cornstarch
1 tablespoon sugar
1/4 teaspoon salt
1/2 cup mild vinegar
2 cups cubed canned or cooked beets

Melt butter. Add cornstarch, sugar, and salt. Blend. Add vinegar. Cook until thick. Add beets, and heat thoroughly.

Serves 6.
Rose Fontenot

I Remember...

when "Mama sewed for us and as we got bigger we made our doll clothes; and then we made, that's how we started learning how to sew. Oh yeah she had a sewing machine. She had bought it, she sold a cow to buy the sewing machine after her and Poppa were married and that's how she bought her sewing machine. Isn't that something? ... She made her own [patterns]. You'd just tell her how you wanted it and she did it. But she sewed so good and she could do lots of needlework, you know. We were busy; she'd crochet little edgings on our stuff."

Corinne Judice

Coleslaw I

1 small head cabbage, shredded
1 small bell pepper, chopped
1 small onion, chopped
1 teaspoon salt
1 teaspoon black pepper
$^1/_2$ cup vinegar

Combine cabbage, bell pepper, onion, salt, pepper, and vinegar. Mix well and chill until ready to serve.

Serves 8 to 10.
Alzena Miller

I Remember...

"... Aunt Marie, she would write for people who didn't know how to write, you know. She'd have a, well, even during the war, like the mothers, their sons were in France and they'd say they didn't know how to write, so she wrote letters for them and when the son wrote back, well, she would read the letters for them."

Helen Gravois

Coleslaw II

1 head cabbage, shredded
1 tablespoon salt
4 tablespoons sugar
3 tablespoons vinegar

Put cabbage, salt, sugar, and vinegar in a large serving bowl. Stir well to mix it good, then serve.

Serves 6 to 8.
Blanche Quebedeaux

that my mother died when I was only 10, and the ladies in my extended family collectively assumed the role of mother. When I would visit my grandparents' house, my grandmother fixed a "nest" with two blankets on the side of her bed where I would sleep. While my "stone deaf" grandfather snored, we would talk, and my grandmother would play with my fingers and hands. "It felt so good. I didn't have that affection you know, anywheres else." My grandmother would also polish my shoes, clean my panties, and make little dresses for me. Those are some of the most important things that I remember about my grandmother.

Marie "Ivy" Ortego

Macaroni Salad

6 eggs
1 package (12 ounces) macaroni
3/4 cup mayonnaise
2/3 cup ground dill pickles
1/2 cup chopped celery
1/2 cup chopped onion tops
1 1/2 teaspoons dry mustard
3 tablespoons lemon juice
2 ounces pimientos, chopped
3 tablespoons pickle juice
2 cloves garlic

Boil and cool eggs. Peel and mash. Then set aside.
Cook macaroni (8 to 10 minutes). Drain and cool.
When cool, add mayonnaise and mashed eggs to
macaroni. Add dill pickles, celery, onion tops, dry
mustard, lemon juice, pimientos, and pickle juice.
Mix well. If not soft enough, add more pickle juice.
Cut garlic in halves and place in salad. Macaroni
salad should age in refrigerator about 8 hours.
Remove garlic before serving.

Serves 10.
Lola Belle Foret

I Remember...

each year when Easter
Sunday arrived, the egg
hunts, *paqueing*, and feast
began. *Paqueing* was not a
casual game, but a serious
competition between
Cajuns of all ages. Our
family and friends would
take turns hitting each
other's eggs until one
cracks and the person with
the stronger egg keeps
both eggs. "Boy when you
broke one you didn't give
it back."

Viola Rider

Baked Macaroni and Cheese

1 pack (16 ounces) macaroni
3 tablespoons butter
3 tablespoons all-purpose flour
2 cups milk
salt to taste
black pepper to taste
red pepper to taste
1/2 pound American cheese, grated
1 cup dry bread crumbs

Preheat oven to 325 degrees. Cook macaroni in boiling water until tender. Drain and rinse. Make white sauce with butter, flour, and milk. Season with salt, black pepper, and red pepper. Add 2/3 cup of cheese, stir until melted. Pour over macaroni in greased 9 by 13-inch baking dish. Sprinkle remaining cheese and crumbs over top. Bake in oven for 30 minutes.

Serves 8.
Rose Fontenot

I Remember...

when "...we helped in the garden and we helped round the cows and we had sheep, the sheep was for the kids and we'd have to round them up to sheer them, and we had horses we rode. We had a happy life. We raised everything. ... We had a farm that supplied all our food except our coffee, sugar, um what else, flour."

Corinne Judice

Hush Puppies

1 bottle (48 ounces) plus 1 tablespoon oil
1 1/2 cups cornmeal
3/4 cup all-purpose flour
3 tablespoons sugar
3 to 4 level teaspoons baking powder
1 onion, chopped
1 egg
salt to taste
black pepper to taste
red pepper to taste
garlic powder to taste
milk (as needed)

Heat bottle of oil in deep pot over medium heat.
Combine cornmeal, flour, sugar, baking powder,
onion, egg, and 1 tablespoon oil. Mix well. Season
with salt, black pepper, red pepper, and garlic powder. Add milk until batter drops well. Drop by
tablespoon into hot grease and fry until done. They
turn golden brown and float.

Serves 6 to 8.
Regina Fontenot

I Remember...

that "my wedding was
very small. In those days,
you didn't have big wed-
dings. It was an all-day
affair. We got married at
seven o'clock in the morning. It was raining, and
they say when it rains you
have a lot of children,
which I did. And in the
evening, they had people
that came over and they
brought cakes. In those
days, the people brought
their cake and they had
coffee, punch, soft drink,
whatever you wanted, no
hard liquor, just the traditional get-together. And it
was nice."

Rita Rodrigue

Breads and Preserves

Pain Perdu (Lost Bread, or French Toast)

3 eggs
¼ cup sugar
½ teaspoon salt
2 cups milk
10 to 12 slices bread
1 to 2 tablespoons oil
syrup (optional)

Beat eggs. Add sugar, salt, and milk. Dip slices of bread in mixture and brown in an oiled, black skillet. You may serve with syrup.

Serves 4 to 6.
Jane Hoffpauir

Preserving Figs

7 pounds figs
8 tablespoons baking soda
5 pounds sugar

Wash figs then add baking soda in a sink of water. Let it soak for about 2 hours. Drain the water and wash them again. Cut the little tails off the figs. In a large pot put the sugar and about 1 or 2 glasses of water then put your figs to cook for about 4 hours. Cook on medium heat. Stir now and then.

Scald your jars with boiling water and boil your lids in a small pot. Make sure the rims of the jars are clean. When the figs are done spoon into the jars and seal them closed.

We eat them with biscuits and I also make sweet dough pies [with them].

Makes 12 pints.
Ella Mae Fontenot

I Remember...

"quilting, I have a friend ... she was quilting since 12 years old and one year we decided a bunch of ladies we'd get together and learn how to do different things and that was one other thing I wanted to learn. So she says I'll help you. ... And I remember telling her I wanted to make the cathedral window, she says 'oh my God that's the hardest one they've got.' ... So she showed me how and I started learning from there and from meeting with others. She'd show us different patterns then I joined the quilt club." They would bring their machines for putting the squares together, but "I'm not a machine quilting person. I liked the hand done." I do it by hand and I am making all the kids one.

Winnie Fernandez

Fig Jam and Berry

2 packages (6 ounces) strawberry gelatin
3 cups sugar
6 cups peeled and mashed fresh figs

Add gelatin and sugar to mashed figs. Stir and cook over medium heat until mixture starts to bubble. Reduce heat to low and cook for 45 minutes. Stir often to keep from sticking.

Makes 3 or 4 pints.
Ella Mae Fontenot

I Remember...

"This [jam] is very good on toast also biscuits or homemade bread. This is nice to put in smaller jars and give as a little gift to a teacher or a neighbor."

Ella Mae Fontenot

Little Yeast Rolls

2 tablespoons sugar
1 tablespoon salt
2 sticks margarine
3 cups warm water
¹/4 cup yeast
4 cups all-purpose flour

Add sugar, salt, and margarine to the water. Add yeast and flour. Mix well. Then start to knead the flour until it makes a bubble in the dough. Let rise about an hour until it is twice its original size.

Preheat oven to 375 degrees. Tear dough into individual rolls and bake for 25 to 30 minutes.

Makes 18 to 24 rolls.
Verna Amedee

I Remember...

when I was growing up we ate biscuits, pancakes, or beignets, served with preserves or syrup for breakfast. The big meal was served at dinnertime; we always ate rice, gravy, meat, and vegetables for lunch. Corn bread and milk, or homemade bread was eaten for supper, which "was no big deal." I continue to cook on a regular basis with Sunday dinners for my family and large holiday celebrations. Now that my children are all married, I share the holidays with the in-laws; we take turns cooking for the extended family.

Versie Meche

Homemade Rolls I

1 packet dry yeast
$^{1}/_{2}$ cup warm water
2 tablespoons lard or corn oil
1 tablespoon salt
1 tablespoon sugar
2 to 3 cups all-purpose flour

Dissolve yeast in warm water. Add lard, salt, and sugar. Mix together well. Add flour until it is mixed to a consistency that suits yourself. Put in an oval pan or dish and let rise to twice its size. With hands work the dough down and let rise once more.

Preheat oven to 450 degrees. When it is ready to cut or make rolls, spray 8- or 10-inch iron skillet with oil before putting the rolls on it. Bake for about 45 minutes or until bread is brown. Serve hot or cold.

Makes 10 to 12 rolls.
Thelma Coles

I Remember...

"I come from the Cajun people, you know. Same pickle bagging string of Cajuns, ... [who] use everything you can use and make. Now we live in a throw-away society, you know. People don't do those kinds of things anymore."

Eva Mae Poirrier

Homemade Rolls II

2 cups warm water
1 pack yeast
3 tablespoons sugar
2 teaspoons salt
3 tablespoons oil
5 cups all-purpose flour
butter (optional)

Mix water, yeast, sugar, salt, and oil well. Add $2^{1}/_{2}$ cups flour and mix. Then mix in remaining flour 1 cup at a time until the dough is hard but not sticky. Let rise until doubled in size.

Then punch and knead. Separate into buns. Put into a 9 by 13-inch greased pan. Let rise again until ready to bake.

Preheat oven to 350 degrees. Bake for 30 to 40 minutes until brown. Brush butter on top of each one if you wish.

Makes 1 to 2 dozen.
Claire Bonin

I Remember...

when we moved to the property on which we now live. While building our new home, I remember sleeping in the barn for five to six weeks. We moved in as soon as the bedroom and kitchen were finished and added on as we had the money.

Belle Fontenot

Homemade Bread

2/3 cup warm water
1 package fast-acting yeast
1 tablespoon salt
3 tablespoons sugar
3 tablespoons cooking oil
1 egg
2 1/2 cups all-purpose flour
butter, as desired

Mix warm water and yeast. Then add salt and sugar. Stir well, then add cooking oil, egg, and flour. Mix well. Then pat flour on your dough. Put in pan and let dough rise until doubles its size.

Then punch it and roll it well with flour. Cut pieces and place in your 9 by 12-inch greased pan. Let rise 1 size larger.

Preheat oven to 325 degrees. Put butter over bread. Bake for about 20 minutes until light brown.

Makes 10 to 12 pieces.
Ella Mae Fontenot

I Remember...

that my family made our own syrup from sugar cane that we grew at home. We made 100 gallons of cane syrup a year. We also often ate biscuits, corn bread, light-bread, salt meat, sausage, bacon, peas, and milk. I usually ate corn bread, biscuits, or homemade bread for breakfast and supper; and the major meal consisting of rice, gravy, and meat was served at noon. "When I was young, I didn't learn too much how to cook. We had to work in the field hoeing, picking cotton, or in school. I learn a lot on my own. I made this recipe myself."

Ella Mae Fontenot

Rising Bread

7 1/2 cups all-purpose flour
1 teaspoon salt
1/2 cup oil
1 package (1/4 ounce) dry yeast
3 cups lukewarm water

Mix 4 cups flour, salt, and oil. Dissolve yeast in lukewarm water. Pour into flour mixture and blend well. Mix in remaining flour 1 cup at a time until dough forms. Cover with a cloth and let rise in warm, draft-free place until doubled in size.

Punch down and knead the dough. Return to the bowl, cover, and let rise again until doubled in size. Grease two loaf pans and place dough in them. Cover and let rise until the dough is coming over the pans.

Preheat oven to 350 degrees. Bake for 50 minutes or until golden brown.

Makes 2 loaves.
Blanche Quebedeaux

I Remember...

One time my daddy bought a rubber tire wagon. Then my parents went visit in Lawtell. That was a big deal. We made a hay ride and picked up all the neighbors. Then we had a little accident, the hitch bent. We washed the wagon and put it up. He [our father] didn't find out until months later when the neighbor said that we had picked up his kids. He told our dad that he had sent some sweet potatoes for him to taste his crop. My dad laughed and fussed a little, but he knew what he had done as a kid. He was only strict on us for morality, but not mischief.

Joyce Brasseux

Nut Bread

2 eggs, well beaten
2 cups brown sugar
2 cups sour milk
4 cups all-purpose flour
1/2 teaspoon salt
2 teaspoons baking soda
1 teaspoon baking powder
1 cup broken pecans

Preheat oven to 350 degrees. Beat eggs and sugar thoroughly. Add sour milk and beat well. Add flour sifted with salt, baking soda, and baking powder. Add in nuts. Bake in 5½ by 10½-inch greased and floured loaf pan for 1 hour. Texture and flavor improves after 12 hours. One of my favorites handed down by my mother 60 years ago.

Makes 1 loaf.
Rose Fontenot

I Remember...

when I was growing up, the other neighborhood children and I lived a secluded life without such modern comforts as a radio or television. "My daddy would play the harmonica, that was our radio. Ella Mae and [my other girlfriends] would come over and we would dance, while my dad played the harmonica."

Versie Meche

Banana Nut Bread

1 cup high-grade shortening
1¹/₂ cups sugar
2 eggs
2 cups all-purpose flour
1 teaspoon baking soda
¹/₄ teaspoon salt
3 large bananas, ripened and mashed
1¹/₂ cups chopped pecans

Preheat oven to 325 degrees. Combine the shortening and sugar in a large bowl and beat until well blended. Add the eggs one at a time, and continue beating. Sift the flour, baking soda, and salt into ingredients and blend well. Add bananas and nuts to the batter and mix well.

Grease and flour a 10-inch tube pan and bake for 55 minutes. Test with toothpick. If not cooked, bake another 5 minutes more and test again.

Makes 1 loaf.
Evon Melancon

Date Loaf

5 cups sugar
2 cups evaporated milk
1 pound dates, chopped
2 cups chopped pecans
2 tablespoons butter

Cook sugar, milk, dates, and pecans on stove over medium heat until it forms a soft ball when a little is dropped into cold water. Add butter; cook on low heat for 5 more minutes. Remove from heat. Beat until almost hard. Turn out on damp cloth, and roll until firm. Store in refrigerator. Slice as needed when cold.

Makes 1 loaf and serves 6 to 8.
Jane Hoffpauir

Whole Wheat Bread

¹/₄ cup plus 2 tablespoons butter or margarine
7 to 8 cups whole wheat flour
2 packs (¹/₂ ounce total) dry yeast
1 tablespoon plus 1 teaspoon salt
1¹/₂ cups milk
¹/₄ cup honey
melted butter or margarine

Combine 6 cups flour, yeast, and salt in a large mixing bowl. Stir well and set aside. Combine milk, 1¹/₂ cups water, butter, and honey in a medium saucepan. Place on low heat stirring constantly until mixture reaches 120 to 130 degrees. Butter does not need to melt. Stir milk mixture into flour mixture. Beat for 2 minutes with electric mixer on medium speed. Let rise in greased bowl until it doubles. Cover bowl with damp cloth while dough is rising.

Then tear in two pieces and roll each in remaining flour. Return them to the bowl and let rise until they have doubled.

Preheat oven to 350 degrees. Bake in two greased and floured 10-inch bread pans for 30 minutes. Baste with butter if desired.

Makes 2 loaves.
Viola Rider

I Remember...

having to ask permission to marry Jeanne. "Aw yes. It was all done on the up and up. I remember, I remember well one day I was at the office and I was thinking I gotta talk to Mr. Dolese if I'm gonna; I wanted to give her an engagement ring so I went to town. I remember it was noon and I went in the, I went in to him and I asked, told him I wanted to talk with him. So he walked back in his office and I told him then that I was thinking of, I wanted to give Jeanne an engagement ring because we thinking of getting married. He said, 'That's nice' and so I went ahead and made arrangements to buy the ring and I gave her the ring."

Jeanne Arceneaux's husband, Lynn Arceneaux

Gingerbread

1/3 cup butter
2/3 cup granulated sugar
1/3 cup molasses
1 egg
1/2 cup hot water
1 2/3 cup all-purpose flour
1/2 teaspoon baking soda
1 teaspoon baking powder
1 teaspoon ground cinnamon
1/2 teaspoon ground ginger
1/2 teaspoon ground cloves
1/4 teaspoon ground nutmeg
chopped pecans and raisins (optional)

Preheat oven to 350 degrees. Cream butter and sugar. Add molasses, egg, and hot water. Mix well. Add flour, baking soda, baking powder, cinnamon, ginger, cloves, and nutmeg. Beat thoroughly. If desired, you can add pecans and raisins at this time. Stir amount desired into the batter. Pour into greased and floured 8 by 8-inch pan and bake 40 minutes. If you want to double the recipe, use a 9 by 13-inch pan. This recipe was my grandmother's.

Serves 6 to 8.
Doris Regan

I Remember...

the Christmas ritual that is unique to my family; we celebrate Jesus' birthday with a cake, candles, and singing. My husband and I and all our children and grandchildren bring a doll baby Jesus outside to the manger display in our yard on Christmas Eve.

Pat Ardoin

I Remember...

My mother died when I was only five and my aunt, who raised me from the age of 10, cooked all the meals; therefore, my cooking experience was limited when I was first married. I remember one instance in particular when my husband had brought home a piece of meat for me to cook. I wasn't home at the time, but upon returning home and finding the piece of meat, I tried to fry it. The piece of pork never browned, it stayed pink. What I did not understand was that the meat was salt cured pork and needed to be boiled. I laughed. "It was too salty to eat." My cooking rapidly improved with experience.

Marie "Ivy" Ortego

Sweet Potato Bread I

4 cups grated sweet potatoes
1 1/2 cups sugar
1 cup cane syrup
1/2 cup margarine or shortening
2 eggs
1 pinch salt
1 1/2 cups all-purpose flour

Preheat oven to 350 degrees. Mix together sweet potatoes, sugar, syrup, margarine or shortening, eggs, salt, and flour. Bake in greased and floured 10-inch bread pan for 35 to 45 minutes. Top should be crispy.

Makes 1 loaf.
Lola Belle Foret

Pain de Patate Douce

2 cups all-purpose flour
2 teaspoons baking powder
$1/2$ teaspoon baking soda
1 teaspoon salt
1 teaspoon ground cinnamon
1 cup boiled and mashed sweet potato
1 cup sugar
$1/2$ cup milk
2 eggs
$1/4$ cup butter
1 cup chopped pecans
1 cup raisins

Preheat oven to 350 degrees. Mix flour, baking powder, baking soda, salt, and cinnamon. Blend in sweet potato, sugar, milk, eggs, butter, pecans, and raisins. Mix well. Pour batter into a greased 10-inch loaf pan. Bake for 45 to 50 minutes.

Serves 6 to 8.
Alzena Miller

I Remember...

that "Mom had a garden of vegetables and flowers in front of the house, and she had two China ball trees on both sides of the house, and we used to rake the leaves and play there." My sister Rita says "We were poor and happy."

Pauline Guidry

Fasting Bread

1 cup boiling water
2 tablespoons margarine
2 tablespoons butter
2 tablespoons sugar
1 tablespoon salt
1 cup cold water
1 package ($^1/4$ ounce) dry yeast
5$^1/2$ cups all-purpose flour
1 large potato, grated

Pour boiling water in bowl. Add margarine and let melt. Add butter, then sugar and salt. Add cold water. Blend in dry yeast and let stand a minute until dissolved. Add the flour alternately with grated potato to gradually form a stiff dough. Knead on floured board until smooth and satiny, 5 to 10 minutes. Place in greased bowl and cover. Place in warm place until doubled in size (about 1 hour).

Cut dough in half and shape it into 2 loaves. Split the tops and place in greased 11 by 6 by 2$^1/2$-inch loaf pans and let rise again until doubled (1 more hour).

Preheat oven to 425 degrees. Bake for 20 minutes, then reduce heat to 350 degrees and cook for 20 to 30 minutes more. I learned this recipe from Helen Pierrotti.

Makes 2 loaves.
Pat Ardoin

Bread Pudding I

6 slices bread
2 cups evaporated milk
2 cups regular milk
4 egg yolks
1 whole egg
1¼ to 1½ cups sugar, to taste
6 tablespoons butter, melted
1 can (20 ounces) crushed pineapple
1 cup raisins
1½ teaspoons vanilla extract
1½ teaspoons almond extract

Meringue:
4 egg whites
8 tablespoons sugar

Preheat oven to 375 degrees. Lightly grease 9 by 13-inch baking pan with a little butter. Line bottom of pan with the bread slices. Pour half of the evaporated and regular milk over the bread and let soak for a while. Mash the bread. Beat egg yolks and whole egg with half of the sugar and pour over soaked bread. Add the rest of the milk and sugar until sweet enough. Add melted butter, pineapple, and raisins. Stir in the vanilla and almond extract.

Bake for 30 minutes or until firm. Make the meringue: Beat the egg whites with about sugar until stiff, forming meringue, and spread over pudding and return to oven to brown. Watch closely not to burn.

Serves 8 to 10.
Hilda Waguespack

I Remember...

when I learned to sew from my mother and older sister and I "never stopped." At 86 years old, I still sew for the public. I do not need a pattern to make a piece of clothing; I make my own pattern and I cut it out. I live on the same property where I was born and raised, and I never invested in air conditioning.

Carrine "Yen" Fontenot

Bread Pudding II

2 eggs
2 tablespoons honey
1 teaspoon vanilla extract
1/2 teaspoon cinnamon
2 cups scalded milk
3 slices whole grain bread, cut into cubes
1/4 cup raisins
1/2 teaspoon ground nutmeg

Preheat oven to 325 degrees. Beat eggs, honey, vanilla, and cinnamon in medium bowl. Slowly stir in scalded milk. Put bread and raisins in 1 1/2-quart casserole dish. Pour milk mixture over and sprinkle with additional cinnamon and nutmeg. Bake for 1 hour.

Serves 4.
Viola Rider

I Remember...

for Christmas "my brothers would go out in the woods and cut [a Christmas tree] you know. If they couldn't find a wild cedar, they'd, they'd cut anything. Sometimes we'd take two or three branches and put them together to make a Christmas tree. Then we would make our orna-ments. You couldn't buy. You ever made a loop, a chain with paper? Yeah, we'd color those little strips. And we'd use cotton you know pieces of cotton that we just would, we had no lights. Popcorn, Momma would pop us popcorn and we'd string that and drape that in the [tree]. Oh yes. We always had a Santa Claus visit."

Jeanne Arceneaux

Bran Muffins

1 cup whole bran flakes
3/4 cup all-purpose flour
1 teaspoon baking soda
3/4 cup buttermilk
1/4 cup oil

Preheat oven to 250 degrees. Mix bran, flour, and baking soda. Add milk and oil. Then mix well. Grease and flour muffin pans. Pour in batter. Bake until done, approximately 1 hour.

Makes 1 dozen muffins.
Alzena Miller

Oatmeal Raisin Muffins

1 1/4 cups all-purpose flour
1 tablespoon baking powder
1 teaspoon salt
1/3 cup sugar
1 cup uncooked rolled oats
1/2 cup raisins
1 egg
1 cup milk
1/2 cup melted fat or oil

Preheat oven to 400 degrees. In a large bowl mix flour, baking powder, salt, and sugar. Stir in oats, and raisins. In a separate bowl, beat egg, milk, and fat or oil. Add this mixture to the first bowl of dry ingredients. Stir just until dry ingredients are wet leaving batter lumpy. Grease muffin pan. Fill half full. Bake for 20 to 25 minutes or until brown.

Makes 15 to 18 muffins.
Verna Amedee

I Remember...

when "we wore stockings all the time, long stockings. So I have a mantle piece in the front, you know, Daddy would tack our long stockings on the mantle [for Christmas] and he always did have us a orange, a apple, and a banana, and some candy. And he'd get a sparkler... He'd have that in there, too. So we'd [the older ones] each have a doll."

Gertrude Stutes

Cinnamon Rolls

1 1/2 packages fast-acting yeast
3/4 cup warm water
2 1/2 tablespoons sugar
2 1/2 tablespoons oil
2 eggs
1 1/2 teaspoon salt
1 teaspoon vanilla extract
4 to 5 cups all-purpose flour
1/2 cup margarine
1 to 2 tablespoons ground cinnamon
1 to 2 cups sugar

Stir yeast in warm water. Add sugar, oil, eggs, salt, and vanilla extract. Stir very well then add 1 cup of flour at a time, stirring well. It will become very hard to stir. Pat with flour a little and make a big ball. Let it rise to double its size.

Then roll out 1/2-inch thick on wax paper about 1/3 of dough at a time. Then melt margarine and apply on dough. Then mix cinnamon and sugar together and sprinkle on dough. Cut dough in strips and roll to make your cinnamon roll. Repeat until dough is used up. Let rise.

Preheat oven to 350 degrees. Then cook for about 8 minutes until very light brown. They will be dry if overcooked. Spread favorite icing on top.

Makes about 18 rolls.
Ella Mae Fontenot

I Remember...

when I was younger. I ate cinnamon rolls that my sister would make. Then one day "I decided I could make some as well as her. So I made my own recipe. And believe me it's very good."

Ella Mae Fontenot

Crescent Rolls

1 package (¹/4 ounce) yeast
1 cup plus 3 tablespoons warm water
2 eggs, beaten
¹/2 cup sugar
¹/2 cup shortening
1 teaspoon salt
4 cups all-purpose flour
butter

Dissolve yeast in 3 tablespoons warm water. Set aside. Mix eggs, sugar, shortening and salt well. Stir in 1 cup warm water. Stir in yeast mixture and add the flour. Mix well. Cover well and put in refrigerator overnight.

Two or 3 hours before baking, roll out dough to ¹/4-inch thick. Cut out saucer-size circles of dough. Spread a small slice of butter on each circle. Roll each circle into crescent roll form. Let rise 2 to 3 hours.

Preheat oven to 350 degrees. Bake for 30 minutes.

Serves 8.
Rose Fontenot

Biscuits I

2 cups all-purpose flour
1 teaspoon baking powder
1 teaspoon salt
⅓ cup shortening
¾ cup milk

Preheat oven to 450 degrees. Mix flour, baking powder, salt, shortening, and milk well. Roll dough to ½-inch thickness. Using the open end of a jar or glass, cut dough into individual biscuits. Place them on a lightly greased flat baking pan. Bake for 10 to 12 minutes.

Serves 6 to 8.
Alzena Miller

I Remember...

how I used to love to visit with my lady friends. "You used to invite a bunch of ladies and you'd cook a meal and then it was the biggest gossiping day that you ever would think of, everybody had something to say. ... About what's goin' on, what went on, and oh yes that was the good old days. Everybody'd visit, right now you don't see nobody. That damn television I call it. I'm, I'm gonna use the word 'damn' because I have three in my house and sometimes I don't have one on but the minute my husband walks in he puts this one on, that one on, and the one in our bedroom."

Rita Rodrigue

Biscuits II

2 cups self-rising flour
1 stick butter
1/4 cup evaporated milk

I Remember...

"I make these biscuits every Sunday morning. My two boys come at 6:30 to have coffee and they bring them back home in Ziploc bags. I am a widow and live alone so I enjoy making them the way they like. I double this recipe so I get about two dozen biscuits. This recipe comes from the hot lunch biscuits, when [my boys] were in school, when butter was plentiful in schools. I do not substitute my butter for margarine or Crisco as [butter] is what they want. They are 52 and 57 years old so I try to keep them happy. One like them thick and one thin so I roll two thickness of dough, but everyone who comes here loves them."

Rose Fontenot

Preheat oven to 350 degrees. Mix flour and butter with a pastry blender until flour resembles small peas. Add evaporated milk slowly so you have the right amount. Evaporated milk is needed to hold dough together. I put milk in the middle and start moving the flour inside until it is all moistened enough to roll. When you can scrape the bowl well, it is time to put dough on a floured board. I pat the dough and then roll it with a small glass rolled into flour first so it don't stick. I use different sizes of glass to cut the biscuits depending if I want to make small biscuits or larger ones. Bake 15 to 20 minutes until they come out a golden brown.

Makes 6 to 7 large biscuits or 1 dozen small ones.
Rose Fontenot

Cheese Biscuits

4 cups all-purpose flour
4 tablespoons baking powder
1 cup oleo (margarine)
2 tablespoons salt
1/2 cup sugar
1 cup shredded cheese

Preheat oven to 425 degrees. Mix flour, baking powder, oleo, and salt. Add 3 cups water and sugar. Then add cheese and mix well. Drop biscuits on the baking sheet. Bake for 15 to 20 minutes.

Makes 18 to 24.
Verna Amedee

I Remember...

"I had a little cough last week. I took a little shot of amaretto and I tell you I slept... Now last night I couldn't stop it. I had something like, something like a ticklish feeling and so I told [my son] Tom, I said I don't think I'm gonna go for a sleeping pill because I don't like to mix things, you know, especially medication, and so I said I think I'm gonna take a little shot. I said 'you want some?' and he says 'yeah.' So there was a little bit left in the bottle, so we, I give him some and I took some and you know it helped. I didn't cough after that. I took it slowly, you know, and let it stay there a while, burn it up."

Hilda Waguespack

Gueydan Couche-Couche

2 cups cornmeal
2 tablespoons sugar
1 tablespoon salt
¼ cup cooking oil or fat
1 cup boiling water

Mix cornmeal, sugar, and salt in a mixing bowl. Mix well. Heat oil in an iron pot. Pour boiling water over dry ingredients slowly while stirring. When the cornmeal holds together, pour into the pot with the hot oil or fat. Cook for 3 or 4 minutes. Cover tightly while cooking. Turn heat to 200 degrees in the oven or to low on the stove. Cook another 15 minutes, stirring occasionally. Serve with milk.

Serves 2 to 3.
Gladys Hebert

I Remember...

when I used to cook Sunday dinners for my children; now my children cook for me. One day "they said 'Mom, you getting too old now. You gonna come to our house, each our turn... you cooked long enough.'"

Henriette Richard

Couche-Couche

1 cup yellow or white cornmeal
4 tablespoons all-purpose flour
1½ teaspoons baking powder
¼ teaspoon salt
1 teaspoon sugar (optional)
¼ cup milk
¼ cup oil

Mix cornmeal, flour, baking powder, salt, and sugar. Slowly add ½ cup water and milk. Mixture will be lumpy. Add oil to skillet. Pour mixture into skillet and cover with tight lid. Cook over medium heat for 5 minutes. Uncover and stir. The mixture will start browning. Cover and cook for an additional 15 minutes. Stir again slowly. By this time the lumps have broken up. May be eaten as a cereal with milk. Especially good with *boudin* and *gratons* (cracklings) and figs or any homemade preserves. Use a black iron skillet to get the true taste of *couche-couche*.

Makes 2 servings.
Velma Reaux

Corn Bread I

1 cup cornmeal
1 cup self-rising flour
1 teaspoon baking powder
1 teaspoon salt
2 tablespoon sugar
2 eggs
2 cups milk
1/2 cup oil

Preheat oven to 350 degrees. Sift together cornmeal, flour, baking powder, salt, and sugar. Then add eggs, milk, and oil. Mix well. Pour into greased 9-inch round black iron skillet or 9 by 9-inch pan. Bake 30 to 40 minutes or until brown.

Makes 1 corn bread.
Viola Rider

I Remember...

when "my grandmother made the best crunchy corn bread in a black iron skillet that she cut and served like a pie. She made this with homemade yellow cornmeal. No one ever found out how she made it. My oldest brother once remarked that he wish she had given us the recipe. She usually went to her kitchen at 4 a.m. before anyone was up. She had to prepare breakfast for the men who had to go to work, meaning her husband and sons. She had four sons. My mother was the only girl. My daddy made delicious biscuits for us but no one knew how he made them. He also got up I think at 3 a.m. and made them before he went to work and left them in a tin container on stove. They were so big and so soft. He did not use a biscuit cutter. He just cut them square. My mother said he used some of her buttermilk to put in them. You could leave them on stove all day and eat them at night and they were still soft and delicious."

Eva Mae Poirrier

Corn Bread II

¹/₄ cup shortening
2 cups white or yellow cornmeal
2 tablespoons all-purpose flour
2 teaspoons baking powder
1 teaspoon baking soda
1 egg
2 cups milk or buttermilk

Preheat oven to 450 degrees. On the stove, melt shortening in a 9-inch round black iron skillet; you will use this skillet to bake the corn bread. In a mixing bowl, sift together cornmeal, flour, baking powder, and baking soda. Then add egg and milk and stir well. Pour batter into hot pan. Bake in oven for 20 to 25 minutes or until brown.

Serves 6 to 8.
Vinice Sensat

I Remember...

"In our home corn bread was a regular for breakfast and supper, mostly for breakfast. If you didn't want that you could fix your own of what you like. We always had milk. For supper, if you didn't want what we had one could fry Irish potatoes or fry a pan of sweet potatoes, etc. Of food, we always had plenty."

Vinice Sensat

Broccoli Corn Bread

10 ounces broccoli, chopped
1 box (8.5 ounces) corn bread mix (preferably Jiffy)
4 eggs
¹/₂ stick butter, room temperature
1 cup grated cheddar cheese
1 teaspoon season-all

Preheat oven to 350 degrees. If using fresh broccoli, steam until tender but not mashable or thaw a box of frozen broccoli. Mix broccoli, dry corn bread mix, eggs, butter, cheese, and season-all. Bake in a 4-quart casserole dish for 30 minutes or until it looks cooked. Very good.

Serves 6 to 8.
Joyce Brasseux

I Remember...

"A Christmas tree was unknown. Boys had home-made toys. Girls had a homemade doll. In your stocking you got a fruit and a nickel if you were good. ... One of my friends says she wanted a Christmas tree and they didn't know how to do it and they didn't have any money. So they, she took her mother's broom and she and her little nephew took the broom and they broke it, broke it up. But, and they had taken the paper that came in the tobacco packs, sort of like uh like aluminum foil, something like that and had made decorations and fixed up her momma's broom. She says her momma was furious. She said she couldn't afford another broom."

Anne Gros

Mexican Corn Bread

1 cup cornmeal
$^1/_2$ teaspoon baking soda
$^1/_2$ cup oil (preferably Wesson)
$^1/_2$ pound cheddar cheese, grated (preferably
   Velveeta because it melts smoother and produces
   less oil residue than other cheeses)
2 jalapeño peppers, chopped fine
1 can (8 ounces) whole kernel corn, drained
$^1/_2$ teaspoon salt
2 eggs
1 cup milk
1 large onion, chopped fine

Preheat oven to 350 degrees. Mix cornmeal, baking
soda, and oil. Sprinkle in cheese. Add jalapeños,
corn, salt, eggs, milk, and onions. Mix well. Place in
a large 9 by 13-inch greased pan. Bake for 45 minutes.

Serves 8 to 10.
Claire Bonin

I Remember...

This recipe tastes "very
good," and was given to
me from my daughter-in-
law Linda. When we get
the family together Linda
is called to bring her
Mexican corn bread. It is
cut in little squares. It is
delicious. Try it and believe
me for special occasions I
know you will enjoy it and
also your family and
friends."

Claire Bonin

Easy Pizza Dough

1 package ($^1/_4$ ounce) active dry yeast
$^1/_2$ teaspoon sugar
1 cup very warm water
$3^1/_4$ cup all-purpose flour
$1^1/_2$ teaspoons salt

Sprinkle yeast and sugar into very warm water. Let stand 10 minutes. Combine flour and salt in a large bowl. Make a well in center. Pour in yeast mixture. Gradually work in flour to form a stiff dough. Turn out on lightly floured surface. Knead about 5 minutes. Place in oiled medium-size bowl. Let stand 45 minutes or until double in volume. Punch down and use as directed.

Makes 1 thick 14-inch round crust or 2 thin 12-inch round crusts.
Vinice Sensat

Pastries, Pies, and Desserts

Crocialles (Beignets)

1 bottle (48 ounces) oil
2 cups self-rising flour
2 tablespoons granulated sugar
1 egg
1¼ cups milk
confectioners' sugar, as desired

Heat oil in a deep pot to 375 degrees. In a bowl,
blend flour and granulated sugar. In another bowl,
blend egg and milk. Add to dry mixture. Beat to a
thick batter. Drop by tablespoon into oil. Deep fry
until golden brown. Drain on absorbent paper.
Sprinkle with confectioners' sugar.

Makes 4 to 5 dozen.
Velma Reaux

I Remember...

the quilting bees that took
place at my grandmother's
house. I used to play under
the quilt and then I
learned to quilt. It takes
patience. There were
always *crocialles* or *'tit
gateau* (doughnuts or
cookies) and "everyone had
coffee and ate and gos-
siped. [They] told who had
new babies, who was get-
ting married, who was
seeing somebody else."

Olga Manuel

I Remember...

"when I was smaller and the others was older, and the young men and ladies used to walk to the end of the road and they'd all meet there at night. Well, I wanted to follow and they wouldn't let us follow. Well we lived in a street that had the grass. You had to cut your path with a cane knife. Well if they had those big long tall grasses there, I'd tie it and when they came walking back they'd trip. You didn't want me to go with you, you were gonna pay for the consequences."

Rita Rodrigue

Beignets

1 bottle (48 ounces) oil
2¹/₂ cups all-purpose flour
1 teaspoon baking powder
1 teaspoon salt
2 tablespoons granulated sugar
1 egg
1¹/₃ cups milk
¹/₂ cup confectioners' sugar

Fill a deep pot ¹/₂ to ²/₃ full with oil. Turn on medium flame or stove setting and let oil heat while you make the dough. Mix flour, baking powder, salt, and granulated sugar. Blend in egg and milk and form into a ball of dough. Roll it out. Pat dough to ¹/₂-inch thickness. Cut in 2-inch squares and fry in hot oil. Flip once. Should turn golden brown when done. Sprinkle with confectioners' sugar before serving.

Serves 6 to 8.
Alzena Miller

Les Oreilles De Cochon (Pig's Ears)

1 bottle (48 ounces) cooking oil or lard
1 cup all-purpose flour
¼ teaspoon salt
1 can (12 ounces) cane syrup

Heat oil in a deep pot over medium heat. Sift flour and salt together. Add sufficient water to make a stiff dough, about ½ cup. Cut off a small portion of dough, about the size of a big marble. On a floured board, roll out each ball very thin. Repeat until all the dough is used. This dough should make about 12 portions.

Drop each portion in hot oil, giving a swift twist in the center of each with a long handled fork. This forms the ear. Fry until golden brown. Remove and drain on paper towel.

In a separate saucepan, boil the syrup until a few drops will form a soft ball when dropped in cold water. Dip each ear into the hot syrup and place on platter to cool.

Makes 12.
Pauline Langlinais

Doughnuts of Long Ago

I Remember...

when "my grandfather lived one mile from our house. Mom would send him cooked food. He loved homemade bread so that was why my favorite cousin Stella [and I] went to take some bread to my grandpa. He asked me to make some doughnuts. Well, I remembered my mom would make some; [I] got everything ready. The dough looked good. Grandpa got the pork lard heating. There were no doughnut cutters. I used a glass and punched a hole with my finger. I told Stella she could cook 'em while I cut out more. I dropped two in the hot fat. Here was the fun. They broke to pieces. Too much baking powder. So I added a little flour to the dough and made cookies. I did learn to make good doughnuts after I married."

Gladys Hebert

1 bottle (48 ounces) plus 1 tablespoon oil (preferably Crisco)
3 cups all-purpose flour
1 cup sugar
1¹/2 teaspoons baking powder
1 teaspoon salt
1 teaspoon ground cinnamon
2 eggs
1 tablespoon vinegar
¹/4 cup milk
powdered sugar, as desired

Heat 1 bottle of oil in a deep pot to 350 degrees. Sift flour, sugar, baking powder, salt, and cinnamon twice. Beat eggs, 1 tablespoon oil, vinegar, and milk. Add liquid mixture to flour mixture. You want a stiff dough. Knead on a floured board. Roll out dough and cut with a doughnut cutter.

Drop doughnuts in the hot oil a few at a time. It takes a few seconds before it will rise to the top of the pot. When golden brown, remove doughnuts from the grease, drain on paper towels, and sprinkle with powdered sugar.

Makes 2 to 3 dozen.
Gladys Hebert

Old-Fashioned Cake Doughnuts

1 bottle (48 ounces) oil
4 1/2 cups all-purpose flour
1/4 teaspoon ground cinnamon
1/4 teaspoon ground nutmeg
1 teaspoon salt
3 1/2 teaspoons baking powder
3 eggs
1 teaspoon vanilla extract
3/4 cup sugar
3 tablespoons butter or margarine
3/4 cup milk

Heat oil in a deep pot over medium heat. Sift together flour, cinnamon, nutmeg, salt, and baking powder. Set aside.

Beat eggs in a separate bowl. Add vanilla, sugar, and butter or margarine. Beat well. Add dry ingredients alternating with milk. Mix into a soft dough. Turn dough onto lightly floured board. Knead lightly. Roll out 1/3-inch thick. Cut with doughnut cutter. Fry in hot oil for about 3 minutes.

Makes 3 to 4 dozen.
Lola Belle Foret

I Remember...

when my adoptive father gave me a pig before Easter and Christmas, which I fattened up and sold to buy a special outfit for the given holiday. "That was fun. Oh boy we had a hard time, but we made it." My adoptive mother made all of my clothes including my underwear until I was 12 years old. She used fertilizer sacks to make sheets and towels and chicken feed cloth bags for dresses. I remember that even if you purchased material, it only cost 10 cents a yard and the supplies for a whole dress including the thread and buttons cost only 35 cents.

Edolia Dupré

I Remember...

when I was first married I mastered an array of domestic tasks which included cooking, cleaning, gardening, and caring for my child and husband as well as keeping the books for the family farm. Otis (my husband) reminds me about the time when my sister and I were helping him check the levees, we found that a levee had busted. In order to stop the water from continuing to flow out of the field, Otis put my sister and me sitting in the busted levee until he returned with the proper tools to fill the gaping hole. I proved helpful in almost any situation!

Belle Fontenot

Crisco Doughnuts

1 bottle (48 ounces) Crisco oil
1/3 cup Crisco shortening, melted
2 eggs, beaten
1 cup granulated sugar, plus additional for serving (optional)
1 cup milk
4 teaspoons baking powder
4 cups all-purpose flour, plus extra flour to roll out dough
1 teaspoon salt
1 teaspoon ground nutmeg
1 teaspoon ground cinnamon, plus additional for serving (optional)
confectioners' sugar (optional)

Heat oil in deep pot for frying to 365 degrees. In a small bowl, mix melted shortening, eggs, granulated sugar, and milk. Set aside. In a separate larger bowl, mix baking powder, flour, salt, nutmeg, and cinnamon. Combine the two mixtures, stirring only until smooth.

Roll dough 1/2-inch thick on floured board. Dough should be soft. Cut with floured doughnut cutter. Fry doughnuts in oil. (Tip: 1-inch cube of bread browns in 60 seconds when oil is the right temperature.) Turn to fry on both sides until golden brown (3 to 5 minutes total). Drain on paper towels or brown paper bags. Sprinkle with cinnamon and sugar or confectioners' sugar before serving. Stores well in large Tupperware containers. Grandkids love these.

Makes 2 1/2 to 3 dozen.
Etheleen Meaux

Doughnuts I

1 bottle (48 ounces) oil
1/3 cup granulated sugar
1 1/2 tablespoons shortening
1 egg, well beaten
1/2 cup milk
2 cups all-purpose flour
2 teaspoons baking powder
1/8 teaspoon ground cinnamon
1/8 teaspoon ground cloves
1/2 teaspoon salt
confectioners' sugar, as desired

Heat oil in deep-fat fryer to 375 degrees. Cream granulated sugar and shortening. Add egg and milk. Mix well. Mix and sift flour, baking powder, cinnamon, cloves, and salt. Add them to liquid mixture and mix thoroughly. Turn out on floured board and roll to 1/2-inch thick. Cut with doughnut cutter. Fry in hot oil until dark brown. Drain on paper. Sprinkle with confectioners' sugar.

Makes 1 1/2 dozen.
Mazel Lassiegne

I Remember...

"I hated the summertime for this reason, because we had to harvest all that food. And we didn't can. We jarred everything. That was so hard. It was hot, and we didn't have air conditioning or anything. It was hot, and you had those hot steaming jars, you know. That's why I said we never suffered from a lack of food, but it was hard work. Boy when we were able to get a freezer that made the [difference], that was the greatest thing. It was so much easier to freeze things than to jar things."

Anne Gros

Doughnuts II

1 bottle (48 ounces) oil
2 eggs
2 cups sugar
1 cup milk
4 cups all-purpose flour
1 tablespoon butter
$1/4$ teaspoon salt
2 teaspoons vanilla extract
4 teaspoons baking powder

Fill a deep pot $1/2$ to $2/3$ full with cooking oil. (We used to use hog lard to fry our food.) Turn on medium flame or stove setting and let oil heat while you make the batter. Mix eggs, sugar, and milk. Add flour, butter, salt, vanilla, and baking powder. Knead into semisoft dough. Roll out dough and cut with doughnut cutter. Fry in deep fat until floating and golden brown. Flip once to brown both sides. Remove from grease and let cool on paper towels or a brown paper bag.

Makes 3 to 4 dozen.
Alzena Miller

I Remember...

when one time a priest slapped a lady and her hat flew down the aisle, because he didn't like short or low-cut dresses. "Now I don't know what [the priest] would say with the way people go to church right now. I'm ashamed of the peoples, me. They go in shorts, yeah, over here. Awwww. When I see that I'm telling you, I can't take it."

Verna Amedee

Cooking With Cajun Women

Homemade Vanilla Ice Cream

5 egg yolks
1 cup sugar
2 large cans (24 ounces total) evaporated milk
  (preferably Carnation)
2 tablespoons vanilla extract
6$^1/_2$ cups whole milk
5 egg whites

Mix yolks with sugar. Add evaporated milk, vanilla extract, and $^1/_2$ cup milk. Fold in beaten egg whites. Pour in ice cream freezer. Add 6 cups milk and stir. Follow the ice cream freezer's instructions for use.

Makes 1 gallon.
Regina Fontenot

I Remember...

that "Momma was very talented. She liked to act in plays... She used to sing, do a lot of singing in French, you know. ... They used to have amateur hours in those days. You didn't have that many places to go." She performed for the amateur hours at church fairs and at St. James High School.

Doris Poirrier

Plain Homemade Ice Cream

I Remember...

when "my mother also taught me this recipe. She made it from scratch without measuring. On Mother's Day, we all went to her house and she prepared dinner for us. She made the homemade ice cream for dessert. I asked her to write a recipe for me and this is what she wrote."

Evon Melancon

$^1/_2$ gallon whole milk
$3^1/_4$ cups sugar
4 eggs
3 tablespoons all-purpose flour
2 tall cans (24 ounces total) evaporated milk
*   (preferably) Carnation*
3 tablespoons vanilla extract
1 bag (8 pounds) ice
1 box (4 pounds) rock salt

Pour whole milk in a pot and bring to a boil. Boil for about 5 minutes. Beat sugar, eggs, and flour in a bowl until completely mixed. Pour boiling milk into this mixture and mix well. Then add evaporated milk. Let cool, then add vanilla. Pour into ice cream freezer. Put ice cream freezer in larger bucket and surround with ice and rock salt. Churn for half an hour in your ice cream maker.

Makes 1 gallon.
Evon Melancon

Custard Floating Islands

6 cups milk
1²/₃ cups sugar
6 eggs, separated
2 tablespoons cornstarch
2 teaspoons vanilla extract
¹/₄ teaspoon cream of tartar

Preheat oven to 350 degrees. Cook milk in large pot until warm. Beat ²/₃ cup sugar, egg yolks, and corn-starch together, and add to milk. Cook on medium heat, stirring constantly until thickened and mixture coats the spoon. Remove from heat; pour into a large bowl, and add vanilla.

In a separate bowl, beat egg whites with cream of tartar until stiff. Add 1 cup of sugar slowly, and beat well. Drop egg white mixture by spoonfuls into a pan of warm water (about 1 inch of water in a 9 by 13-inch pan). Bake for 20 minutes.

Then spoon egg white "islands" over custard and refrigerate.

Serves 6 to 8.
Hilda Waguespack

I Remember...

when tenant farmers grew cotton and corn for shares on our farm. All the neighborhood kids would go and pick cotton "and we'd made fun out of it. We enjoyed doin' it. ... Momma used to chord it for her quilts."

Corinne Judice

Easy Peach Crumble

1 can (29 ounces) peaches
³/4 cup brown sugar
¹/2 cup all-purpose flour
¹/2 teaspoon ground cinnamon
¹/4 cup butter or margarine

Preheat oven to 375 degrees. Place peaches in a lightly greased 9-inch pie plate. In a mixing bowl combine sugar, flour, and cinnamon. Add butter, small pieces at a time. Mix with a pastry blender until mixture resembles coarse meal. Sprinkle mixture over the peaches. Bake for 25 minutes.

Serves 4.
Viola Rider

Peggy's Peach Cobbler

1 large can (15 ounces) sliced peaches, undrained
2 cups biscuit mix (preferably Bisquick)
6 tablespoons hot water
1 cup plus 1 tablespoon sugar
$^1/_2$ cup oleo (margarine)
1 teaspoon ground cinnamon

Preheat oven to 375 degrees. Pour peaches and juice in greased 9 by 12-inch pan. Combine biscuit mix, hot water, and 1 cup sugar. Spoon onto peaches. Dot with pats of oleo. Combine cinnamon and 1 tablespoon sugar, and sprinkle over top. Bake for 45 minutes or until golden brown.

Serves 10 to 12.
Mazel Lassiegne

I Remember...

that "café au lait is as simple as burning sugar and don't let it burn too much, then you put coffee in it then you put milk and let it boil. And that was so good, I can still taste it how good that was."

Delna Hebert

Blackberries and Dumplings

2 cups fresh blackberries
¹/₂ cup sugar
¹/₂ cup flour
1 teaspoon baking powder
1 dash of salt
¹/₄ cup milk

In a pot, combine blackberries, ²/₃ cup water, and ¹/₄ cup sugar. Bring to a boil. In a bowl, combine flour, ¹/₄ cup sugar, baking powder, salt, and milk to make dumplings. Mix well. Drop by spoonfuls in boiling berry mix. Cover and cook over medium heat for 10 to 15 minutes or until done. Double if using more berries.

Serves 4.
Doris Regan

I Remember...

when we used to dye our Easter eggs with peach leaves which turned the eggs green, onion skins for a yellowish hue, and beets which stained the eggs a beautiful shade of burgundy. "Dad kept an egg that wasn't broke, kept it on the shelf for next year, for good luck."

Lois François

Blackberry Cobbler I

2 cups sugar
1 quart berries
cornstarch as needed
1 cup all-purpose flour
1 teaspoon baking powder
1 pinch salt
1 egg
2 tablespoons butter
1 teaspoon vanilla extract
2 to 3 tablespoons water or milk

Preheat oven to 350 degrees. Cook 1 cup sugar, $^{1}/_{2}$ cup water, and berries in a pan on top of the stove until it boils well or microwave for 3 to 4 minutes. Add cornstarch to thicken as needed. When done pour the berries into a 9 by 13-inch casserole dish.

In a separate bowl, mix 1 cup sugar, the flour, baking powder, salt, egg, butter, vanilla, and the water or milk to make your batter. Drop the batter in the berries the same way that you would dumplings. Bake for 30 to 40 minutes or until golden brown. Converts easily to a sugar-free cobbler by substituting Equal for sugar and still tastes good, too.

Makes 1 cobbler.
Regina Fontenot

Blackberry Cobbler II

1 quart blackberries, sweetened
1 cup plus 2 tablespoons all-purpose flour
1 1/2 teaspoons baking powder
1/2 teaspoon salt
3/4 cup sugar
4 tablespoons shortening
1/2 cup milk
1/2 teaspoon vanilla extract
1 egg

Preheat oven to 350 degrees. Pour blackberries into 8 by 8-inch pan. Put flour, baking powder, salt, sugar, shortening, milk, vanilla, and egg in a bowl and mix for 3 minutes. Then drop by spoonfuls over berries. Bake for 30 minutes or until center is baked. I always use a toothpick to check the center. Other fruit may be used.

Makes 1 cobbler.
Doris Regan

I Remember...

the strap that my mom had hanging on the wall. I remember that one day my sister and I decided to bury the strap in the hog pen not realizing that the hogs would rout it up. When my mom found the strap she gave us both a healthy spanking. "Just bickering was enough to drive a mother crazy with six of us."

Viola Rider

Instant Cobbler

1 stick oleo (margarine)
1 cup sugar
1 cup self-rising flour
$^1/_2$ cup milk
1 cup apple filling

Preheat oven to 350 degrees. Melt oleo in 9-inch pie pan. Mix sugar, flour, and milk, and pour in middle of pan. Then pour apple pie filling in center and bake for 30 to 45 minutes.

Makes 1 cobbler.
Joyce Brasseux

I Remember...

when for a time one of my chores included hoeing but my adoptive father did not like my hoeing and left me to do the household and barnyard chores. I washed and ironed the clothes and cleaned the house and by 10 years old was cooking all the meals. Without indoor plumbing, various methods of acquiring water were used for bathing, cooking, and cleaning. I remember that the pond water was pre-ferred for washing clothes to the well water, and I placed large tubs outside to collect rainwater for washing dishes. I also made many batches of lye soap and "that was fun."

Edolia Dupré

Sweet Dough for Pies

³/4 cup shortening (preferably Crisco)
1¹/4 cups sugar
¹/4 cup milk
2 eggs
1 teaspoon vanilla extract
2 teaspoons baking powder
3 cups flour

Preheat oven to 325 degrees. Mix, sugar, milk, eggs, and vanilla. Add baking powder and 2 cups flour. Mix well. Use the extra cup of flour to adjust dough consistency as necessary and to roll out dough. You may need to work them together by hand. It is very thick. Grease and lightly flour two 9-inch pie pans. Roll out dough ¹/4- to ¹/2-inch thick on floured surface. Form crusts with dough in the pie pans. Pour in your favorite filling. You can use any kind of preserves or pie fillings, for example, fig, sweet potato, or stove cooked pudding (not instant). Place the rest of the rolled out dough on top of the filling and pinch at the edges. Then cook for about 30 minutes. Check with a toothpick and the crust should be golden brown.

Makes 2 pies crusts.
Ella Mae Fontenot

I Remember...

when I sold pies to make extra money for my family. I baked and sold many sweet dough pies with my friend, Bessie. Once in a two-day baking spree, we baked 101 pies. These treats were sold for $3 a piece and before I stopped making them I earned $4 per pie.

Edolia Dupré

Sweet Dough for Pies or Tarts

3 cups all-purpose flour
1 teaspoon of baking powder
1 cup sugar
1 teaspoon salt
1 teaspoon vanilla extract
2 tablespoons oil (preferably Crisco)
1/2 cup milk
2 eggs
1 to 2 pints fruit preserves

Preheat oven to 350 degrees. Mix flour, baking powder, sugar, and salt. Add vanilla extract, oil, milk, and eggs. Mix well. If you use too much liquid your dough will not be holding firm enough to knead. Put dough on floured board and roll it out.

For tarts, measure the size of your pie with a milk bowl. Press firmly to cut dough. For half moon tarts, put your favorite fruit on one half, fold the empty side closed and press the edges with a fork. Repeat until all dough is used. Cook for 10 to 12 minutes on a greased cookie sheet.

For regular round pies, make the same batter and roll half the dough out on a floured surface. Measure the size of the dough you need to cut with the 9-inch pie plate you will use. Press firmly to cut dough. Repeat, so you'll have two pie crusts. Place the dough in the bottom of the pie plate and fill with fruit preserves or custard. Cover the top with strips of dough and bake for about 30 minutes or until golden brown.

Makes 2 to 3 dozen tarts or 2 pies.
Gladys Hebert

Miracle Pie Crust

¹/₃ cup oil
1¹/₂ cups all-purpose flour
3 tablespoons cold water
¹/₂ teaspoon salt

Preheat oven to 350 degrees. Mix oil, flour, water, and salt together and roll out. Grease and flour your pie plate. Mold your dough to the inside of the pie plate, forming a pie shell. Bake for 15 to 20 minutes or until golden brown.

Makes 1 pie shell.
Mazel Lassiegne

I Remember...

"Frank, I wouldn't trust [to cook anything]. I don't think he could boil an egg without overdoing it most probably, but he was good at helping me cut the seasoning. If the kids were coming like for Sunday or something we'd make the big chicken stew and stuff or spaghetti and he'd cut all the seasoning for me. He'd cut up the potatoes for the potato salad, so that's the way he'd help. So far as cooking, unt unh."

Verda Bellina

Never-Fail Pie Crust

1¹/₄ cups shortening
3 cups all-purpose flour
1 teaspoon salt
1 egg, beaten
5 tablespoons cold water
1 tablespoon vinegar

Cut shortening into flour and salt. Mix well. Combine egg, water, and vinegar. Pour liquid mixture into flour mixture all at once. Blend with spoon just until flour is all moistened. Form into 2 portions. This pastry can be rerolled without toughening. Will keep in refrigerator for 2 weeks, until you are ready to fill the pie crust (for some fillings you may cover with a layer of dough, or you have enough dough for two open-faced pies) and bake the finished pie. This dough works well with my Louisiana Sweet Potato Pie (recipe follows).

Makes two 9-inch pie crusts or one 9-inch double crust.
Mazel Lassiegne

I Remember...

"You see there are certain things of long ago that I would like to go back to: family, family get together. ... You don't set the table anymore, everybody grabs a bite and some of them are at the TV eating some of [them] have TV tray and another one is eating. Over here I eat more with the family than anywhere else because when I eat over here, well the table is set and everybody sits around it. Although we sit around the table but it's like cafeteria-style; the dishes are not put on the table."

Delna Hebert

Louisiana Sweet Potato Pie

I Remember...

when "you didn't take a full bath every day that's for sure. You washed what was the dirtiest and that was it, I promise you. And I've had more than one doctor tell me that people nowadays bathe too much because they wash the oils off their bodies. You can wash yourself without taking a big bath. And I promise you that's what we used to do. Let me tell you I had four children and I used to bathe my four children in a bucket of water. I'd put that water in there, first came the face, all the faces were clean, stand in line. The boys would go first and the girls would go next. I used to have clean children."

Delna Hebert

1¹/₂ cups yams, fresh or canned
²/₃ cup dark brown sugar
¹/₂ teaspoon salt
¹/₄ teaspoon ground allspice
2 eggs, beaten
1 tablespoon lemon juice
1 cup whole milk
1 unbaked 9-inch pie shell
1 cup whole or chopped pecans (for decorating)

Preheat oven to 450 degrees. Mix yams, brown sugar, salt, allspice, eggs, lemon juice, and milk thoroughly. Fill pie shell with mixture and bake in oven for 15 minutes. Reduce heat to 325 degrees and bake 30 minutes longer. Remove and decorate with pecans in any fashion that you choose. Cool before serving.

Serves 6.
Mazel Lassiegne

Sweet Potato Pie

2 eggs
juice from $^1/_2$ orange
$^1/_2$ cup milk
2 tablespoons shortening, melted
2 cups cooked mashed sweet potatoes
1 teaspoon ground cinnamon (optional)
$^1/_2$ teaspoon salt
$^1/_2$ cup corn syrup
1 teaspoon grated orange rind
1 (9-inch) graham cracker pie shell (preferably
  Nabisco Honey Maid)

Preheat oven to 350 degrees. Beat eggs. Combine
with juice, milk, shortening, sweet potatoes, cinnamon, salt, syrup, and orange rind. Mix well. Bake
35 minutes in graham pie shell using usual recipe
on graham cracker box. You can also use a ready-
made graham cracker pie shell.

Makes 1 pie.
Viola Rider

Sweet Potato Delight

¹/₂ cup butter
2 eggs
3 cups mashed cooked sweet potatoes
1 teaspoon vanilla extract
¹/₃ cup milk
1 cup sugar

Topping:
1 cup light brown sugar
¹/₂ cup all-purpose flour
1 cup chopped pecans
¹/₃ cup butter

Melt butter. Beat eggs slightly. Add to well mashed potatoes. Add vanilla extract, milk, and sugar. Mix well. Pour in well buttered pan.

Preheat oven to 350 degrees. Make the topping: Mix brown sugar, flour, and pecans well. Melt butter and add to topping mixture. Mix until butter is absorbed. When done, pour over potatoes. Bake for about 20 minutes or until brown.

Serves 4.
Dorothy Bryant

I Remember...

"Momma used to tell us, 'If you make your work your pleasure, it's not work.' And 'Now don't be lazy today, because if you're lazy, it's going to take you longer to do what you have to do.' Momma was humorous."

Corinne Judice

Coconut Yam Delight

3 medium yams
1/2 cup hot water
1/3 cup well packed brown sugar
1/4 teaspoon salt
3 tablespoons butter, melted
1/4 cup shredded coconut

Preheat oven to 350 degrees. Cook yams on a baking pan or directly on the oven rack for 1 1/2 to 2 hours, until skin is tender. Peel and cut in halves. Arrange in shallow pan.

Combine hot water, sugar, salt, and butter. Pour over yams. Bake in oven for 15 minutes, basting occasionally. Sprinkle top with coconut and bake 10 minutes longer or until a golden brown.

Serves 3 to 4.
Pauline Langlinais

I Remember...

when growing up, my average day entailed hoeing in the morning, changing my clothes before walking a mile to school; and after school, returning home for the baked sweet potato snack my mother always had waiting and then on to more hoeing. Even with all the work back then I still believe "everybody was always happy. We had a better life than today."

Carrine "Yen" Fontenot

Apple Pie

3¹/₂ cups diced fresh apples
4 tablespoons all-purpose flour
1¹/₄ cups sugar
1 tablespoon butter (not margarine), melted
1¹/₂ teaspoons ground cinnamon
1 unbaked 9-inch pie shell

Preheat oven to 450 degrees. Mix apples, flour, sugar, butter, and cinnamon well and put in an unbaked pie shell. Bake for about 45 minutes on second rack in oven.

Makes 1 pie.
Thelma Coles

I Remember...

when we used to "wash with a scrub board. I still have a scrub board. Yeah we had a scrub board and uh and then we had to heat water. They used to use a big iron kettle out in the yard that they would heat the water and like the white clothes, they would boil it, you know. Then they would use a broomstick and raise or a good stout stick and they would raise that clothes out of that hot water and put it in a big iron in a big galvanized kettle, tub and they would rinse it before they'd put it on the line so it was snow white when they washed it."

Jeanne Arceneaux

Coconut Cream Pie

$^{1}/_{2}$ cup sugar
5 tablespoons all-purpose flour
$^{1}/_{8}$ teaspoon salt
$^{1}/_{4}$ cup cold milk
$1^{1}/_{2}$ cups scalded milk
3 egg yolks
1 teaspoon vanilla extract
1 cup shredded coconut
1 baked 9-inch pie shell

Meringue:
3 egg whites
$^{1}/_{2}$ cup sugar
$^{1}/_{2}$ teaspoon vanilla extract

Blend sugar, flour, and salt with cold milk. Then cook this mixture on a medium heat in a pot on the stove, stirring constantly. Add scalded milk, turn the heat down a little, and continue cooking on low heat until thick. Add beaten egg yolks, then cook 2 minutes longer. Remove from range. Add vanilla and coconut. Cool, then pour into baked pie shell. Set aside.

Preheat oven to 350 degrees. In a separate dish, fluff egg whites. Then add sugar and vanilla in slowly while beating continuously until mixture forms peaks. When ready, cover top of pie with meringue. Slip in hot oven for about 2 minutes to brown meringue.

Makes 1 pie.
Thelma Coles

I Remember...

"we would sit at the table, nobody would eat before the whole gang was there." Rita, my sister, says "You could sit but you wouldn't eat. And we were served ... [Mom] was the last one to sit down." "But [Mom] would, this is how she would say that 'If you eat one by one you never have enough for the last one. But if you eat all at one time, you have enough.' And that's how we were raised.'"

Pauline Guidry

Heavenly Cream Pie

1 can (14 ounces) condensed milk
1 large container (16 ounces) whipped topping
  (preferably Cool Whip)
1 large can (16 ounces) crushed pineapple, drained
¹/₃ cup lemon juice
2 cups chopped pecans
2 (9-inch) graham cracker pie shells

Mix milk, whipped topping, pineapple, lemon juice, and pecans together well. Pour in ready-made graham crackers crusts. Serve chilled.

Makes 2 pies.
Joyce Brasseux

I Remember...

Cajun women supplemented the work of *traiteurs* by exchanging many home remedies that would cure common illnesses. Some of the most common remedies were spider webs to clot blood from an open cut; Mamou tea, Mamou cough syrup (made from the mamouth plant's red seeds or roots boiled with sugar or honey); whiskey and honey for coughs and the common cold; and "cataplasm," "poultice," or mustard plasters, which was placed on the chest for colds and on muscles to keep them warm and avoid cramping. I credit my mother's and grandmother's constant application of mustard packs with saving me from the grips of polio when I was three years old.

Olga Manuel

Custard Pie

3 eggs
5 tablespoons sugar
¹/₄ teaspoon salt
2¹/₂ cups scalded milk
1 unbaked 9-inch pie shell
¹/₈ teaspoon ground nutmeg

Preheat oven to 450 degrees. Beat eggs slightly. Add sugar, salt, and scalded milk. Mix well. Pour into pie shell. Sprinkle lightly with nutmeg. Bake for 5 minutes. Then lower heat to 350 degrees and bake for 20 to 30 minutes longer. When cooked, let cool. Serve hot with ice cream or Cool Whip.

Makes 1 pie.
Thelma Coles

I Remember...

"we always had our, what we called our truck patch: big rows of beans and peas, and we had tomatoes, okra; and we'd have to go out there and pick all of that and then Momma would can all that. She had a pressure cooker she even canned meat lots of times."

Corinne Judice

Graham Cracker Fruit and Nut Dessert Rolls

1 box graham crackers or 1 box graham cracker crumbs (save 1/2 cup for coating)
2 cups raisins (yellow and black combined may be used for coloring)
2 cups chopped pecans
1 medium bottle (16 ounces) red cherries
1 small bottle (12 ounces) green cherries
1 can (14 ounces) condensed milk

Crush 2 1/2 stacks of graham crackers and mix with raisins, pecans, red and green cherries and condensed milk. Blend all ingredients well. Break mixture into three pieces and form each piece into a 8-inch-long roll about 1 1/2 inches in diameter. Then crush the remaining 1/2 stack of crackers and coat each dessert roll with the crumbs. Note: you can make as many dessert rolls as you want in any shape. Wrap rolls in foil, cool in refrigerator. These dessert rolls preserve well. Slice and serve as needed.

Makes 3 dessert rolls.
Pauline Langlinais

I Remember...

"one time we were playing a bunch of girls, children, and I went to jump across a ditch and I missed the, the shoulder on the other side and I fell in the ditch. And there was a broken bottle in the bottom of the ditch, and I fell right on my foot. And we were all barefeeted; we didn't wear shoes like we do today. So I went over to my aunt's who lived right next-door to us in town and she took some kerosene and she poured in that, oh my goodness. I saw stars. Well that was the remedy, that was the remedy."

Jeanne Arceneaux

Chocolate Yummy

*¹/₂ package (8 ounces) chocolate sandwich cookies
  (preferably Oreos)*
*1 container (16 ounces) whipped topping
  (preferably Cool Whip)*
1 cup confectioners' sugar
1 package (8 ounces) cream cheese
3 cups milk
1 package (3 ounces) chocolate instant pudding
1 package (3 ounces) vanilla instant pudding
chocolate morsels (as desired)

For the crust, crush chocolate sandwich cookies in
a ziptop bag and pour cookie crumbs in the bottom of a 9 by 13-inch Corningware dish. Mix 1 cup
whipped topping, powdered sugar, and cream
cheese. Spread on crust. Mix milk with puddings.
Spread on top of the first, white layer. Then top
with rest of the whipped topping and chocolate
chips. Cover with Saran Wrap and refrigerate.

Makes 1 platter.
Regina Fontenot

I Remember...

"My daddy never went to
school; he learned with us.
He learned how to read
and write while we were
in school. And I mean he
could take a paper and
read it from back, front to
back, just from us, you
know, studying and listen-
ing to everything. That's
what I say, if he'd of had
an education, he'd of been,
he'd of been smart."

Elmina Landry

Lemon Icebox Pie

1 cup condensed milk
¹/₂ cup lemon juice
2 egg yolks
1 baked 9-inch pie shell
2 egg whites
¹/₂ cup sugar
1 teaspoon cream of tartar

Mix condensed milk, lemon juice, and egg yolks
well in mixer. Let stand to thicken. Then pour into
crust that is cooked and brown. In a separate bowl
make a meringue by beating egg whites, sugar, and
cream of tartar until meringue is real stiff. Cover
pie with meringue and put it in broiler for a few
minutes to brown the meringue. Watch it close so
it doesn't burn.

Makes 1 pie.
Elva Ardoin

I Remember...

the Great Depression very
well. "Well, I tell you, for
us it was not so bad
because my father always
had work and as he could
get groceries wholesale
also; that helped. And my
uncle had a big garden,
and we had cows, so we
had, you know, the neces-
sities and not much money
but enough to get by. But
some people were very
poor."

Helen Gravois

"Tante" Angel's Sweet Pie Dough Fig Tarts

1 cup sugar
$^1/_2$ cup milk
2 eggs
$^1/_2$ cup oleo (margarine)
$3^1/_2$ cups all-purpose flour
$^1/_2$ teaspoon ground nutmeg
$^1/_2$ teaspoon salt
$^1/_2$ teaspoon ground cinnamon or allspice
2 teaspoons baking powder
1 to 2 pints fig preserves

Preheat oven to 425 degrees. Mix sugar, milk, eggs, and oleo. Add flour, nutmeg, salt, cinnamon or allspice, and baking powder. Add more flour if dough is too soft. Roll out small amount on floured board. Cut out with a 3-inch cutter (I use a small pot cover). Use about 1 teaspoon of fig preserves on one half of the circle. Fold over the other half and crimp edges with a fork dipped in flour. Place on cookie sheet. Bake for 10 to 12 minutes. Other fruits may be used for the filling.

Makes 3 to 5 dozen tarts depending on how thin you roll the dough.
Etheleen Meaux

I Remember...

that we did not have any running water. We had to walk from the back porch to pump water to wash clothes, bathe, and cook. We even kept a cup outside to get water to drink. In the summertime, my mom would fill the large bathing tub with water and leave it outside. By nightfall the water was nice and warm and baths were taken outside.

Rose Fontenot

Sweet Dough Pie with Custard Filling

1 cup sugar
¹/₂ cup butter
1 egg
¹/₄ cup milk
2 cups all-purpose flour
2 teaspoons baking powder
1 teaspoon vanilla extract

Custard Filling:
2 cups milk
1 cup sugar
¹/₂ cup flour
1 teaspoon pure vanilla extract or 1 tablespoon
vanilla flavoring

Preheat oven to 350 degrees. Mix the sugar and butter until well beaten. Add egg. Beat well. Add milk alternately with flour. Add baking powder and vanilla extract. Mix well. It should be firm enough to roll. (This dough can be made in advance and put in the refrigerator for a couple of days before you have to finish making your pie.) Roll a little less than half of the dough on a floured board or sheet so it doesn't stick. Roll about ¹/₈-inch thin to fit the size of your pie plate. Fit into a greased and floured 9-inch pie plate. Repeat for second pie. Make sure and leave enough dough for a lattice top, about ¹/₃ of the dough.

Make the custard: Put milk, sugar, flour, and vanilla in a saucepan and boil slowly on a really low setting. Stir constantly or custard will stick to the pot and burn and you will have to start over. After 5 to 10 minutes the custard should thicken and is ready

when I met my husband. He wrote me a letter and all my friends didn't want me to date him. They wanted me to stay at school with them and he was at a different school. So my friends helped me to write him a letter back, "and I married him anyway."

Pauline Langlinais

to pour in your pie shells. I make strips with a knife to make a lattice to cover the filling. Bake for 30 to 40 minutes or until dough is cooked to a golden brown.

Makes 2 small pies.
Rose Fontenot

Cakes

Sad Cake

1 box (1 pound) light brown sugar
4 eggs
1/2 cup oil
1 teaspoon vanilla extract
1 package (6 ounces) biscuit mix (preferably
   Bisquick)
1 cup chopped pecans

Preheat oven to 350 degrees. Cream sugar, eggs,
and oil. Add vanilla. Then blend in biscuit mix and
pecans. Grease and flour a 9 by 13-inch pan. Bake
in oven for 30 minutes.

Serves 10 to 12.
Belle Fontenot

I Remember...

during the Great
Depression, when people
ate just as well as before
and the clothing was the
same: scantily dressed. I
remember hearing about
men who could not find
work and if they did, the
pay was around 50 cents a
day, but the farmers ate
well, helped each other,
and were generous with
vegetables.

Annie Taylor

I Remember . . .

the *boucheries* well. "Oh yeah that was a big day, the *boucheries*. All the neighbors would come help. It was always a cold day, because for that meat to hang out, for them to work with it and cut it. Sometimes we had two a year. That was a big thing that butchering. ... [The ladies] would help. They would cook for the men that was doing the meat cutting and all this and making the cracklings and the sausage. Momma always was the head of the sausage. And the men would fix the bacon and get it all ready, and then [Momma] used to salt meat in a big old jar."

Corinne Judice

Upside-Down Cake

2 lemons
6 tablespoons freshly squeezed lemon juice
2 eggs
$^2/_3$ cup granulated sugar
1 teaspoon vanilla extract
1 cup all-purpose flour
$^1/_2$ teaspoon baking powder
$^1/_4$ teaspoon salt
$^1/_3$ cup butter
$^1/_2$ cup brown sugar

Preheat oven to 350 degrees. Cut lemons and squeeze until you extract 6 tablespoons of lemon juice. Set juice and fruit pieces aside. Beat eggs until lemon colored, while gradually adding granulated sugar. Beat in at once lemon juice and vanilla extract. Sift together flour, baking powder, and salt and beat in at once. Melt butter in a heavy 10-inch skillet or baking dish. Sprinkle brown sugar evenly over butter. Arrange lemon pieces in attractive pattern on the butter sugar coating. Pour batter over the lemons and bake in oven for approximately 30 minutes. Once cooled, serve straight from the pan. This recipe was given to me by Effie Lahaye in the '50s.

Makes 1 cake.
Rose Fontenot

Poor Man's Cake

1 cup brown sugar
1 cup hot water
1 cup raisins
1 heaping tablespoon shortening
1 teaspoon ground cinnamon
1 teaspoon ground nutmeg
2 cups all-purpose flour
$^1/_2$ teaspoon baking powder
$^1/_2$ teaspoon salt
$^1/_2$ teaspoon baking soda

Preheat oven to 300 degrees. Boil brown sugar, hot water, raisins, shortening, cinnamon, and nutmeg for 5 minutes. Let cool. Add flour, baking powder, and salt to mixture. Then add baking soda, which has been dissolved in 2 tablespoons of water. Bake in a 9 by 13-inch greased and floured pan for 1 hour. Check with toothpick. Top should be golden brown.

Makes 1 cake.
Lola Belle Foret

I Remember...

when I fed all the animals—the pigs, cows, horses, and chickens. Growing up I helped my adoptive parents raise and care for 30 to 40 chickens for the purpose of selling the eggs. At the time a dozen eggs brought 25 cents, which was then spent on household items.

Edolia Dupré

Plantation Pound Cake

1 yellow cake mix
4 eggs
1 container (8 ounces) sour cream
³/4 cup oil
1 cup sugar
1 small can (3.5 ounces) coconut
1 teaspoon vanilla extract

Preheat oven to 325 degrees. Mix cake mix, eggs, sour cream, oil, sugar, coconut, and vanilla extract well together. Put in greased and floured 10-inch Bundt pan. Bake for 1¹/2 hours or until done.

Makes 1 cake.
Joyce Brasseux

I Remember...

When I was just a baby, my birth mother died, which left my father with four young children. My family was separated and I was adopted by "two strangers," who had no children of their own. [My adoptive family raised me and I called them mother and father.] My birth father remarried and had ten more children with his new wife; "I forgive him, but he could have done better than he did." I managed to stay in touch with my father, especially when I was older. I visited my brothers and sisters as often as possible, and I love them very much. I enjoyed cooking for them when they visited.

Edolia Dupré

Syrian Cake

1 box (1 pound) brown sugar
3 eggs
2 cups all-purpose flour
2 tablespoons milk
$^1/_2$ teaspoon salt
1 teaspoon baking powder
1 teaspoon vanilla extract
3 cups chopped pecans
8 ounces dates, chopped (optional)

Preheat oven to 350 degrees. Mix sugar, eggs, flour, and milk. Add salt, baking powder, vanilla, and pecans. Mix well. Add dates if desired. Cook in a greased and floured 9 by 13-inch pan for 30 to 45 minutes or until done. It should be golden brown. Poke it with a toothpick, and if it comes out clean the cake is done.

Makes 1 cake.
Hazel Pousson

I Remember...

when everyone was very conservative. "You know, something [*talking about furniture pieces*] had to last forever. [My parents] were conservative like everybody had to be." During the Great Depression, I remember that shoes were rationed and my family made do with what was available on the farm.

Lessie Deshotel

Plain Cake

1 cup shortening (preferably Crisco)
2 cups sugar
4 eggs
1 cup milk
1 teaspoon vanilla extract
3 cups all-purpose flour
6 teaspoons baking powder

Preheat oven to 375 degrees. Mix shortening, sugar, eggs, and milk. Then add vanilla, flour, and baking powder. Mix well. Grease and flour 4 round 9-inch pans. Pour batter into pans and bake for about 30 minutes.

Makes 1 large 4-layer cake or 2 double-layer cakes.
Evon Melancon

I Remember...

"an old aunt of mine gave me this recipe when she was about 88 years old. She said whenever there was a wedding in the family, she always used this recipe to make the cakes. She said this was much cheaper than using the store-bought cake mix. She said any filling and frosting could be used with [Plain Cake]."

Evon Melancon

Seven-Minute Frosting

2^1/$_4$ cups sugar
1^1/$_2$ tablespoons light corn syrup
3 large egg whites
1^1/$_2$ teaspoons vanilla extract

Combine sugar, corn syrup, and egg whites in top of double boiler and mix well. Cook over boiling water for 3 minutes. (Be sure your sugar melts.) Then, remove from fire but leave over hot water. Beat with rotary beater for 7 minutes or until a consistency to spread. Add vanilla and blend well. (Additional note for high humidity or if frosting is not thick enough: You can put the frosting in the oven to dry and beat it for 12 minutes, instead of 7, if it is above 70% humidity.)

Makes enough for 1 to 2 cakes depending on the type and size.
Mazel Lassiegne

Ella Mae's Cake

I Remember...

that my father represented
the mindset of the time
when he turned to my
future husband and lec-
tured, "'Now you are mar-
rying a child (he was 23
years of age and I was 16)
and you are going to have
to finish raising her.' I
thought 'no way sweetie.'"
Mom said "[marriage] can
be happy, work at it."

Joyce Brasseux

2³/₄ cups sugar
1¹/₂ sticks margarine or butter
¹/₂ cup shortening (preferably Crisco)
3 teaspoons baking powder
1¹/₂ teaspoons vanilla extract
1 teaspoon salt
4 eggs
1¹/₄ cups milk
4 cups all-purpose flour

Preheat oven to 250 degrees. Stir sugar, butter,
shortening, baking powder, vanilla extract, salt,
and eggs well. Add your milk then add your flour 1
cup at the time. Mix well. Bake in 3 greased and
floured 9-inch cake pans for 1¹/₂ hours. Use your
favorite filling. I either make a homemade coconut
custard or pineapple custard filling.

Makes 1 cake and serves 14.
Ella Mae Fontenot

Cake I

¹/₂ cup sugar
1¹/₂ teaspoons ground cinnamon
1 can (20 ounces) apple pie filling
1 can (20 ounces) crushed pineapple
1 can (1 pound) yams, mashed
1 box yellow cake mix
¹/₂ cup butter, melted
1 cup coconut
¹/₂ cup chopped pecans

Preheat oven to 350 degrees. Mix sugar and cinnamon then set aside. In 9 by 13-inch greased and floured baking pan, spread apple pie filling and sprinkle ¹/₃ of cinnamon and sugar over it. Spread one layer of crushed pineapple with juice over pie filling and sprinkle sugar and cinnamon. Then spread yams and sprinkle remainder of sugar and cinnamon. Sprinkle dry cake mix over yams, and pour melted butter over cake mix. Sprinkle coconut and pecans over cake. Cook for 30 to 35 minutes.

Makes 1 cake and serves 14.
Ella Mae Fontenot

I Remember...

when my husband was fighting in World War II. I spent nine months as a welder and an office clerk in a New Orleans shipyard before deciding to quit and return home. Bed bugs were the problem and I refused to live in such filth. After about nine months I decided I had enough and moved back home and lived with my parents until I found another job working at the hospital. I didn't ask my husband. "I just told him, sha. He was overseas. I'd do what I wanted."

Ella Mae Fontenot

I Remember...

Cake II

1 stick margarine, at room temperature
1 box yellow cake mix
4 eggs
1 cup chopped pecans (optional)
1 cup coconut (optional)
1 container (8 ounces) cream cheese
1 box (1 pound) powdered sugar

Preheat oven to 350 degrees. Blend the softened margarine with yellow cake mix, 1 egg, and 1 tablespoon water. You can add chopped nuts or coconut or both to the crust mixture, if desired. Pour into 9 by 13-inch greased and floured pan to form a crust/bottom layer. In a bowl, blend cream cheese with 3 eggs and the box of powdered sugar. Beat well and pour over the crust. Bake for 35 to 45 minutes.

Makes 1 cake.
Rose Fontenot

One-Egg Cake

2 cups sifted all-purpose flour
2 teaspoons baking powder
¼ teaspoon salt
4 tablespoons butter (or shortening)
1 cup sugar
1 egg, unbeaten
¾ cup milk
1 teaspoon vanilla extract

Preheat oven to 350 degrees. Sift flour, baking powder, and salt together. Cream butter and sugar well. Add egg and flour mixture alternately with milk. Beat well. Add vanilla. Bake in a 9 by 13-inch pan for 50 minutes. When cool add your favorite icing if desired.

Makes 1 cake.
Vinice Sensat

No-Egg Raisin Cake

2 cups sugar
1 cup butter or margarine
1 pound raisins
2 cups coconut
1 cup chopped pecans
3 to 3^1/$_2$ cups all-purpose flour
2 teaspoons baking powder
^{1}/$_2$ teaspoon baking soda
1 teaspoon vanilla extract

Filling:
2 cups sugar
2 cups milk
1 cup coconut

Preheat oven to 350 degrees. Boil sugar, butter, raisins, 1^1/$_2$ cups water, coconut, and pecans for 3 minutes. Let cool. When cold add ^{1}/$_4$ cup cold water. Then add flour, baking powder, baking soda, and vanilla extract. Line two 9-inch cake pans with wax paper. Pour in batter and bake for 25 to 30 minutes.

Make the filling: Mix sugar, milk, and coconut. Then cook in a saucepan over medium heat until slightly thick. Let cake cool a little and then put the filling between the cake layers.

Makes 1 cake.
Lola Belle Foret

I Remember...

when I met my future husband at a *fais-do-do* in Ville Platte. My mother had taken me and I remember dancing to French music accompanied by a fiddle, a guitar, piano, and accordion. He and I dated for two years before I married him when I was merely 16.

Edolia Dupré

Coconut Cake

1 box yellow cake mix

Topping and Filling:
1 can (8 ounces) Pet evaporated milk
1/2 cup whole milk
5 envelopes Equal
2 tablespoons sugar
2 tablespoons batter from cake
coconut (as desired)
1 teaspoon lemon or vanilla extract
1 tablespoon butter

In a bowl, prepare cake mix as directed on the box and set aside 2 tablespoons of batter for filling. Bake remaining cake batter as directed on cake mix box in 2 round 9-inch pie pans.

Make the filling: Cook Pet milk, whole milk, Equal, and sugar in pot on medium to low heat. When very hot, add 2 full tablespoons of cake batter to mixture until thick enough (not too thick because it will be too dry). Add coconut as desired to this mixture. Add lemon or vanilla extract to taste. Add butter at the end. Note: Without coconut, the filling is called *bouillie au lait*. If you make a one layer cake, use as a topping. For multiple layers, use as a filling and frosting.

Makes 1 cake.
Freddie Parent

I Remember...

We ate a lot of seafood growing up, got the shrimps in the river. We used a cage, a sky box with a hole [funnels] on both ends, just like the crawfish cage. We also ate crabs and crawfish. Mom made stews and gumbos. "And when we were small we'd go, they, it wasn't too far where we'd live and uh. When momma and daddy would go and we'd follow them and go fish with our little bucket."

Pauline Guidry

Layer Cake

2 cups sugar
$1/2$ cup oil
1 cup milk
1 teaspoon salt
1 teaspoon baking powder
2 eggs
$2^1/2$ cups all-purpose flour
1 can (21 ounces) coconut or strawberry filling

Preheat oven to 350 degrees. Mix sugar, oil, milk, salt, baking powder, and eggs. Then add flour. Mix and stir well. Pour in two 9-inch round greased and floured cake pans and bake for 25 to 30 minutes or until toothpick comes out clean, when put in center of cake. Layer it with coconut or strawberry filling in the middle.

Serves 8.
Blanche Quebedeaux

I Remember...

when my mother had employed a lady to help in the house ... "but with our mother that didn't count, [the hired help] had her chores and we [the children] had ours. ... You know, I thank the good Lord for my father and mother, because they taught us how to live."

Claire Bonin

Carrot Cake

2 cups sugar
4 eggs
1¹/₂ cups oil (preferably vegetable oil)
3 cups grated carrots
2 cups all-purpose flour
1 teaspoon salt
2 teaspoons baking soda
3 teaspoons ground cinnamon

Filling:
1 pound powdered sugar
1 stick oleo (margarine), at room temperature
1 bar (8 ounces) cream cheese, at room temperature
2 teaspoons vanilla extract
2 tablespoons heavy cream
1¹/₂ cups chopped pecans

Preheat oven to 350 degrees. In a large bowl cream
sugar, eggs, oil, and carrots. In a small bowl mix
flour, salt, baking soda, and cinnamon. Then mix
contents of both bowls together. Place batter in 3
greased and floured round 9-inch cake pans. A 3-
layer cake takes 2 cups mix in each baking pan.
Bake for 30 to 35 minutes.

Make the filling: Mix powdered sugar, oleo, and
cream cheese. Add vanilla, cream, and pecans. Mix
well. Spread on hot cake between each layer and
on top.

Makes 1 cake.
Claire Bonin

I Remember...

I used to think that babies
came on trains. "We were
as green as grass."

Mildred LeJeune

Louisiana Fig Cake

2 large eggs
4 tablespoons sugar
1 cup oil (or melted shortening or margarine)
2 teaspoons vanilla extract
2 cups plus 6 tablespoons all-purpose flour
1 teaspoon salt
1 teaspoon baking soda
2 teaspoons baking powder
ground nutmeg to taste
ground cinnamon to taste
1 quart cooked and mashed figs

Preheat oven to 350 degrees. Mix eggs, sugar, oil, and vanilla extract. Add flour, salt, baking soda, baking powder, nutmeg, and cinnamon. Mix well. Add in figs and blend well. Pour in greased and floured 9 by 13-inch pan and bake for 40 to 50 minutes at 350 degrees.

Makes 1 cake.
Lola Belle Foret

I Remember...

when "my momma would raise a lot of eggplants, the green ones. She'd even raise the celery. We'd go to the woods and get some moss and put around the celery to make it tender. All kinds of vegetables. We didn't have too many fruits but my grandpa had fruits. Figs, he had huge fig trees and we'd get all the figs we wanted."

Gladys Hebert

Fig Cake I

1 teaspoon vinegar
2/3 cup milk
2 cups all-purpose flour
1 teaspoon baking soda
2 teaspoons salt
1 teaspoon ground cinnamon
3 eggs
2 cups brown sugar
1 stick oleo (margarine), melted
2 cups chopped pecans
1 cup mashed figs

Preheat oven to 350 degrees. First mix vinegar with milk and set aside. Then make a dry mixture of the flour, baking soda, salt, and cinnamon and set aside. Then mix the eggs, brown sugar, oleo, pecans, and figs in a third bowl. Gradually add to this third bowl the vinegar and milk alternately with the dry mixture. Mix well then place batter into a greased 9 by 13-inch cake pan 45 minutes or until done. Test with a toothpick or until brown.

Makes 1 cake.
Claire Bonin

I Remember...

when I was a child, I helped my parents both inside and outside the house. I picked peas, cotton, figs, and peaches and I even used an old time "*traineau*" to pick cucumbers, cantaloupe, watermelons, and tomatoes. Two of my daily duties included emptying every chamber pot in the morning and cleaning the milk cow.

Odile Hollier

Fig Cake II

1 quart cooked figs
2 eggs
1 cup oil
2 cups all-purpose flour
1 teaspoon baking soda
1 teaspoon baking powder
1 cup chopped pecans

Preheat oven to 250 degrees. Mix figs, eggs, and oil. Stir in flour, baking soda, baking powder, and nuts. Pour batter in a 9 by 13-inch greased pan. Bake for 45 minutes or until done.

Serves 8 generously.
Alzena Miller

I Remember...

we ate "a lot of syrup but there was no honey in those days. But after we were married, there was one of Bruce's [my husband's] cousins that had a rice mill, so if we'd brought a bag of rice, a sack of rice, he'd mill it, and there was a truck from around Marksville that would come down with some syrup the best syrup, cane. So they'd give you 12 gallons of syrup for a sack of rice so that lasted us a whole year."

Gladys Hebert

Cooking With Cajun Women

Fig Cake III

1 pint fig preserves
1 box yellow cake mix
$^{1}/_{2}$ cup oil
$1^{1}/_{2}$ cups chopped pecans
3 eggs

Preheat oven to 350 degrees. Pour fig preserves into blender. Cover processor and chop figs. Place cake mix in bowl. Blend in 1 cup water. Add figs, oil, pecans, and eggs. Beat for 2 minutes. Place in greased and floured 10-inch tube pan. Bake for 45 minutes or until cake tests done.

Makes 1 cake.
Viola Rider

Fresh Apple Cake

3 cups peeled and chopped apples
1 cup chopped pecans
2 teaspoons vanilla extract
3 eggs
1¼ cups oil (preferably Crisco)
3 cups all-purpose flour
1 teaspoon salt
2 cups sugar

Topping:
1 cup brown sugar
1 stick margarine
1 teaspoon vanilla extract
¼ can (3 ounces) evaporated milk

Preheat oven to 250 degrees. Stir apples, nuts, vanilla extract, eggs, oil, flour, salt, and sugar all together. Pour in 9 by 13-inch greased and floured pan. Bake for 1½ hours.

For topping, cook brown sugar, margarine, vanilla, and evaporated milk to full boil. Beat and cool. Spread on top of warm apple cake.

Makes 1 cake and serves 14.
Ella Mae Fontenot

I Remember...

that oftentimes all we could afford was the material from the feed and fertilizer sacks. It made the nicest little dresses and shirts, and sturdy sheets, blankets, and pillow cases.

Belle Fontenot

Fresh Pear Cake

1¼ cups oil
2 cups sugar
3 eggs
1 teaspoon baking soda
1 teaspoon salt
3 cups all-purpose flour
3 cups peeled and chopped pears
1 cup chopped pecans
2 teaspoons vanilla extract

Topping:
1 cup brown sugar
1 stick butter or margarine
¼ cup evaporated milk
1 teaspoon vanilla extract

Preheat oven to 250 degrees. Mix together oil, sugar, and eggs. Add baking soda, salt, flour, pears, pecans, and vanilla extract. Mix well, and pour in a 9 by 13-inch greased and floured pan. Bake for about 1½ hours or until done.

While pear cake is baking, make your topping. Mix sugar, butter or margarine, evaporated milk, and vanilla extract in a pot and heat to a full boil. Beat and cool. Spread on warm pear cake.

Serves 14.
Ella Mae Fontenot

I Remember...

when we went to house parties and dances. "We had an old Model T without the glasses and boy we'd get in there and it was cold sometimes and raining, but that wouldn't stop us from going to the dances. And I went to the dances until I couldn't dance no more." I also enjoyed playing cards since I was a little girl. "A Cajun likes to have a good time you know. The old ones don't want to play for money, [they] keep points. It's not fun if you don't play for money. Anyway, it's a penny."

Pauline Langlinais

that I was an "old maid" whose mother and sister did all the cooking. I worked in the yard with the animals, swept and scrubbed the house, sewed and worked professionally; "I did other things and I never did cook. So when my sister died quite suddenly in 1972, I had to open a cookbook and learn how to cook you know. But I did it; I learned how to cook."

Eva Mae Poirrier

Banana Layer Cake

³/₄ cup butter
1¹/₄ cups sugar
2 eggs, beaten
2¹/₂ cups all-purpose flour
1¹/₄ cups ripe, mashed bananas
1 teaspoon baking soda
1 teaspoon baking powder
¹/₄ cup sour milk or buttermilk
1 teaspoon vanilla extract

Preheat oven to 375 degrees. Mix butter, sugar, and eggs. Add flour, bananas, baking soda, baking powder, sour milk or buttermilk, and vanilla extract. Mix well until you have a smooth batter. Pour into 2 greased and floured 9-inch pans and bake 25 to 30 minutes or until golden colored. Test with a toothpick. If it comes out clean, the cakes are done. Use whatever icing you wish when cooled.

Makes 1 cake.
Thelma Coles

Easy Lemon Bundt Cake

*1 box lemon cake mix (preferably Duncan Hines
    Supreme Lemon)*
¹/₂ cup sugar
4 eggs
1 cup apricot nectar
¹/₂ cup oil (preferably Crisco)

Preheat oven to 350 degrees. Combine cake mix,
sugar, eggs, nectar, and oil. Mix well and pour into
greased and floured Bundt pan. Bake for 45 minutes.

Makes 1 cake.
Evon Melancon

Lemon Pound Cake

*1 box lemon cake mix (preferably Duncan Hines
  Deluxe)*
1 package (3 ounces) lemon instant pudding
$^1/_2$ cup oil (preferably Crisco)
1 cup water or milk
3 or 4 eggs

Glaze:
1 cup confectioners' sugar
1 or 2 tablespoons lemon juice

Preheat oven to 350 degrees. Mix cake mix, instant
pudding, oil, water or milk, and eggs. Bake in
greased and floured 10-inch pan for 45 to 50 minutes. To make cupcakes, line pans and bake for 30
minutes. May also bake as regular 2-layer cake.
Check with toothpick to see if cake is done.

Make glaze for cake by mixing confectioners' sugar
and lemon juice. Pour over cooled cake.

***Makes one 10-inch or 2-layer cake or
24 cupcakes.***
Etheleen Meaux

I Remember...

I boarded and worked for
two years in a Ville Platte
restaurant. Without my
parents' permission, I
dated Abbie for two years
before we were wed by a
Ville Platte judge. Contrary
to tradition, Abbie and I
notified my parents after
the civil ceremony and had
our marriage blessed a
couple weeks later. I
remember my father's
reaction, "That paper
doesn't do me any good,
I don't know how to read."
In time my parents
accepted their new son-
in-law. Abbie and I
enjoyed a happy loving
marriage that produced
four children.

Ella Mae Fontenot

7-Up Cake

1 box yellow cake mix
1 package (3 ounces) Jell-O instant pineapple or
*   lemon pudding mix*
4 eggs
³/₄ cup oil
1 bottle (10 ounces) 7-Up

Frosting:
1 small can (8 ounces) crushed pineapple and juice
1 stick butter
1 cup sugar
2 eggs
2 tablespoons all-purpose flour
1 can (3.5 ounces) flaked coconut

Preheat oven to 350 degrees. Put cake mix, Jell-O or pudding mix, eggs, oil, and 7-Up in a bowl and mix. Bake in 3 greased and floured 9-inch round cake pans for 25 to 30 minutes.

For frosting, mix pineapple and juice, butter, sugar, eggs, and flour. Mix and cook over medium heat until thick. Let cool. Add coconut. Spread between layers and on top.

Makes 1 cake and serves 14.
Ella Mae Fontenot

I Remember...

"going to and from school at the Ursuline Convent in New Orleans. It was by train. And I remember once my daddy tried [to come visit me at school]. At the time we didn't have paved roads, or not even gravel roads. It was mud you know, and he had so much trouble. He said, 'never again.' He had even put chains on the tires you know, to try to get through. That was in the '20s. So actually all the time during those years boarding there at school [travel to and from home] was by train."

Hilda Waguespack

1-2-3-4 Cake

1 cup margarine
2 cups sugar
4 eggs
3 cups all-purpose flour
3 teaspoons baking powder
3/4 cup milk
1 teaspoon vanilla extract

Filling and Topping:
1 large can (16 ounces) crushed pineapple with juice
1 tablespoon sugar
2 teaspoons cornstarch
1 pat (tablespoon) margarine

Preheat oven to 325 degrees. In a large mixing bowl cream margarine. Add sugar and blend well. Beat eggs in one at a time. In a separate bowl sift flour and baking powder together. Add sifted dry ingredients, alternately with the milk and vanilla extract, to the original large mixing bowl. Beat until well mixed. Pour into three 8-inch cake pans, which have been greased and floured. Bake for about 20 minutes. Test before removing from oven. When cake cools a little spread pineapple filling between the layers and on top of the cake.

Make the filling: Place pineapple, sugar, cornstarch, and margarine in a saucepan. Cook over medium heat until it reaches consistency of a thick pudding. Remove from heat. When cool reserved 1/2 cup for topping and spread remaining filling between cake layers. Then use the 1/2 cup of reserve topping to frost the cake.

Makes 1 cake.
Lola Belle Foret

I Remember...

"Well don't get married until you're 50 years old, because life is too hard when you get married. ... I had a bad husband." He was not a beater, but he didn't want anything to do with me and the kids and he had girlfriends. "He wouldn't tell 'hi' to those kids [when they came for Sunday dinner]. That would get me mad enough to kill him. If I had a hard time with that man. ... If there's a hell like they say there is [and] I believe there is, I guess he's scratching his old butt over there."

Edolia Dupré

Cooking With Cajun Women

Dump Cake

1 can (20 ounces) crushed pineapple
1 can (21 ounces) cherry pie filling (or any fruit)
1 box yellow or white cake mix
1¹/₂ sticks oleo (margarine)
¹/₂ cup chopped pecans (or favorite nuts)

Preheat oven to 350 degrees. Grease 9 by 13-inch cake pan. Add ingredients in layers. Pour pineapple in pan. Pour pie filling. Pour dry cake mix evenly over fruit. Cut slices of oleo evenly over dry cake mix. Sprinkle nuts over top. Bake for 40 to 45 minutes.

Serves 10 to 12.
Belle Fontenot

I Remember...

when we used to make the *veillée*. At night, we would gather with neighbors on the porch and visit. There was always a good storyteller, who told ghost stories, "*defunt*" tales (accounts of dead relatives), or Civil War stories about jayhawkers who raided local farmsteads.

Olga Manuel

Fruit Cocktail Cake

2 cups sugar
2 cups all-purpose flour
2 teaspoons baking soda
2 eggs
1 can (15 ounces) fruit cocktail

Preheat oven to 350 degrees. Mix sugar, flour, and baking soda. Then add eggs and fruit cocktail. Blend well. Pour into a 9 by 13-inch greased pan. Bake 30 to 35 minutes or until done.

Serves 8 generously.
Alzena Miller

I Remember...

that my adoptive mother was better suited for the outside work. "She worked in the field like a horse. ... Anything a man could, she could do it herself." I remember that my adoptive mother maintained a large garden; "you name it she had it." My adoptive parents did not plant rice commercially, but they did throw a little seed and hoped the rain would come and they might harvest a patch of providence rice, enough to eat.

Edolia Dupré

Fruit Cocktail (or Pineapple) Cake

1 box yellow cake mix
1 can (16 ounces) fruit cocktail or
    crushed pineapple, undrained
2 eggs
$2^1/2$ cups coconut
$1/2$ cup brown sugar
$1/2$ cup granulated sugar
$1/2$ cup butter or oleo (margarine)
$1/2$ cup evaporated milk

Preheat oven to 325 degrees. Mix cake mix, cocktail
or pineapple, eggs, and 1 cup coconut. Pour into
greased and floured 9 by 13-inch pan and sprinkle
brown sugar on top. Bake 30 to 45 minutes or until
done and golden brown.

While the cake is baking, bring granulated sugar,
butter or oleo, and evaporated milk to a boil on the
stove. Boil for 2 minutes. Add $1^1/2$ cups coconut to
the mixture. Then spoon over hot cake.

Makes 1 cake.
Joyce Brasseux

I Remember...

During the Great
Depression, I had to
extend credit to some of
my customers, who were
in need. When I finally
collected, I paid the
wholesaler and I remember
not having enough left
over to save in the bank. I
did manage to set enough
money aside to pay my
husband's doctor bills.

Carrine "Yen" Fontenot

Festive Fruit Cake

1 can (12 ounces) whole candied cherries
1 can (8 ounces) candied or dried pineapple rings
1 box spice cake mix (preferably Duncan Hines Deluxe)
$^1/_2$ cup finely chopped walnuts
1 package (3.5 ounces) instant vanilla pudding mix
4 eggs
$^1/_3$ cup oil
1 teaspoon ground cinnamon
$^1/_2$ teaspoon ground cloves
$^1/_2$ teaspoon ground nutmeg
$^1/_2$ teaspoon ground ginger
1 cup orange juice

Topping:
2 tablespoons lemon juice
1 $^1/_2$ cups sifted powdered sugar

Preheat oven to 350 degrees. Grease and flour a 10-inch Bundt or tube pan. Set aside 6 whole cherries and 2 pineapple rings for decoration. Finely chop remaining cherries and pineapples and place in a large bowl. Add cake mix, walnuts, pudding mix, eggs, oil, cinnamon, cloves, nutmeg, ginger, and orange juice. Mix at medium speed for 2 minutes. Pour into prepared pan. Bake for 45 to 55 minutes. Cake is done when toothpick inserted in center comes out clean. Cool on rack for 25 minutes then remove from pan. Cool completely.

Then mix lemon juice with powdered sugar. Drizzle over cool cake. Halve the 6 cherries and place them on the cake. Cut leaf shape out of pineapple rings and place around cherries. Store in airtight container.

Makes 1 cake.
Hazel Pousson

I Remember...

My husband worked in a grocery store before venturing off to create his own meat market/convenience store. I remember that when I was pregnant my husband used to bring home watermelons for me. I would eat half of a watermelon during the course of a day and finish the other half during the night.

Marie "Ivy" Ortego

Fruit Cake

3 packages (96 ounces total) chopped mixed
   candied fruits and peels
1 package (16 ounces) candied cherries
2 boxes (30 ounces total) white raisins (golden)
27 ounces shelled walnuts
56 ounces shelled pecans
2 bottles (16 ounces total) imitation vanilla flavoring
5 cups all-purpose flour
2 teaspoons baking soda
2 teaspoons baking powder
2 teaspoons ground nutmeg
2 teaspoons ground cinnamon
18 eggs
6 sticks (1½ pounds) butter
5 cups sugar

Preheat oven to 250 degrees. Put the dried fruits,
cherries, raisins, walnuts, and pecans in a large
dishpan. Pour vanilla extract on dried fruits. Pour
flour, soda, baking powder, nutmeg, and cinnamon
on fruits and mix well with hands. Beat eggs, butter, and sugar in mixer until very fluffy, then pour
on floured fruits, and mix very well until grimy.
Finally, grease four 10-inch loaf pans heavily,
preferably with Pam. Then pack cakes into the pans
well. Bake in oven for about 2 ½ hours.

When done let cakes cool in same pans you cooked
them in. Cover cakes with foil while still hot. When
cooled then take out of pan and wrap with foil and
Handi Wrap. Store in cabinet for weeks—do not
put in fridge.

Makes 4 cakes.
Elva Ardoin

I Remember...

"We was poor." My hus-
band and I had saved
$5,000 and it took all of it
to build the house. "And
we didn't believe in bor-
rowing. We had cried. We
had no more money." My
mom would bring us gro-
ceries from their store and
feed us so that we could
save money for the house
and that was back when a
big bag of groceries cost
$1.50 to $2. A big roast
cost 15 cents and would
last all week.

Pauline Langlinais

Ginger Cake

2 eggs
1 cup syrup
$^1/_2$ cup margarine
$^1/_2$ cup hot water
$1^1/_2$ cups all-purpose flour
1 teaspoon baking soda
1 teaspoon ground ginger
$^1/_4$ teaspoon salt

Preheat oven to 350 degrees. Beat eggs with syrup. Add margarine. Beat. Add hot water. Beat well. Add flour, baking soda, ginger, and salt. Cook in a greased and floured 9-inch Bundt pan or regular pound cake pan. Bake for approximately 30 minutes.

Makes 1 cake.
Rose Fontenot

I Remember...

making our own cream and butter. "We had a little churn and then we used to do it in a jar; just take your cream and keep moving the jar back and forth, after while your butter would form."

Corinne Judice

Oatmeal Cake

1 cup old-fashioned oats
1 1/2 sticks margarine
1 1/4 cups boiling water
1 cup granulated sugar
1 cup brown sugar
2 eggs
1 1/3 cups all-purpose flour
1/2 teaspoon salt
1 teaspoon baking soda
1 teaspoon baking powder
1/2 teaspoon ground nutmeg
1 teaspoon ground cinnamon

Frosting:
6 tablespoons margarine
1/4 cup cream
1/2 cup sugar
1/2 cup coconut
1 teaspoon vanilla extract
1 cup chopped pecans

Preheat oven to 350 degrees. Place oatmeal and margarine in a large mixing bowl. Pour in boiling water. Cover, and let stand for 20 minutes. Then add white and brown sugar and eggs. Add flour, salt, baking soda, baking powder, nutmeg, and cinnamon. Blend together. Bake in greased and floured a 9 by 13-inch pan for 1 hour.

Make the frosting: Melt the margarine. Add cream, sugar, coconut, vanilla, and pecans. Mix well. Spread on cooled cake. Place under broiler for about 5 minutes. Watch carefully not to burn icing. Remove and serve.

Makes 1 cake.
Evon Melancon

I Remember...

when I met my husband through a friend. My friend had a picture of me in his wallet and my husband saw it. He said that he would like to meet me and we got married the day after my graduation. I wanted to quit in April to marry him, but my mom made a deal with me to wait.

Jean Brasseaux

Pecan-Date Loaf Cake

I Remember...

"My mother used to make fruit cakes but I do not make these and I do not know how she made them. I know she made them at least a month before Christmas and wrapped them in brown paper and would open [the] paper every now and then and sprinkle a little whiskey on them. I do not drink at all and I did not like the taste of whiskey. I do not sprinkle anything on my pecan-date loaf cake."

Eva Mae Poirrier

1 pound dates, chopped
2 1/2 cups coarsely ground pecans
1 cup sugar
1 cup all-purpose flour
1/4 teaspoon salt
2 teaspoons baking powder
4 eggs, separated
1 teaspoon vanilla extract
2 ounces red candied cherries (optional)
2 ounces green candied cherries (optional)

Preheat oven to 250 degrees. Combine dates and nuts. Sift sugar, flour, salt, and baking powder over dates and nuts. Stir until thoroughly mixed. In a separate dish, beat egg yolks until foamy (save egg whites for later), and add vanilla. Then add to date-pecan mixture and blend thoroughly. Fold in stiffly beaten egg whites. Dough should be kind of stiff. Hint: To make cake look festive, add cherries cut in half to the pecan-date mixture.

Pack dough in greased and waxed-paper lined 9 by 5 by 3-inch loaf pan. Bake in oven for 2 1/2 hours. Remove cake from oven, turn over loaf onto a cookie sheet, and remove wax paper. This is an easy cake to make for Christmas.

Makes 1 cake.
Eva Mae Poirrier

Heavenly Hash Cake

2 teaspoons vanilla extract
2 cups sugar
2 sticks oleo (margarine), melted
4 eggs, slightly beaten
1 1/2 cups self-rising flour
4 tablespoons unsweetened cocoa powder
1/2 cup chopped pecans
1 package (10.5 ounces) miniature marshmallows

Icing:
1 pound powdered sugar
4 tablespoons cocoa powder
8 tablespoons evaporated milk
4 tablespoons melted oleo

Preheat oven to 350 degrees. Mix vanilla, sugar, oleo, and eggs. In a separate bowl, mix flour, cocoa, and pecans then add to first mixture. Mix gently, but don't beat. Pour into greased 13 by 9-inch pan. Bake in oven for 30 to 35 minutes. Remove from oven and cover with miniature marshmallows (or large ones cut in half, cut-side down on hot cake.)

Make the icing: Heat sugar, cocoa, evaporated milk, and oleo. Pour over hot cake after it is covered with marshmallows, not before.

Makes 1 cake.
Etheleen Meaux

I Remember...

"We raised cattle so we had all the meat we needed. We didn't have to buy any and we had the rice we needed and we had all the vegetables that we needed. [My husband] would take care of one to make it very nice to butcher and his brother said 'why don't you sell that one? You'd get a better price for it and get another one in the field.' He said, 'yes, but I want to have good meat too.'"

Hazel Pousson

I Remember...

"Since I had the stroke it's hard to walk with a cane and I cannot stand for long, but I love to cook but most of all I love to bake. I have a rocking chair in front of my stove so I can sit every few minutes. I never buy anything at a bakery as my cakes are better. The boys says 'this is not air cake.' It is heavy with all the fillings I put between the layers."

Rose Fontenot

Red Velvet Cake

2 bottles (2 ounces total) red food color
3 tablespoons chocolate drink powder (preferably Nestlé's Quik)
$^1/_2$ cup shortening
$1^1/_2$ cups sugar
2 eggs
1 cup buttermilk
$2^1/_4$ cups all-purpose flour
$^1/_4$ teaspoon salt
$1^1/_2$ teaspoons vanilla extract
1 tablespoon vinegar
1 teaspoon baking soda

Frosting:
3 tablespoons all-purpose flour
$^3/_4$ cup milk
6 tablespoons butter
6 tablespoons shortening
$^3/_4$ cup sugar
1 teaspoon vanilla extract
whole pecans for garnish

Preheat oven to 350 degrees. Make a paste with food coloring and chocolate flavoring. In a separate bowl, combine shortening and sugar. Cream until fluffy. Then add eggs. Next add paste and blend well. Add buttermilk. Mix. Add flour, salt, and vanilla extract, and blend thoroughly. Fold in vinegar and baking soda. Pour into two well greased and floured round 9-inch cake pans. Bake for 25 to 30 minutes.

Make the frosting: Combine flour and milk in small saucepan. Cook on low heat to a thick consistency. Cool thoroughly. Combine butter, shortening, sugar, and vanilla in separate bowl. Blend with mixer until fluffy. Combine the two mixtures. Mix until peaks form. Spread between layers and over cake. Garnish with pecans.

Makes 1 cake.
Pat Ardoin

I Remember...

"my Mom's food. I used to like everything she fixed. Her biscuits were out of this world. Her cornbread, her cakes from scratch. And she would fix 'em some kind of uh, what can I call that. Anyway it was fixed with fruit and she'd make like a sauce over it, a sweet deal, a custard like, you know and cover that with that. Aw, no wonder I was fat. That was so good. It was like a dumpling but it was made with biscuit dough but she would put preserves of some kind in there and serve that with the sauce. Lord that was terrific. Her dressings, aw, she made some good dressings. And vegetables. Well the vegetables, she was just an ordinary. Her eggplants were better than anybody else I ever ate."

Anne Gros

I Remember...

when "Mom used to make her homemade soap in the yard in a big old black pot; and she'd make her soap and when it would get hard, she'd turn it over and she'd cut it in pieces." Mama used to make some for the baths; it was lighter and white. "Making soap was a pretty day."

Corinne Judice

Mock Red Velvet Cake

1 box German chocolate cake mix
1 bottle (1 ounce) red food color

Topping and Filling:
1 can (12 ounces) evaporated milk
1 cup sugar
$^1/_4$ cup cornstarch
$^1/_2$ stick butter
1 teaspoon vanilla extract

Prepare cake mix and bake according to directions on box. Before baking, stir in the red food coloring. I use 3 greased and floured 9-inch cake pans.

When cake is cold I make a rich cream pudding for topping and filling. Boil milk and sugar. Dissolve cornstarch with $^1/_2$ cup water and mix slowly with hot milk, sugar, and butter until thick. Take off of heat and add vanilla extract. Put aside and when cooled, put between layers and on top of cake. You can let some filling fall over the side of the cake. Very good.

Makes 1 cake.
Rose Fontenot

Mahogany Cake

1 cup unsweetened cocoa powder
1 cup boiling water
3 tablespoons vinegar
1 cup sour milk
4 cups sugar
4 eggs
1 cup oil
4 cups all-purpose flour
2 teaspoons baking soda
1 jar (16 ounces) cherries, undrained
1 teaspoon ground cinnamon
1 teaspoon ground nutmeg

Preheat oven to 325 degrees if you are making one large cake or to 350 degrees if you are making two Bundt cakes. Dissolve cocoa in boiling water and set aside. Add vinegar to sour milk. Then mix cocoa mixture with vinegar and sour milk. Add sugar, eggs, oil, flour, and baking soda. Mix well. Slice cherries. In a mixer, mix cherries and juice, cinnamon, and nutmeg. Cook covered in a small blue roaster at 325 degrees for about 1 1/2 hours or until done. You can also use two 10-inch greased and floured Bundt pans and cook at 350 degrees for 1 hour or until done. If using Bundt pans when done remove from the oven, cover with aluminum foil and let cool. Covering it while cooling keeps the cake moist.

Makes 1 large or 2 small cakes.
Elva Ardoin

I Remember...

we had "a nice wedding, not a big wedding like they have now, family and just a few friends, and just a little reception at the house. And I wore my sister's dress. My sister had been married just a few years before me and she had a beautiful dress and it fit me so why not."

Helen Gravois

I Remember...

a time when my father was unable to work after falling into a cotton gin, and the barn needed a new roof. Our neighbors brought food, everyone pitched in, and by the end of the day a new roof covered the barn. No money was exchanged, for payment came later when the favor was returned in kind. This is what we call a *coup de main*, giving a helping hand.

Odile Hollier

Chocolate Filling

1 cup sugar
4 heaping tablespoons all-purpose flour
1/2 cup semisweet chocolate morsels
1 1/2 cups milk
1 tablespoon butter
1 teaspoon vanilla extract

Mix sugar and flour. In a separate microwaveable bowl, melt chocolate chips in the microwave oven. Stir sugar and flour mixture into the melted chocolate. Blend in milk, butter, and vanilla. Then bring to a boil and stir until thick.

Makes enough filling for 1 cake.
Belle Fontenot

Tunnel-of-Fudge Cake

3 sticks (1¹/₂ cups) butter, softened
6 eggs
1¹/₂ cups sugar
2 cups all-purpose flour
1 box powdered chocolate fudge frosting (preferably
    Betty Crocker) or homemade frosting described
    on next page)
2 cups chopped walnuts

Preheat oven to 350 degrees. Beat butter at high
speed until fluffy. Add eggs, one at a time.
Gradually beat in sugar. Beat until fluffy. Hand-stir
in flour and frosting mix, and chopped walnuts.
Bake in greased and floured 10-inch Bundt pan for
55 to 60 minutes. When done top is shiny. Cool in
pan for 2 hours before taking out.

Makes 1 cake.
Elva Ardoin

I Remember...

when my mother made
feather beds from the
feathers of her own chickens. Because my mother
raised chickens, we always
had a source of meat and
eggs. Also, the money
collected from the sale of
chicken eggs "bought a lot
of things in the kitchen."
When I was first married, I
raised chickens as well.

Versie Meche

I Remember...

"Powdered chocolate fudge frosting can no longer be found in local grocery stores. My friend came to the rescue with this homemade frosting mix. It has allowed me to keep making one of our family favorites—Tunnel-of-Fudge Cake. ... This was one of Elva's [my mother-in-law's] specialities. ... My son, Kevin, always loved when his MoMo Elva made this cake, and now, I can continue the tradition.

Pat Ardoin

Homemade Frosting Mix

1 box confectioners' sugar
$1/2$ cup unsweetened cocoa powder (preferably Hershey's)
2 to 3 tablespoons butter
1 tablespoon all-purpose flour

Mix together powdered sugar, cocoa, butter, and flour.

If you cannot find a box of powdered chocolate fudge frosting by Betty Crocker, use this recipe to make a similar mixture for the Tunnel-of-Fudge Cake on page 309. I learned this recipe from Kerry Higginbotham.

Makes enough for 1 cake.
Pat Ardoin

Butterscotch Marble Cake

1 box white or yellow cake mix
1 package (3 ounces) instant butterscotch pudding
1/2 cup oil
4 eggs
1/2 cup chocolate syrup
1/3 to 1/2 cup confectioners' sugar

Preheat oven to 350 degrees. Mix cake mix, dry pudding, 1 cup water, oil, and eggs in a large bowl at medium speed. Pour 2/3 of batter into well-greased and floured 10-inch Bundt pan. With remaining 1/3 batter, mix chocolate syrup and pour evenly over the first layer of batter. Bake for 1 hour. Cool 30 minutes then remove and sprinkle with powdered sugar. This is a very moist cake.

Serves 8 to 10.
Belle Fontenot

I Remember...

that "each cook has their own little secret ways... a certain family way. ... We all know our cooking is the best, we argue points of putting in there. [For instance,] I don't like bay leaves, and I tell others it doesn't help." Furthermore, Cajun women are easily insulted when someone interferes with the preparation of a special recipe, or if a guest does not eat a hearty serving of each entrée.

Olga Manuel

Gateau de Sirop (Cake Syrup)

1 cup sugar
2 cups dark cane syrup (preferably Steen's)
³/4 cup lard or oil
2 eggs
4 cups all-purpose flour
2 cups boiling water
2 teaspoons baking soda
2 teaspoons vanilla extract
pecans (optional)

Preheat oven to 350 degrees. Dissolve baking soda in the boiling water. Mix sugar, syrup, lard, and eggs. Beat well. Then add flour and boiling water with baking soda. Add vanilla extract. Bake for about 1 hour in a 9 by 13-inch greased and floured pan.

Makes 1 cake.
Pauline Langlinais

I Remember...

that even though my formal education ended in the seventh grade, I managed to keep all the books for the store my husband and I owned, run it alone after he took ill, care for a sick husband and my young children, and tend to the house and yard. "I'd cut the grass and would have to stop and go in to wait on customers." Furthermore, I enjoyed working with the people and had enough education to oversee the store. "When I went to school I went to learn." My close friend, Ella Mae Fontenot says, "[Carrine] did like me, she hustled and bustled all her life."

Carrine "Yen" Fontenot

Syrup Cake I

1 cup sugar
1 teaspoon baking soda
1 cup dark cane syrup (preferably Steen's)
$^1/_2$ cup cooking oil
2 eggs
2 cups all-purpose flour
1 cup boiling water
2 teaspoons vanilla extract

Preheat oven to 375 degrees. Blend sugar, baking soda, cane syrup, and oil. Beat in eggs one at a time. Blend in flour and boiling water. Add vanilla extract. Beat well. Bake in a greased and floured 9 by 13-inch pan for 25 to 35 minutes or until cake springs back.

Makes 1 cake.
Lola Belle Foret

I Remember...

when I would make pralines, sometimes neighbors would play a joke and take them off the window seal. Other common pranks were putting syrup in good shoes left out on the porch or stopping up the chimney. These tricks were played and reciprocated in good fun.

Viola Rider

Syrup Cake II

$2^{1}/_{2}$ *cups sifted all-purpose flour*
$^{1}/_{2}$ *teaspoon baking soda*
$1^{1}/_{2}$ *teaspoons baking powder*
$^{1}/_{2}$ *teaspoon salt*
1 teaspoon ground ginger
1 teaspoon ground cloves
1 teaspoon ground cinnamon
$^{1}/_{2}$ *cup shortening*
$^{1}/_{2}$ *cup sugar*
2 eggs, beaten
$^{1}/_{4}$ *cup dark cane syrup (preferably Steen's)*
1 teaspoon unsweetened cocoa powder (optional)
1 cup chopped pecans or nuts (optional)

Preheat oven to 350 degrees. Sift flour, baking soda, baking powder, salt, ginger, cloves, and cinnamon into a bowl and set aside until later.

In another bowl, cream the shortening and sugar until fluffy. Add eggs. Then add the previously sifted dry ingredients alternately with the syrup and 1 cup water. (If you would like it darker put cocoa in the water and pour in dough.) Beat enough to mix thoroughly. Add chopped pecans or nuts if desired. Pour into a well greased $12^{1}/_{2}$ by $7^{1}/_{2}$ by 2-inch pan and bake for 40 to 45 minutes.

Makes 1 cake.
Claire Bonin

I Remember...

"this recipe was given to me by my mother about 75 years ago. I am now 89 years old and still make it. My family loves it.... After supper my brother, Priest Monsignor Daniel Bernard, as a boy would help me clean the kitchen after we served our parents the meal so we could play checker, cards, or domino, or play the piano and sing."

Claire Bonin

Honey Cake

1 cup sugar
1/2 cup honey
3/4 cup oil
2/3 cup milk
1 1/2 cups all-purpose flour
1 teaspoon vanilla extract
1 teaspoon baking powder
1 teaspoon baking soda

Preheat oven to 250 degrees. Blend sugar, honey, oil, and milk. Add flour, vanilla, baking powder, and baking soda. Mix well. Pour into a 9 by 13-inch greased pan. Bake for about 1 hour.

Serves 8 generously.
Alzena Miller

I Remember...

that "at first Momma didn't want me to sew on her machine. She was afraid that I would break it. So one day she went to Grandpa's to see about him. He was kind of sick. And I had a piece of material she had bought for me. It was a blue check. Pretty. So I took it out. My sister was so rough on me. She said 'What you gonna do with that?' I said, 'I'm going to make me a jumper.' She said 'You know. Momma don't want you to fool with her machine.' I said, 'Mamma's not here.' And so I cut my jumper out and sewed it and by the time she come back I was hemming it by hand."

Gladys Hebert

Cookies and Candies

Old-Fashioned Tea Cake

2 sticks butter
2 cups sugar
4 eggs
2 teaspoons baking powder
$1/2$ teaspoon soda
$1/2$ teaspoon salt
7 cups all-purpose flour
$1/4$ cup milk
1 teaspoon vanilla extract

Preheat oven to 375 degrees. Cream butter and sugar well. Add eggs one at a time, beating well. Then add sifted baking powder, baking soda, salt, and flour. With first cup of flour, add milk and vanilla extract with enough of the remaining flour to get the proper consistency for rolling dough. Cut in shapes. Bake on a greased cookie sheet until light tan. Store in tight container.

Makes about 90 cookies.
Mazel Lassiegne

I Remember...

"My mom used to put the cookies in a pillowcase and tie it tight. They would stay fresh a long time. A long time ago people didn't have cookie jars to save the cookies."

Mazel Lassiegne

Old-Fashioned Sugar Cookies

¹/₂ cup shortening
1 cup sugar
2 eggs
3 cups all-purpose flour
¹/₄ teaspoon salt
3 teaspoons baking powder
¹/₂ cup milk
1 teaspoon vanilla extract

Preheat oven to 250 degrees. Cream shortening and sugar. Add eggs and mix well. Add flour, salt, baking powder, milk, and vanilla. Knead into a semi-soft dough. Use cookie cutters or the open end of a coffee cup to cut out cookies. Place on a flat cookie sheet and bake for about 1 hour or until done.

Makes 2¹/₂ to 3 dozen.
Alzena Miller

I Remember...

when we used to have fresh farm eggs and homemade butter. "Yes, oh yes, Momma would pick the eggs, and when we had what we needed, you see, and then she'd milk six and seven cows every day, and she'd skim the milk. She'd skim the cream, and so we had homemade butter."

Gladys Hebert

Sugar Cookies

1 cup sugar
¹/₂ cup butter
1 egg
¹/₄ cup milk
2 cups all-purpose flour
2 teaspoons baking powder
1 teaspoon vanilla extract

Preheat oven to 350 degrees. Mix the sugar and
butter until well beaten. Add egg. Beat well. Add
milk, alternating flour and milk, plus baking powder and vanilla extract. Mix well. It should be firm
enough to roll. Roll dough on floured board or
sheet so it doesn't stick. Roll the dough out thinly
and cut with a cookie cutter. Place on a greased
cookie sheet. Bake for approximately 20 minutes. I
always check the oven to be sure they do not overcook.

Makes 16 cookies.
Rose Fontenot

I Remember...

"This recipe was given to
me in 1938, the year I got
married, by Rose Mae
Landreneau, Claude
Landreneau's wife, and it
was copied on sheet of
paper for years. When I
was able to buy me a
cookbook, I transferred
them into it in the 1950s.
Cookies and pies come out
a golden brown when
cooked. People used butter
in the 1930s as cows were
milked, cream picked up
over the milk bowls and
shake to make butter. No
money to buy."

Rose Fontenot

Fig Cookies I

1 stick butter
2 eggs
1$^1/_2$ cups sugar
3 cups all-purpose flour
$^1/_2$ teaspoon baking soda
$^1/_2$ teaspoon ground cinnamon
1 cup fig preserves

Preheat oven to 375 degrees. Mix together butter, eggs, and sugar. In a separate bowl, mix together flour, baking soda, and cinnamon. Then add all together. Add fig preserves, mashed fine by hand. Mix well. Then drop by teaspoon on greased and floured cookie sheet. Bake for 15 minutes or until top is brown. (Bakes fast.)

Makes 4 to 6 dozen, depending on the size cookies you make.
Claire Bonin

I Remember...

when I was growing up, my mother suffered from diabetes and had full-time help from "a colored woman" woman named Emily King, who lived in the house with the family. "She was a treasure." My siblings and I cried when Emily got married. Some of us persisted in our refusal to accept her absence; we would go and stay at Emily's new house until bedtime, when her husband would bring us home. I remember how we hated Emily's husband because he took her from us.

Odile Hollier

Fig Cookies II

2 cups sugar
¹/₂ cup butter
1 cup mashed figs
1 cup chopped pecans
1 teaspoon baking soda
3 cups all-purpose flour
3 eggs

Preheat oven to 375 degrees. Mix sugar, butter, and figs. Add pecans, baking soda, flour, and eggs. Mix well and spoon on cookie sheet. (Do not grease.) Bake for 15 to 20 minutes.

Makes 5 to 6 dozen, depending on the size cookies you make.
Evon Melancon

Ma Mère Cookies

1 cup butter
2 cups sugar
2 eggs
$^1/_2$ cup milk
6 cups all-purpose flour
1 tablespoon baking soda
1 teaspoon salt

Butter and Cream Frosting:
1 pound confectioners' sugar
$^1/_2$ cup oleo (margarine)
3 tablespoons milk
$1^1/_2$ teaspoons vanilla extract
$^1/_2$ cup shortening

Preheat oven to 350 degrees. Mix butter and sugar. Add eggs and milk. Mix in flour 2 cups at a time. Add baking soda and salt. Roll out dough and cut out cookies with cookie cutters. Bake for 7 to 10 minutes.

Make the frosting: Beat $^1/_2$ pound of powdered sugar with oleo. Gradually add milk. Add vanilla extract, shortening, and the remaining powdered sugar, stirring until frosting is mixed. Frost cookies when they are cool.

Makes 3 to 4 dozen.
Verna Amedee

I Remember...

when we were young, "chores, oh yes, we had chores. Chores, if we had chores. Yes indeed! Well, we'd help Momma here around the house, you know. And we had cows and we had chickens and we had a garden so we had to we had to help with that, you know. Then when we got old enough, you know, she'd let us iron the clothes and clean house, wash the dishes. We didn't have dishwashers in those days."

Jeanne Arceneaux

Sour Cream Cookies

2 cups all-purpose flour
1 teaspoon ground nutmeg
$^1/_2$ teaspoon baking soda
1 teaspoon baking powder
$^1/_2$ cup shortening (preferably Crisco)
1 cup brown sugar
1 egg
$^1/_2$ teaspoon salt
$^1/_2$ cup sour cream
$^1/_2$ cup any chopped nut meat

Preheat oven to 375 degrees. Sift flour, nutmeg, baking soda, and baking powder together. In another bowl, cream shortening, sugar, egg, and salt. Beat well. Blend both mixtures together with sour cream. Then add nuts. Bake cookies on a greased cookie sheet for 10 to 15 minutes.

Makes 2$^1/_2$ dozen cookies.
Thelma Coles

I Remember...

that "my grandmother, my mother's mother, was an excellent cook on a wood stove. How did she do that, I don't know. But she made like dove jambalayas, you know. She used to make the best boiled dinner that I have ever eaten. She used to take like cabbage and potatoes and carrots and corn... and I think they used to put a little piece of salt meat in there when they boiled it all together."

Eva Mae Poirrier

Seven Layers Cookies

$^1/_2$ stick butter
1 cup graham cracker crumbs
1 small can (3.5 ounces) flaked coconut
1 pack (6 ounces) chocolate morsels
1 pack (6 ounces) butterscotch chips
1 can (14 ounces) condensed milk
1 cup chopped pecans

Preheat oven to 325 degrees. Melt butter in a 9 by 12-inch baking pan. Add ingredients by layers, in order listed. Make a layer of graham cracker crumbs. Add a layer of coconut flakes. Sprinkle a layer of chocolate chips and then one of butterscotch chips. Pour condensed milk over the chips. Sprinkle pecans over the entire dish. Bake for about 30 minutes. Let cool, then cut into squares.

Makes about 30 pieces.
Belle Fontenot

I Remember...

that sometimes one woman was more adept at a task than another, so they would trade services in order to complete the tasks more efficiently. For instance, my aunt sewed for my mom and in return, my mother cleaned my aunt's house. When the sewing and cleaning were complete my aunt and mother collaborated on quilts, while I watched and learned. "They had to let me have a needle. ... Miss nosy [speaking of myself] had to have her own needle. ... I was always the type that if somebody else can do it, I can too and [quilting's] fun."

Joyce Brasseux

Refrigerator Nut Cookies

¹/₂ cup butter
1 cup brown sugar
3 eggs, beaten
1 teaspoon vanilla extract
2 cups sifted all-purpose flour
2 teaspoons baking powder
¹/₂ teaspoon salt
1 cup finely chopped nuts

Preheat oven to 350 degrees. Cream butter and brown sugar. Add eggs and vanilla extract. Sift flour, baking powder, and salt together; add nuts and combine with first mixture. Stir well. Chill and form into rolls. When it becomes solid, cut across in thin slices, about ¹/₄ inch. Bake for 10 to 15 minutes. Allow to become crisp on the cookie sheet. Very old recipe.

Makes 48 cookies.
Mazel Lassiengne

I Remember...

"We'd play, I remember with my neighbor and my cousins we'd play hide and seek in the corn, my daddy used to raise corn and that was fun for us, we'd wait late in the evening when it wasn't hot."

Winnie Fernandez

that my mother cared for her husband, bore 12 children, gardened, raised chickens, sewed, cooked, cleaned, and quilted. I have a deep appreciation and love for my mother; "I still miss her. ... I don't know how she did it. She had grandchildren older than her last kid. ... She sewed as long as her eyes let her [she was a diabetic]. ... She did housework and she taught us how to work." My mother organized quilting bees in the attic of the "old house." I used to wait on them with coffee and cookies and continued quilting after I married.

Odile Hollier

Cookies

$^1/_4$ pound butter, melted
1 cup sugar
3 eggs, slightly beaten
$^1/_2$ teaspoon nutmeg
$^1/_2$ teaspoon ground cinnamon
2 teaspoons vanilla extract
6 to 7 cups sifted all-purpose flour
6 to 7 teaspoons baking powder

Icing:
2 egg whites, unbeaten
$1^1/_2$ cups sugar
dash of salt
$1^1/_2$ teaspoons light corn syrup
$1^1/_2$ teaspoons vanilla or almond extract

Beat butter and sugar together until creamy. Add eggs, nutmeg, cinnamon, and vanilla. Mix well. Then sift the flour and baking powder into the batter, 1 teaspoon to 1 cup at a time. Dough should be a little soft but not sticky.

Preheat oven to 400 degrees. Grease cookie sheet. Roll dough to about $^1/_4$-inch thickness on a floured board and cut. Bake until cookies turn golden brown, about 10 minutes.

Make the icing: Combine egg whites, sugar, salt, 5 tablespoons water, and corn syrup in top of double boiler mixing thoroughly. Place over boiling water. Beat constantly until sugar is completely dissolved. Remove from boiling water and beat at high speed of electric mixer until icing stands up in peaks. Add vanilla or almond extract and mix. This icing

may be divided before adding the vanilla if you want to use different extracts and colorings. Use this as a topping for the cookies.

Makes 6 to 7 dozen depending on the size of the cookies.
Hilda Waguespack

Gumdrop "Orange Slice" Cookies

2 cups all-purpose flour
20 orange slice candy, chopped small
1 cup chopped pecans
4 eggs
2¹/₂ cups dark brown sugar
¹/₄ teaspoon salt

Preheat oven to 350 degrees. Take a little of the flour, and mix with candy and pecans so they won't stick together. Mix well your eggs, brown sugar, salt, and the remaining flour. Add this to orange slices and pecans. Mix well. Pour into 9 by 13-inch greased pan. Bake 40 to 45 minutes or until golden brown. Allow to cool a little then cut into bars.

Makes 18 to 24 pieces, depending on size.
Pauline Langlinais

I Remember...

that I grew up the daughter of a tenant farmer and spent a large portion of my adult life as the wife of a tenant farmer. The first house my husband and I lived in was rented from the landowner and furnished with iron beds, feather mattresses that my mother made using chicken feathers, and cowhide chairs and rockers, which my nephew, Joey Soileau from Grand Prairie, still makes.

Versie Meche

Graham Goodies

24 graham crackers
2 sticks oleo (margarine)
1 cup light brown sugar
1 cup chopped pecans

Preheat oven to 350 degrees. Break crackers in half to make 48 cookies. Place crackers on cookie sheet. In saucepan, bring oleo and brown sugar to a boil and boil for 2 minutes until it makes a syrup. Stir in pecans. With teaspoon, cover each cracker with syrup. Bake for 10 minutes. Remove from pan as soon as baked.

Makes 4 dozen.
Etheleen Meaux

I Remember...

that I worked as a nurse before I married and began having children; This was during the Depression and I was making $1 per day. I managed to buy a bed, living, and dining room set before my wedding. I still have the pieces in my home, and they are as good as new. "We had to work for what we got."

Odile Hollier

I Remember...

when my brother served in the Navy during World War II. People from around here sent cookies sealed in cans to the young men overseas.

Lessie Deshotel

Peanut Butter Squares

1 cup all-purpose flour
$^1/_2$ cup granulated sugar
$^1/_2$ cup firmly packed brown sugar
$^1/_2$ teaspoon baking soda
$^1/_4$ teaspoon salt
$^1/_2$ cup butter or margarine, softened
$^1/_2$ cup crunchy or smooth peanut butter
1 egg, lightly beaten
1 cup quick-cooking oats
1 package (12 ounces) semisweet chocolate morsels
$^1/_2$ cup powdered sugar
$^1/_4$ cup smooth peanut butter
3 to 5 tablespoons milk

Preheat oven to 350 degrees. Combine flour, granulated sugar, brown sugar, baking soda, salt, butter, $^1/_2$ cup peanut butter, egg, and oats in large mixing bowl. Mix well. Press dough into a lightly greased 9 by 13-inch pan. Bake for about 30 minutes or until golden brown. Remove from oven and sprinkle with chocolate morsels. Let stand until morsels melt then spread evenly.

Combine powdered sugar, smooth peanut butter, and enough milk to make a thin consistency. Beat well; drizzle over peanut butter squares. Cut into 2-inch squares.

Makes 24 squares.
Viola Rider

Divinity Fudge I

$^1\!/_2$ cup cold water
3 cups sugar
$^1\!/_2$ cup corn syrup
1 pinch salt
3 egg whites
$1^1\!/_2$ cups pecans

Combine water, sugar, corn syrup, and salt. Cook to a soft boil. Beat egg whites until stiff. Pour $^1\!/_2$ of syrup mixture over egg whites. Beat constantly. Pour the rest of syrup mixture until thick. Add pecans and mix well. Roll out on a greased pan or wax paper. Let cool and cut into squares.

Makes 2 to 3 dozen.
Verna Amedee

I Remember...

the most important thing I learned from my parents "would be the everything around the religion side ... and good manners, etiquette of all sorts, you know, coming up, I was saying that ... I said when meal time came, everybody, I mean the whole family had to be at the table, and the grace was said and everybody remained at the table excepting maybe one or two of my sisters who would get up, you know, and bring in the dishes, you know, but after that they sat down and nobody would leave the table ..., not like now, we had to stay there and grace after meals was said all together and then we could leave the table."

Hilda Waguespack

Divinity Fudge II

3 cups sugar
¹/2 cup light corn syrup
¹/8 teaspoon salt
2 egg whites
1 cup chopped pecans
¹/2 teaspoon vanilla extract

Cook sugar, syrup, ²/3 cup water, and salt over medium heat to 252 degrees or hard ball test in cold water. Beat egg whites at high speed for 3 minutes. Reduce speed to low and beat as you slowly pour syrup mixture into egg whites. Continue beating until glossy. Continue beating as you add pecans and vanilla until peaks are formed. Drop on waxed paper from a teaspoon. Let cool.

Makes about 2 dozen pieces.
Hilda Waguespack

Patience Fudge

3 cups sugar
1 can (12 ounces) evaporated milk
4 tablespoons butter
2 teaspoons vanilla extract
1 cup finely chopped pecans

In one pot, dissolve 1 cup of sugar over medium heat. In another pot, put 2 cups of sugar, milk, and butter and mix well. Cook over high heat until mixture begins to boil, stirring constantly. Then lower the heat but continue stirring. When the first cup of sugar is completely dissolved, add it to the mixture and continue cooking until a bit of the mixture forms a soft ball in cold water. Remove from heat. Add vanilla. Beat until mixture gets heavy and loses its gloss. Add pecans; mix well and pour into a buttered pan. Let cool. Cut into squares.

Makes about 2 dozen pieces.
Hilda Waguespack

I Remember...

that from the age of 10 I attended church with my aunt and uncle, with whom I lived. When my uncle did not bring us in the buggy, my aunt and I walked to church. We would wear our everyday shoes while walking and then change into our Sunday shoes before entering the church.

Marie "Ivy" Ortego

Chocolate Fudge

2 cups sugar
3 tablespoons unsweetened cocoa powder
3 tablespoons light corn syrup (preferably Karo)
1 tablespoon all-purpose flour
²/₃ cup milk
¹/₃ stick butter
1 teaspoon vanilla extract
1 cup chopped pecans

Make sure skillet is clean. Mix sugar, cocoa, corn syrup, flour, and milk. Cover and cook until sugar is boiling, stir often. Remove lid and continue cooking and stirring. Test readiness by spooning out a teaspoonful and drop in water. If it hardens, it is ready. Stop sink up, and fill with water. Put a large pot in sink and put the pot you were cooking with in the larger pot to cool. Keep stirring while adding butter, vanilla, and pecans. When it starts to cool, beat and pour into buttered square dish. Then allow to cool until it is hardened. Cut into squares.

Makes 1 pound.
Dorothy Bryant

I Remember...

my home economics teacher once advised us on "how to keep our man happy. (Now girls, you primp up and you fix up to get a man and if you want to keep him you've got to keep doing that.") She also warned "Don't ever both of you get mad at the same time. If you get mad and you see he's not going to give in walk out and vice versa."

Joyce Brasseux

Cocoa Fudge

3 cups sugar
$^3/_4$ cup unsweetened cocoa powder
$^1/_4$ teaspoon salt
2 cups evaporated milk
4 tablespoons light corn syrup
3 tablespoons butter
2 teaspoons vanilla extract
1 cup chopped pecans

Combine sugar, cocoa, and salt. Mix well. Add milk, corn syrup, and butter. Cook over low heat, stirring continuously until mixture begins to boil. Then continue boiling without stirring until a bit of the mixture forms a soft ball when dropped into cold water. Remove from heat. Add vanilla, and beat until mixture thickens and loses its gloss. Mix in pecans. Pour into a buttered pan. When cool, cut into squares.

Makes about 2 dozen pieces.
Hilda Waguespack

I Remember...

my First Communion well. Unfortunately I was suffering with measles on the important day, but tradition was not abandoned. I was not allowed to eat after midnight and recall a few of my friends even fainted during the service. My aunt was waiting for me with a large piece of cake, which I thoroughly enjoyed after the ceremony finished.

Marie "Ivy" Ortego

Old-Fashioned Praline

2 cups granulated sugar
¹/₂ cup brown sugar
³/₄ cup milk
1 stick oleo (margarine)
2 cups halved or chopped pecans
1 teaspoon vanilla extract (optional)

Combine white sugar, brown sugar, and milk. Cook over medium heat until sugar is dissolved and mixture begins to boil. This will take about 10 minutes. Add oleo and pecans and continue to cook until a spoonful of the mixture forms a small ball when dropped in cold water. Remove from heat. (At this point, you can add vanilla, if desired.) Beat until candy shows signs of thickening. Drop by spoonfuls on waxed paper, which has been buttered. Let cool.

Makes 2 dozen.
Mazel Lassiegne

I Remember...

"when we were first married all I could do was make coffee and boil water. I tried to cook cabbage thinking all I have to do is boil it. I wasn't successful. I threw it away. My neighbor told me her dog had died because it had eaten the cabbage. Ha! The dog was about ready to die. I was teased about and still do today. But later I really learned how to cook."

Elia Bodin

Creamy Pralines

2 cups sugar
¹/₂ cup light corn syrup
¹/₂ cup evaporated milk
¹/₂ teaspoon baking soda
¹/₄ cup margarine or butter
2 cups chopped pecans
1 teaspoon vanilla extract

Mix sugar, syrup, milk, baking soda, and margarine in a heavy saucepan. Cook until a medium hard ball forms in cool tap water (or 238 degrees). Remove from heat. Add pecans and vanilla. Stir until mixture loses gloss and begins to thicken. Drop by tablespoons on waxed paper. Let cool.

Makes 2 dozen.
Vinice Sensat

I Remember...

"We made a lot of pralines in my young days. Of peanuts and pecans, whichever we had. We loved to make candy such as pralines, divinity, and fudge."

Vinice Sensat

My Favorite Pecan Praline

1 stick margarine
2 cups granulated sugar
1 cup brown sugar
1 teaspoon vanilla extract
1 small can (12 ounces) evaporated milk
2^1/$_2$ tablespoons light corn syrup (preferably Karo)
1 pinch salt
3 cups halved or chopped pecans
1 bag (10.5 ounces) miniature marshmallows

Mix together margarine, white sugar, brown sugar, vanilla extract, evaporated milk, corn syrup, salt, and pecans. Cook at medium heat all together until it forms a ball when a small amount is dropped in cold water. Beat a while. Then add 2 handfuls small marshmallows. Beat until it is mixed. Drop by spoonful on wax paper. Let cool.

Makes 3 to 4 dozen.
Joyce Brasseux

I Remember...

going to school and all the other children had a piece of candy so I would charge a piece at the Corner Store across the street and the next time my father went to the store, he had to pay for it. I also remember when I sold the family eggs to the grocer, I would use a few pennies to buy candy and my parents never found out. I definitely had a sweet tooth.

Carrine "Yen" Fontenot

Pecan Pralines

1 cup brown sugar
1 cup granulated sugar
¹/2 cup evaporated milk
2 tablespoons oleo (margarine)
1 cup chopped pecans
1 teaspoon vanilla extract

Combine sugars and milk. Cook until sugars are dissolved and mixture begins to boil, about 10 minutes. Add oleo and pecans and continue to cook until mixture forms a small ball when dropped in cold water. Remove from heat and add vanilla extract. Beat until candy shows signs of thickening. Drop by spoonfuls on waxed paper, which has been buttered. Let cool.

Makes 1 to 2 dozen.
Viola Rider

I Remember...

that "[my mother] loved to cook, and she liked gardening. She loved gardening. That's how I learned to cook real young. She'd put the stuff on the stove and say 'You take care of it now. I'm going outside' That's how I learned to cook real young."

Rose Thibodeaux

Sesame Seed Praline

4 cups sesame seeds
4 cups sugar
1 cup milk
³/₄ stick butter or margarine
pinch of salt
1 large tablespoon light corn syrup

Parch sesame seeds in heavy, dry skillet on medium heat, stirring constantly until brown. Set aside to cool. Combine sugar, milk, butter or margarine, salt, and syrup in heavy saucepan and cook to a soft ball stage (drop a small amount in cold water). Stir in parched seed and continue to stir until it holds shape. Pour on a well-greased cake pan. When cold, break into pieces.

Makes 3 to 4 dozen.
Lola Belle Foret

I Remember...

that like many Cajun women, I did not use recipes. I just cooked "from my head." Some of my favorite meals include etouffée, jambalaya, chicken dishes, seafood, and barbecue. I also enjoy making cakes and sweet dough pies filled with either lemon or blackberries. My children have enjoyed many Sunday dinners and holiday meals cooked in my kitchen. We always sat around the dinner table; and on special occasions, the meal was eaten in shifts with the adults eating first.

Mildred LeJeune

Pralines I

3 cups sugar
¹/₄ cup butter
1 cup Carnation evaporated milk
¹/₂ teaspoon vanilla extract
3 cups coarsely ground pecans

Mix sugar, butter, and cream and cook on medium heat until it forms a soft ball when you drop a spoonful in cold water. Take off fire and beat counting to 120. Then put in vanilla and pecans and blend well together quickly. Then drop by spoonfuls on wax paper. Hint: The wax paper should be placed on top of a layer of newspapers. Let them cool before serving or save in a container for later.

Makes 3 dozen.
Eva Mae Poirrier

I Remember...

"I did make pralines when I was quite young and I still make a lot of that today to give people as gifts. Of course when I was young they were made with home made butter that my mother made and the cup of cream used in the pralines was skimmed from big bowls of cows' milk after cream had come to top of bowl. We had a lot of cows that my oldest sister milked. I never could milk a cow. I never could learn as I do not think I had enough strength in my small hands. I am putting here the recipe for the pralines I make today. ... We have a lot of pecan trees on our place and I also make a pecan-date loaf cake that people like."

Eva Mae Poirrier

Pralines II

1 cup heavy cream
1 pound brown sugar
2 tablespoons margarine
2 cups halved or chopped pecans

Mix cream and brown sugar. Microwave high for 13 minutes. Add margarine and pecans. Mix well. Beat until firm. Place a sheet of aluminum on a flat baking pan. Drop teaspoons at a time about 1 inch apart. Let cool.

Makes 2 to 3 dozen.
Verna Amedee

I Remember...

when I was 17 and in the seventh grade, I decided to quit school. "[My mother] was willing because she could use me at the house instead of sending me to school and failing." I did not start school until I was nine years old, because we lived too far away; and I failed the fourth grade, because I had missed a lot of school during the harvest. After quitting school, I began to forget what I had learned so I decided to start reading the newspaper and it helped me to remember.

Blanche Quebedeaux

Pralines III

1 cup evaporated milk
2½ cups sugar
2 tablespoons butter
1 teaspoon salt
2 tablespoons light corn syrup (preferably Karo)
1 teaspoon vanilla extract
2 to 3 cups halved or chopped pecans

Bring milk and 2 cups sugar to a boil. Then reduce
heat. Meanwhile in another heavy saucepan, on
medium heat, caramelize ½ cup sugar to a deep
golden brown. Then add this to the milk and sugar
mixture (it will be lumpy but quickly dissolves).
Continue cooking on medium and stir constantly
until it dissolves and comes to a boil. Add butter,
salt and corn syrup. Cook until it reaches a soft ball
stage (when dropped in cold water). Stir in vanilla
and add pecans. Remove from heat and let set a
few minutes. Then beat until it begins to thicken
and starts to lose its gloss. Quickly drop by spoonfuls onto waxed paper or buttered cookie sheets.
Let cool.

Makes about 2 dozen.
Velma Reaux

I Remember...

when my oldest brother
worked in the fields and
saved up so we could get
electricity and a radio. We
loved it. "We thought that
was fabulous. Of course
today, if those old people
could come back today
and see that box in our
house, the TV, I think they
would get afraid, you
know."

Eva Mae Poirrier

Caramel-Pecan Candy

6 small bars (9.3 ounces total) milk chocolate or
   dark chocolate
1 bag (14 ounces) caramels
1 tablespoon butter
2 cups finely chopped pecans

Put chocolate in top of double boiler to melt. Put
caramel, butter, and 1 tablespoon water in top of
second double boiler to melt. When caramels are
completely dissolved, add pecans and mix well.
Remove from heat and let cool just enough to han-
dle. Using a small spoon, pick up enough of the
caramel mixture to form a small, flattened ball.
Then place it on a large piece of wax paper to hard-
en. Continue making small pieces with the rest of
mixture. When balls have hardened dip them in the
melted chocolate and put on wax paper to dry and
harden.

Makes 4 to 5 dozen.
Hilda Waguespack

I Remember...

that for an earache we
would put tobacco juice or
the juice of boiled cabbage
in the infected ear, and
that was our medicine.

Marie "Ivy" Ortego

Pecan Macaroons

2 egg whites
$1/2$ teaspoon cream of tartar
2 cups dark brown sugar
1 teaspoon vanilla extract
$3^1/2$ cups finely chopped pecans

Preheat oven to 350 degrees. Beat egg whites until stiff, then slowly add cream of tartar. Slowly add brown sugar. Add vanilla. Lastly, stir in pecans. When well mixed, drop spoonfuls on greased cookie sheet. Bake in oven for about 15 minutes.

Makes approximately 3 dozen.
Elma Oubre

I Remember...

that my mother used to make homemade lye soap by combining lye, hog lard, and the bones of salt pork in a large black pot, which she stirred with a large wooden paddle until the mixture thickened. Then my mother would spread the soap out on a flat surface, let it cool and harden, and then cut into bars. My mother made two batches a year for the family. I helped wash clothes with a scrub board, milk cows, harvest vegetables, plow the fields, and gather eggs. In addition to collecting the eggs, I was responsible for bringing them to trade for groceries at the local store. I remember always having one egg to buy some candy.

Ella Mae Fontenot

I Remember...

On the day of my wedding my husband and I put in a full day's work before rushing off to dress and marry. My husband was a mailman and worked until 1:30 p.m., and we were married at 4:00 p.m. I worked in the operating room as a nurse and left the hospital at 2:30 p.m., walked two blocks to my sister's house, dressed, and then went to church to meet my soon-to-be husband.

Odile Hollier

Pecan Crisp or Russian Balls

1 cup butter or oleo (margarine)
$1/2$ cup sugar
1 teaspoon vanilla extract
2 cups all-purpose flour
1 cup chopped pecans
powdered sugar, as desired

Preheat oven to 350 degrees. Cream butter and sugar. Add vanilla extract. Work in flour and nuts. Chill if desired then roll into balls, about 1 inch. Bake for 20 to 30 minutes or until slightly browned. Cool slightly and roll in powdered sugar. Store in tightly covered container.

Makes about 5 dozen.
Etheleen Meaux

Rice Krispies Treat

4 cups crisp rice cereal
1 jar (7 ounces) marshmallow cream (preferably
  Kraft)

Spray a 9 by 13-inch pan with coating (oil) spray. In
a large mixing bowl, mix cereal and warm marshmallow cream together. Make sure cereal is all
coated. Press mixture in the pan. Refrigerate. Cut
as desired.

Serves 8.
Verna Amedee

I Remember...

for my First Communion I
had a white dress and a
"veil and a crown. ... Now
they dress any kind of way.
You don't know who's
making their First
Communion. And, you
know, the priests asked
us questions, and he'd
ask, to make our First
Communion, he asked how
old Jesus Christ was when
he was dead, when he
died. I'm the only one that
answered. You know how
old he was? Thirty-three
years old, 33."

Henriette Richard

Old-Fashioned Peanut Brittle

1 tablespoon butter or margarine
1¼ cups salted peanuts
¼ teaspoon salt (optional)
2½ cups granulated sugar (preferably Domino)

Melt butter or margarine in small saucepan over very low heat. Add peanuts and salt. Allow to warm. Place sugar in large thick skillet over medium heat. Stir continuously until sugar caramelizes into golden brown syrup. Stir peanuts into syrup quickly. Pour onto large buttered surface at once. With big spoon, stretch and pull candy into thin sheet. Allow to cool. Break into pieces.

Makes about 1½ pounds.
Dorothy Bryant

I Remember...

when my husband asked my parents for permission to marry me. My mother counseled, "Make the best of it. Life's not easy and you have to work at it." My father gave me fair warning when he said, "It's for life and you're not coming back unless he is beating you." And he has never hit me yet so I cannot go home. "So many times I wanted him to [*laughs*]," so I could go visit for a while.

Joyce Brasseux

Peanut Soda Candy (Brittle)

2 cups raw peanuts
2 cups sugar
1/2 cup light corn syrup (preferably Karo)
1/2 cup hot water
1 tablespoon baking soda

Combine peanuts, sugar, corn syrup, and water in large (at least 4-quart) saucepan. Cook over high flame until peanuts begin to parch. (They will pop and turn light brown colored.) It takes 15 minutes. Stirring well. Add baking soda and pour into a large greased pan (cookie sheet). Let cool then break into pieces and store in jars.

Makes about 1 gallon.
Etheleen Meaux

I Remember...

"Do not double this recipe. [I remember when] a friend tried to double the recipe. Everything was okay until he added the baking soda. It bubbled all over the pan, stove, and floor. What a mess."

Etheleen Meaux

Popcorn Balls

$^1/_2$ cup popcorn
2 to 3 tablespoons oil, enough to grease pot bottom
2 cups cane syrup

Put corn and oil in a 4-quart pot, cover, then heat. After popcorn finishes popping, remove extra kernels. Hint: Do not put corn after the oil is hot. While the oil is heating, the corn cooks, and it leaves no leftover kernels.

In a separate pot cook cane syrup until it spins a fine thread when you lift a spoonful of the syrup. It's ready to pour on about 2 gallons of popped popcorn. Mix well. When cool enough, wet your hands and make balls.

Makes about 2 gallons.
Gladys Hebert

I Remember...

when I was in grade school we played under the schoolhouse. In order to get to school I either walked or sometimes my teacher picked me up, and I was able to ride in a horse and buggy. On one of my many walks to school I saw something white in the bushes and thought it was dogs. Scared, I refused to proceed until someone passed by and showed me that the white image was merely ducks on the levee.

Lessie Deshotel

Caramel Popcorn

2 or 3 batches popcorn
2 cups raw peanuts
2 cups sugar
$1/2$ cup light corn syrup (preferably Karo)
$1/2$ cup hot water
1 tablespoon baking soda

Pop 2 or 3 batches of popcorn in an air popper and set aside. Combine peanuts, sugar, corn syrup, and hot water in large (at least 4-quart) saucepan. Cook over high flame until peanuts begin to parch. (They will pop and turn light brown colored.) It takes 15 minutes. Stirring well, add baking soda, then pour over popcorn in a large dishpan and stir. Let cool. Do not double recipe, or mixture will boil over. Makes good crackerjacks.

Makes about 2 gallons.
Etheleen Meaux

I Remember...

during the early part of my marriage my husband farmed and I helped out whenever possible. I worked in the fields until my first child was born and again when my children were old enough, we would pick cotton together to buy clothes for the school year. I remember getting up at 4:30 a.m. to start picking cotton and that the school year was delayed until the harvest was collected.

Viola Rider

Resource Guide

Assorted Products

Cajun Creole: Makes the world a little spicier
Since 1978. Only the Best Coffee, Spices, and Those Incredible Cajun Creole Hot Nuts
   Cajun Creole Products, Inc.
   5610 Daspit Road
   New Iberia, LA 70563
   www.cajuncreole.com
   Phone: 1-800-946-8688

Cajun Grocer.com: One-stop shopping!
   Worldwide Delivery
   www.cajungrocer.com
   U.S. Phone: 1-888-CRAWFISH

CAJUNTRADING.COM: The Flavor of South Louisiana Delivered to Your Door!
   E-mail: sales@cajuntrading.com

New Orleans Showcase, Inc.: The Best of New Orleans Shipped Directly to You!
Delicious Cajun Food, Wonderful Cookbooks, Unique Gift Sets, Mardi Gras King
Cakes and more.
   www.NewOrleansShowcase.com

Rouses: Louisiana's Best Cajun Specialty Meats, Gourmet King Cakes, and more
   www.rouses.com
   Phone: 1-800-688-5998

Sauces, Seasonings, and Mixes

Bruce's Sweet Potato Pancake Mix
www.brucefoods.com

CaJohns Fiery Foods: Flavor with Fire
   www.cajohns.com
   Phone: 1-888-703-FIRE

Crazy Charley Sauces
Crazy Cajun Enterprises, Inc.
Phone: 1-877-TO-CAJUN (862-2586)
E-mail: cajun@jps.net

Grant Fruit Processing:
Juices for Sauces, Jellies & Syrups, Jams, and Jellies
8484 Hwy. 165
Pollock, LA 71467
www.grantfruit.com
Phone: 1-866-765-2230

J & S Foods: Hot Sauce, Spices, Gumbo, Jambalaya, & Etouffée Mixes
www.jandsfoods.com
Phone: 1-800-97LAHOT (1-800-975-2468), Fax: 504-821-8874

Jack Miller's: The Bar-B-Que Sauce with a Cajun Accent
www.jackmillers.com
Phone: 1-800-646-1541   Fax: 318-363-4784

Private Label Products: Hot Sauces, Seasonings, and Jellies
P.O. Box 74514
Metairie, LA 70033, USA
www.hotsaucegifts.com
Phone: 1-800-429-4624

REX: Crab Boil, Fish Fry, Spices, Seasonings, and Sauces
P.O. Box 29323
New Orleans, LA 70129
www.rexfoods.com
Phone: 1-800-344-8314

Slidell Spice O' Life: Spice Up Your Food With Something New & Exciting
35096 Hwy 433
Slidell, LA 70460
www.spice-o-life.com
Phone: 1-888-533-1999

Tabasco: Hot Sauces
www.TABASCO.com
1-800-634-9599

Zatarain's
82 First Street
P.O. Box 347
Gretna, Louisiana 70053
www.zatarain.com
Phone: 504-367-2950

Seafood and Fish

America's Mail-Order Cajun Connection: Seafood's Our Specialty, plus Sausage, Jambalaya, Gumbo, and more!
www.nuawlins.com
Phone: 1-800-NU-AWLINS

Live Crawfish: Your complete provider of live, select, Louisiana crawfish
www.livecrawfish.com
Phone: 1-866-LA-CFOOD

Louisiana Fish Fry Products: Bring the Taste of Louisiana Home!
www.louisianafishfry.com
Phone: 1-800-356-2905   Fax: 225-356-8867

Vincent Piazza Jr. & Sons Seafood: A trusted name in the seafood business for over 100 years. Gourmet Seafood to your Door!
www.piazzaseafood.com
Phone: 1-866-3-shrimp

Meats

The Corner Store
"The Best Specialty Meat Market Around." You can always find fresh hot *boudin*, cracklings, sausage, and any cut of meat. They'll cut and season it for you ahead of time; just call before you come to pick it up.

5112 Vidrine Road
Ville Platte, LA 70586
Phone: 337-363-4298

Rice

Cajun Country: Falcon Rice Mill, Inc.
Crowley, LA
www.falconrice.com
Phone: 1-800-738-7423

Mahatma and Water Maid: From the heart of Louisiana comes the best-selling rice in America
www. mahatmarice.com

Cakes and Pies

Gambino's The Real Bakery: The King of King Cakes
Phone: 1-800-GAMBINO, 1-800-426-2466

Lea's Lunchroom: Pie Capital of Louisiana
Highway 71
P.O. Box 309
Lecompte, LA 71346
Phone: 318-776-5178   Fax: 318-776-5715
E-mail: leaspies@aol.com

Maurice's King Cakes
www.mardigraskingcakes.net
www.mauricefrenchpastries.com
Phone: 1-888-285-8261, Fax: 504-885-1527

Fruits and Nuts

Fresh Louisiana Peach's
Mitcham's Orchards
    1926 Mitcham Orchard Road
    Ruston, LA 71270
    Phone: 318-255-3409

Natchitoches Pecans, Inc.
    At Little Eva Plantation
    439 Little Eva Road
    Cloutierville, LA 71416
    Phone: 1-800-572-5925

Sources for Louisiana Citrus
To find a grower who ships, contact:
Plaquemine Parish Economic Development District
    P.O. Box 937
    Belle Chasse, LA 70037-0937
    Phone: 504-394-0018

Pots and Utensils

Baldwin-Taylor Hardware: It's Time for a Louisiana Crawfish Boil!
For all your outdoor Cajun cooking needs, including aluminum boiling pots,
burners, replacement baskets, Dutch ovens, cast iron cookware, jambalaya pots,
turkey fryers, and stainless steel pots.
    4301 Jefferson Hwy
    New Orleans, LA 70121
    www.cajunliving.com
    Phone: 1-800-833-8704, 504-833-9700

Real Cajun Cookin' Spoons
    P.O. Box 73051
    Baton Rouge, LA 70874
    Phone: 1-800-349-6278

Smoke Chef™ by Southern Pride Bar-B-Q systems, Inc.
3240 Hwy 152
Homer, LA 71040
Phone: 318-353-2210   Fax: 318-353-6313

Index

D

E

FROM HIPPOCRENE'S
CAJUN LIBRARY:

CAJUN FRENCH-ENGLISH/ENGLISH-CAJUN FRENCH DICTIONARY & PHRASEBOOK

Clint Bruce and Jennifer Gipson

At the heart of Cajun culture is a fascinating dialect of French that has survived the forces of Americanization and is still spoken by over 250,000 residents of Louisiana.

With a historical overview and an introduction to the language, this book answers many common questions about Cajun French. The preface by David Cheramie, executive director of the Council for the Development of French in Louisiana (CODOFIL), offers the viewpoint of an influential leader in the movement to preserve Louisiana's unique linguistic heritage.

- Pronunciation guide
- Basic grammar
- Frequently Asked Questions about Cajun French
- 3,800 dictionary entries
- Essential phrases

Clint Bruce and Jennifer Gipson, both *summa cum laude* graduates of Centenary College of Louisiana, are active contributors to the state's French Renaissance. Bruce received his bachelor's degrees in French and Latin and accepted a Fulbright scholarship to research Acadian literature in New Brunswick, Canada. Gipson completed degrees in French and music and received CODOFIL's Domengeaux scholarship to study translation at the Université Catholique de Paris.

3,000 ENTRIES • 160 PAGES • 3 3/4 x 7 1/2 • 0-7818-0915-0 • $11.95PB • (93)

FROM HIPPOCRENE'S
FRENCH LIBRARY:

HIPPOCRENE CHILDREN'S ILLUSTRATED FRENCH DICTIONARY

"Here comes a completely new English-French Dictionary for small children, ages 5-10. With 500 words illustrated in beautiful colors and with nice pictures, this dictionary covers all aspects of everyday life: animals, flowers, games ..."

—*Journal Français*

- for ages 5 and up
- 500 entries with color pictures
- commonsense pronunciation for each French word
- French-English index

500 ENTRIES • 94 PAGES • 8 1/2 x 11 • 0-7818-0847-2 • $11.95PB • (663)

FRENCH-ENGLISH DICTIONARY OF GASTRONOMIC TERMS
Bernard Luce
20,000 ENTRIES • 500 PAGES • 5 1/2 x 8 1/2 • 0-7818-0555-4 • $24.95PB • (655)

TREASURY OF FRENCH LOVE POEMS, QUOTATIONS AND PROVERBS
Bilingual
Edited and translated by Richard A. Branyon
128 PAGES • 5 x 7 • 0-7818-0307-1 • $11.95HC • (344)
AUDIOBOOK: 0-7818-0359-4 • $12.95 • (580)

TREASURY OF CLASSIC FRENCH LOVE SHORT STORIES
Bilingual
Edited by Lisa Neal
159 PAGES • 5 x 7 • 0-7818-0511-2 • W • $11.95HC • (621)

FRENCH-ENGLISH / ENGLISH-FRENCH
DICTIONARY & PHRASEBOOK
5,500 ENTRIES • 233 PAGES • 3 3/4 x 7 1/2 • 0-7818-0856-1 • $11.95PB • (128)

BEGINNER'S FRENCH
Marie-Rose Carré
465 PAGES • 5 1/2 x 8 1/2 • 0-7818-0863-4 • $14.95PB • (264)

OTHER **HIPPOCRENE COOKBOOKS**
FROM THE AMERICAS

A TASTE OF HAITI

Mirta Yurnet-Thomas & The Thomas Family

With African, French, Arabic and Amerindian influences, the food and culture of Haiti are fascinating subjects to explore. From the days of slavery to present times, traditional Haitian cuisine has relied upon staples like root vegetables, pork, fish, and flavor enhancers like *Pikliz* (picklese, or hot pepper vinegar) and *Zepis* (ground spices). This cookbook presents more than 100 traditional Haitian recipes, which are complemented by information on Haiti's history, holidays and celebrations, necessary food staples, and cooking methods. Recipe titles are presented in English, Creole, and French.

180 PAGES • 5 1/2 x 8 1/2 • 0-7818-0927-4 • $24.95HC • (8)

A TASTE OF QUEBEC, SECOND EDITION

Julian Armstrong

First published in 1990, A Taste of Quebec is the definitive guide to traditional and modern cooking in this distinctive region of Canada. Now revised and updated, this edition features over 125 new recipes and traditional favorites, along with highlights on up-and-coming new chefs, the province's best restaurants, notes of architectural and historical interest, and typical regional menus for a genuine Quebecois feast. With photos illustrating the people, the cuisine, and the land sprinkled throughout, this is the food lover's guide to Quebec.

200 PAGES • 8-PAGE COLOR INSERT • 7 3/4 x 9 3/8 • 0-7818-0902-9 • $16.95PB • (32)

FRENCH CARIBBEAN CUISINE

Stéphanie Ovide

Preface by Maryse Condé

This marvelous cookbook contains over 150 authentic recipes from the French islands of Guadeloupe and Martinique. Favorites such as Avocado Charlotte, Pumpkin and Coconut Soup, Fish Crêpes Saintoise, and Fish Court Bouillon will beckon everyone to the table. The author has spent many hours traveling, researching, and cooking all over the French islands to give her readers a real taste and appreciation of what French Creole cuisine is about.

The book would not be complete without its chapter on favorite drinks, featuring the famous Ti Punch. Also included are an extensive glossary of culinary terms that will familiarize home cooks with various exotic fruits, vegetables, and fish, as well as a list of websites that specialize in Caribbean products and spices.

232 PAGES • 6 x 9 • 0-7818-0925-8 • $24.95HC • (3)

OLD HAVANA COOKBOOK
CUBAN RECIPES IN SPANISH AND ENGLISH

Cuban cuisine, though derived from its mother country, Spain, has been modified and refined by locally available foods like pork, rice, corn, beans and sugar, and the requirements of a tropical climate. Fine Gulf Stream fish, crabs and lobsters, and an almost infinite variety of vegetables and luscious, tropical fruits also have their places on the traditional Cuban table. This cookbook includes over 50 recipes, each in Spanish with side-by-side English translation—all of them classic Cuban fare and old Havana specialties adapted for the North American kitchen. Among the recipes included are: Ajiaco (famous Cuban Stew), Boiled Pargo with Avocado Sauce, Lobster Havanaise, Tamal en Cazuela (Soft Tamal), Quimbombó (okra), Picadillo, Roast Suckling Pig, and Boniatillo (Sweet Potato Dulce), along with a whole chapter on famous Cuban cocktails and beverages.

123 PAGES • 5 X 7 • LINE DRAWINGS • 0-7818-0767-0 • $11.95HC • (590)

Prices subject to change without prior notice. To purchase HIPPOCRENE BOOKS contact your local bookstore, call (718) 454-2366, or write to: HIPPOCRENE BOOKS, 171 Madison Avenue, New York, NY 10016. Please enclose check or money order, adding $5.00 shipping (UPS) for the first book, and $.50 for each additional book.